NIKKI GEMMELL has written five novels. Her critically acclaimed fiction, including the international bestseller *The Bride Stripped Bare* as well as *Cleave* and *The Book of Rapture*, has been translated into many languages. Until recently she lived with her husband and children in London and worked as a successful journalist for the *Mail on Sunday*'s *you* magazine. She has now returned with her family to her native Australia.

Also by Nikki Gemmell

Shiver

Cleave

Lovesong

The Bride Stripped Bare

Pleasure: An Almanac of the Heart

The Book of Rapture

Why You Are Australian

With My Body

NIKKI GEMMELL

FOURTH ESTATE · London

Fourth Estate
An imprint of HarperCollins*Publishers*
77–85 Fulham Palace Road,
Hammersmith, London W6 8JB

This Fourth Estate paperback edition published 2012
This production 2012

First published in Great Britain by Fourth Estate in 2011

ISBN: 978-0-00-792991-7

Printed in Great Britain by Clays Ltd, St Ives plc

PROLOGUE

You begin.

It feels right. At his desk. On his chair. His typewriter is the only thing left of him in the room. The ink ribbon is fresh – the metal letters cut firm and deep – as if he has placed it for this moment, just for you. You start slow, clunking, getting used to the heft of the old way. Working laboriously on the beautiful, antique machine for if you make a mistake you can't go back and you need these pages methodical, neat. You type with his old Victorian volume by your side, that he gave you once – *A Woman's Thoughts About Women* – that logged within its folds all that happened in this place, that breathed life, once. You relive the dialogue of his handwriting and yours jotted in the margins and the back, don't quite know what you're going to do with all the work; at this stage you're just collating, filching everything that's needed from this notebook whose pages are bruised with age and grubbiness and life, luminous life: sweat and ink and rain spots; sap and dirt and ash; the grease from a bicycle and a silvery snail's trail and a cicada wing, its fragile, leadlit tracery. You reap his words and yours and then the Victorian housewife's, her lessons about life, her guiding voice. She will lead you through this. *Tell the truth and don't be afraid of it*, she soothes. Yes.

Writing to understand.

And as you work you feel a presence, a hand in the small of your back, willing you on. Every person who's ever loved and lost, every person who's ever entered that exclusive club – heartbreak. Your little volume always beside you, the book you came here to bury, to have the earth of this valley receive as one day it will receive your own flesh, you are sure – lovingly, gratefully, because it is so, right, you are part of it.

But first this book must serve another purpose.

You feel strong, lit.

Whole.

Writing to work it all out.

You have never told anyone this. No one knows what you really think. It has always been extremely important to never let them know; to never show them the ugliness, brutality, magnificence, selfishness, glory; never give them a way in. It has always been important to maintain your equilibrium, your smile, your carapace at all times. You could not bear for anyone to see who you really are.

But now, finally, it is time. With knowing has come release. It has taken years to get to this point.

I

'Even in sleep I know no respite'

Heloise d'Argenteuil

Lesson 1

Let everything be plain, open and above-board.
Tell the truth and don't be afraid of it.

You think about sleeping with every man you meet. You do not want to sleep with any of them. Couldn't be bothered anymore. You are too tired, too cold. The cold has curled up in your bones like mould and you feel, in deepest winter, in this place that has cemented around you, that it will never be gouged out. You live in Gloucestershire. In a converted farmhouse with a ceiling made of coffin lids resting on thatchers' ladders. It is never quite warm enough. There are snowdrops in February and bluebells in May and the wet black leaves of autumn then the naked branches of winter clawing at the sky, all around you, months and months of them with their wheeling birds lifting in alarm when you walk through the fields not paddocks; in this land of heaths and commons and moors, all the language that is not your language for you were not born in this place.

Your memories scream of the sun, of bush taut with sound and bleached earth. Of the woman you once were. She is barely recognisable now.

You do not know how to climb out, to gain traction with some kind of visibility, as a woman. To find a way to live audaciously. Again.

Lesson 2

The house-mother! Where could you find a nobler title,
a more sacred charge?

Your husband, Hugh, will be home late. Ten or so. This is
not unusual. He works hard, as a GP, and you cherish that,
the work ethic firm in him; he will not let his family down.
There's always something he has to do at the end of the day,
paperwork, whatever.

It is good Hugh is home late, what you want. You seize
those precious few hours between putting the children to
bed and his homecoming for yourself. The soldering time.
When you uncurl, recalibrate. Draw a bath and dream of
being unclenched, of standing with your face to the sky in the
hurting light, opening out your chest and filling up your bones
with warmth. Becoming tall again, vivid-hearted, the woman
you once were.

You have a good girl's face. Young, still. But Hugh detected
something underneath, early on he sniffed it out like a
bloodhound. Something ... unhinged ... under the smile.
Something coiled, waiting for release.

He'll never find it. You have been locked away for so long
and your husband does not have the combination and never

will, now, has no idea what kind of combination is needed; he thinks all is basically fine with his marriage. You've both reached a point of stopping in the relationship. Too busy, too swamped by everything else.

You are the good doctor's wife. All wellies and Range Rovers, school runs and Sunday church and there is a part of you that your husband will never reach and that elusiveness used to addle him with desire; what went on, once, in your life.

'Tell me your thoughts,' he used to say. 'What are you thinking?' But you couldn't let on, ever, didn't want this good man scared off: he must never know the rawness of the underbelly of your past. This one was marriage material: respectability, kids, the rose-bowered cottage; nothing must jeopardise it.

The magnificence, ugliness, beauty, power, transcendence – when you were unlocked. That Hugh will never know, for you did not marry him for that; he cannot lay you bare like you were laid bare once.

Some men know how, but most don't.

Lesson 3

She is forever pursued by a host of vague adjectives,
'proper', 'correct', 'genteel', which hunt her to death
like a pack of rabid hounds

Your children are just back from school. Outside is icy-white but it is frost, not snow, a brittle blanket of stillness that clamps down the world. The frost has not melted in the mewly light of the previous few days. The kids champ at the bit inside, they want to be out in the light, before it is gone; almost. You let them loose. They spill through the kitchen door, run. Storming into the crisp quiet, roaring it up; bullying the frost, its deathly stillness.

You smile as you stare through the window at your boys – so much life in them. Such shining, demanding, insistent personalities, all so different. You make another cup of tea, the last of the day or you won't sleep; green tea because so many dear friends are getting ill now – three at the moment, with breast cancer. And with your mother's history you have to be careful of that.

You're so tired, you have four boys if you count the one you're married to and the exhaustion is now like an alien that's nestled inside your body, sucking away all your energy. It's an exhaustion that stretches over years, since your first child, Rexi, was born; the exhaustion of never being in control anymore, of never completely calling the shots. Once, long ago, as a single career woman, you did. You dwelled within a white balloon of loveliness, in the city, loved your beautifully pressed, colour-ordered clothes and regular weekend sleep-ins, your overseas trips and crammed social life.

But now this. A tight little world of Mummyland, symbolised by a mountain of unsorted clothes on the floor at the end of the bed. You can get the clothes into the washing machine. You can get them out. You can arrange them over the radiators to dry. You can collect the dried clothes and put them in a heap ready for sorting. But you cannot, cannot, get the clothes back into their cupboards and drawers. Until that pile at the end of the bed becomes a volcano of frustration and accusation and despair; ever growing, ever depleting you. Until sometimes, alone, you are weeping and you barely know why, your hands clawed frozen at your cheeks. 'I can't do it.' Sometimes you even say it to your children, horribly it slips out – 'It's too hard, I can't do this' – bewildering them.

You weren't this woman, once; despised this type of woman, once.

You are lonely yet desperate for alone; it's so hard to get away from your beloved Tigger-boys, to steal moments of blissful alone from everyone dependent upon you. You feel infected with sourness, have lost the sunshine in your soul. You do not like who you have become; someone reduced.

Yet you are so fortunate, have so much. You know this, despairingly. Cannot complain but are locked in your demanding little world of giving, giving, giving to everyone else, all the time; trapped.

Lesson 4

Lost women

You have not slept with your husband since the birth of your third son two years ago. This doesn't bother you. It is a relief. If it bothers Hugh he no longer expresses it. You've both stopped talking about your lack of a sex life, the joshing has gone, the teasing; he never talks about it now. He used to snuffle about, playful, trying to unlock his little librarian with her knee-length tweed skirts and demure shirts, unleash whatever it was that was underneath. Now, you suspect, he's as exhausted as you.

Almost every night it's musical beds, a different combination of child next to you with Hugh squeezed into various dipping mattresses. Recently you've been waking every night, around 3 a.m., hugely, violently. Roaming the house, banging the walls with clenched fists; harangued by sleeplessness, needing to reclaim yourself. Heart thudding, knowing you will not be able to sleep for several hours and then tomorrow will be no better and perhaps worse. Oh for a full, deep, rich sleep, with nothing to wake you the next day, no demands, squabbles, wants. Oh for that sated sleep of deeply satisfying sex. Tenderness, a shiver of a touch.

You love Hugh, of course, feel for him deeply, but would

be happy to be celibate from now on. You look at some of the school dads around you and just know they'd be 'dirt' – cheeky, playful, a bit of rough – and it's always the divorced ones; there's something unfettered, loose, lighter about them. But you'd never do anything about it. Don't need sex anymore. You wonder at the shine of those women who are man-free by choice: some widows and divorcees you've seen over the years, nuns, septuagenarians; those precious few who no longer seek out men and are strong with their decision and lit with it. You recognise that glow.

Unencumbered.

Men, for you, have fulfilled their purpose; you have children, are sated. Once, long ago, you were made tall and strong by the shock of someone who cherished women and was not afraid of them, who revered their bodies. Men like that are extremely rare and when a woman finds one she recognises profoundly the difference in the lovemaking and is forever changed; that man becomes a paragon by which all others are measured and you are lucky, so lucky, to have found it, once. You have girlfriends who never have.

Lesson 5

That season of early autumn, which ought to be the most
peaceful, abundant, safe and sacred time
in a woman's whole existence

A memory slicing through your life.

That you slip out every night like a billet-doux hidden in a pillowcase, that you've carried through all your adult years. A memory of exquisite shock: that your body was cherished once. Not used but thrummed into life. His touch – you are addled by the remembering even now, after all these years. His touch – sparking you awake, God in it. And his voice. Is that what we remember most potently, out of all the senses, long after someone has gone? You can still recall the exact way he spoke your name when he was deep inside you, moving almost imperceptibly, the nourishment of it. You have pocketed that voice in your memory long after the sharpness of his features has faded.

In no way did he want to reduce you; that above all you remember. His singular aim: to empower you, lift you, unlock you. Teach you to know your body, what it is capable of. How many men give women that gift?

Another country. Another life.

A world away from this one, now, sipping your green tea as you stare out the window at 4.30 p.m., your life ticking by, your knuckles white around the mug. It'll be teatime soon, followed by the pleading to get the homework done, the dragging from screens, the nagging to have showers, do teeth; all the plea-bargaining, negotiating, cajoling in your life, the relentless exhaustion of it.

Lesson 6

Married women have cast their lot for good or ill,
having realised in greater or lesser degree
the natural destiny of our sex

Hugh and you are bound by an unspoken acknowledgement that you'll never split – you're in this together, for life. When you married him you were aching for love, something transporting; he was a friend who had you laughing deep into the night and so it would work, yes. You've always cherished his evenness. Were never uncomfortable with him, even in silence – the test of a true connection. You are so fortunate to have him, you know this, you must never forget it.

You do not like the way he kisses. Do not know how to tell him this, could never hurt him. It will not change. It's gone on too long. It cannot be taught. How can you say to someone you love that they lack tenderness? It's impossible to learn, to acquire. You could endure it pre-children, he offered so much else – filling up the glittery loneliness of yet another Saturday night by yourself, another New Year's Eve; his sturdy, charming presence quelling all those awkward questions on Christmas Days and all the weddings and baby showers you were suddenly going to. Your saviour, you know it.

Yet it feels like the only thing that unites you now is the children. You dream of another, a girl – the bliss of her – but just couldn't be bothered; with Hugh, you're both beyond all that. You never talk about it. About anything.

He is an Englishman who boarded from the age of seven and from then onward was taught not to trust his feelings; to shut down. He craved his mother, was overwhelmed by grief and loneliness yet all the time was told that his family wanted this, it was for the best. So he learnt from very young not to trust his deepest instincts, to bury far inside what he really thought. He has carried these lessons through life; expects it of others. He never changes towards you – is warm, playful – but doesn't want all the emotion, the mess of it.

He calls you Vesuvius to his Pompeii. When all your raging, swamping frustrations blurt out. When a voice in you snaps in the thick of the exhaustion, a voice you've never heard before, a woman you don't recognise, at your husband and your children; a voice of anger and ugliness. You fear your beloved boys will hold its tone somewhere in their memories for the rest of their lives and you're ashamed of that but still, occasionally, it roars out. Yet you love them to distraction, it's a swamping that's greedy, wild, voluptuous; every night in prayer you thank God for the gift of them.

Motherhood, the complexity of it. The richness, the depletion, the incandescence. The despair, the loneliness.

Lesson 7

She has ceased to think principally of herself and
her own pleasures

Once, for a long period, you never had an orgasm. You
had surrounded yourself with a boundary of no; your body
recoiling, in shock, at what men would do. Or wouldn't. Their
ignorance, clumsiness, lack of finesse. Your body in shock at
what was the smarting truth: that some of these men didn't,
actually, like women very much. Wanted to chip away at them,
deplete them, make them vulnerable and weak; were afraid of
them. And your entire body retracted at the knowing, like a sea
anemone flinched.

But then the lover from long ago, who gave you your first
orgasm. Taught you to surrender. And now, at your age, if you
can't have transcendent sex you're not going to have it at all. It's
as simple as that. You're too old for anything else.

Hugh, God love him, is good at sleep. He doesn't snore or smell,
he wings you close on the rare occasions you find yourself in
the same bed as him and you love the protectiveness of it. You
may have lost your taste for sex but you will never lose your
desire for shared sleep.

With Hugh.

To the outside world you are blissfully married, one of those rare couples that works.

Lesson 8

Marriage: to resign one's self totally and contentedly into the hands of another; to have no longer any need of asserting one's rights or one's personality

---

You were born in mountain country, north of Sydney, a place assaulted by light. High hill country with ground leached pale by the sun and tap water the colour of tea and you always looked down when walking through tall grass, because of snakes, and at dusk the hills glowed pink with the force of the sun, trapping the heat under your skin, in the very marrow of your spine; that could not be gouged out. Whispering you back. Home. To a tall sun, a light-filled life.

When you were eighteen you climbed down from your high mountain place. Went to university and became a lawyer, in Sydney, the Big Smoke. Winged your way to London in your mid twenties: restless, fuelled by curiosity, eager to gulp life. After several years of hard work there was the expat's dilemma of wanting to return to Australia but unable to decide when; of meeting Hugh – the man who did not excite you but sheltered you; of one thing leading to another and now you are in this rain-soaked island for life, staring at a mountain of washing by your bed and dreaming of the roaring light. After the second bouncy boy the decision was mutual: a move to the west country, the Cotswolds, for space and fresh air, a better life. Your dream of a partnership in the law firm fell away under the demands of motherhood; after the first maternity leave you never went back, lost your professional confidence and now your children cram every corner of your life. You are driven by perfection and ambition as a mother, just as you were driven as a lawyer. Everything you do you dive into completely, attacking with a ferocious will to succeed and hating it when you fall short. Which you do now, often, to your distress.

Hugh has said it's good you're Australian in this place; your accent can't be placed, you can slip effortlessly from lower class to upper, can't be pinned down. You know it's good Hugh is not Australian for he can't nail the broad flatness of tone that any Aussie East Coaster would recognise as originally from the sticks. The bush has never been completely erased from your voice; wilfully some remnant clings to it. Your vowels have been softened by Sydney, yes, but they still carry, faintly, the red-neck boondocks in their cadence. England hasn't left a trace.

You will always be an outsider here. You revel in not-belonging, enjoy the high vantage point. Marvel, still, at the strict sense of place, of class they cannot breach – the fishing and shooting, the villas in France, the stone walls that collect the cold and the damp, the wellies even in July, the jumpers in August, the hanging sky like the water-bowed ceiling of an old house. How can it hold so much rain, cry so much? Days and days and days of it and at times you just want to raise your arms and push up the clouds, run. Hugh will never move to Australia, he has a blinkered idea of it as the end of the earth and deeply uninteresting, really – that the only culture you'll find there is in a yoghurt pot.

You can see your whole future stretching ahead of you now until your body is slipped into this damp black earth, the years and years of sameness ahead. Once, long ago, you never wanted to be able to do that, curiosity was your fuel, the unknown. You carry your despair in you like an infection that cannot be shaken.

But now. A dangerous will inside you to crash catastrophe into your life, somehow, God knows how – or with whom. It's been brewing for years; it's something about reaching your forties and seeing all that stretches ahead. You've never been fully unlocked with Hugh and bear responsibility for that, entirely.

For always wearing a mask. For not being entirely honest. For never showing him your real self.

Lesson 9

Unhappiness of soul — a state of being often as
unaccountable as it is irrational

'How are you?' the lovely, cheeky Bengali man in your
newsagency asked before school pick up today.

You replied, distracted, 'I have no idea.'

The ultimate flaky mum, you know he thought.

But it was the truth. You have no idea. Have lost the woman
you once were. Cannot simplify your life. Had so much energy
for so much, once; now your days are taken up with so many
bitsy, consuming, domestic things. You catch yourself talking
aloud as you walk away down the High Street. Is it madness
or preoccupation or mere motherhood. In a window reflection
you gasp at yourself scowling, jaw set. There's the niggle that
now you're married you are somehow less. Just the little wife.
Hugh doesn't mean to convey that but he does. There's a subtle
and discernible loss of confidence, so insidious, as you lean on
another for so much and you never did that, once. As you have
somehow allowed over the years your petrol tank to be filled and
restaurant dinners to be decided for you, sweets secreted to your
kids, Nintendo Wiis gleefully bought behind your back, theatre
tickets purchased for plays you don't like.

You cannot explain how circumstances have closed over you, how you became a woman who lost her voice.

But you know there's only one person who can haul you out.

It is five o'clock.

The potatoes have to be peeled and the toilet unblocked; it's probably a plastic toy, it's becoming a habit with Pip, your youngest.

You have to change this life, somehow, or something in you will implode like a depth charge way beneath the surface.

Lesson 10

There are very few families whose internal mismanagement
and domestic unhappiness are not mainly the fault
of the mistress

Nine p.m. Just the dishwasher to unpack now and then you'll
draw your bath and unclench, at last, in the warmest room in
the house, the main bathroom.

The phone. Susan. A mum from the boys' school and you
don't know how it came to this: a Susan so entwined in your
life. Rexi is friends with her eldest, Basti. You met when the
boys were in the same nursery and then they moved to primary
school together, have known each other for years. It is assumed.
But you became friends before you realised how unsettling she
is. A mother with an overdeveloped sense of her own rightness,
with everything, and there's something so undermining about
that.

Every conversation, to Susan, is a form of competition; there
must always be the moment of triumph. When she's first seen
every morning, at the school gate, she forces you to say how
lovely her little girl looks, to compliment.

'Look at Honor, she dressed herself today, doesn't she look
gorgeous?'

'Where's Honor, is she hiding on my shoulders?'

'Isn't she beautiful?'

Yes of course, and you are a woman who does not have a daughter but it would never cross Susan's mind that the keenness for a girl once sliced through you like a ragged bit of tin; you can't deny there was a moment of disappointment at each subsequent son who appeared from your womb – just a moment, wiped as soon as you held them to your breast. And now, every day at the school gate, there is the ritual noticing of what you do not have, every day this conversation you have somehow allowed in your life.

Susan is obsessed by her children. Like no other woman you know. Always talking about how good her Basti is – at maths, swimming, art, he's just swum four laps, helped plant her herb garden, is never sick, always good – not one of those naughty ones.

You always cringe at this – your boys are boys, you adore them but they are not always the best; often your heart is in your mouth when your family is with other people, about what may be said, knocked over, who may be shouted at. Susan is critical of your Rexi whenever he's had a play date. Always, on the doorstep when you pick him up, you have to submit to her little ritual of complaint. The only time you can ever remember her complimenting your eldest was when she said, in wonder, 'He's good looking ... now.' Now. Your beautiful, sunny, ravishing boy, from day one.

'Rex didn't eat his food ... wouldn't play with Honor ... was very loud ...'

You have allowed it, for so long – Susan's reward for taking one son off your hands, for giving you a blessed break; it means one less child for a few hours and you both know how needed that is in your life, a tiny sliver of extra space.

Lesson 11

A state of sublime content and superabundant gaiety —
because she always had something or other to do.
If not for herself, then her neighbour.

It is nine-fifteen and Susan is still on the phone and inwardly,
at her voice, there is a tightening in your stomach, a knot —
what has her Basti excelled at today, what triumph has to
be endured? And your head is full of the 'Shout Book' you
have just discovered under your middle child's bed. Jack has
recorded, meticulously, every time he is yelled at. By you. In
writing neater than it's ever been at school.

> *Saturday: 14th January. 2 times.*
> *Sunday: 15th January. AMAZING. Nothing.*
> *Monday: 16th January. 3 times.*

Devastation. Today it was all to do with him wearing a good
shirt to his grandmother's tomorrow, for her birthday tea.

'I hate that button shirt so much it makes me walk backwards,'
he had shouted.

You laughed at the time and later jotted it down; for what,
God knows. You had to laugh, they give you so much and

don't even know it. These bouncy, shiny little scamps fill every corner of your life, plump it out; you love them so consumingly but you're not sure they believe it, Jack most of all, your middle child you worry will one day slip through the cracks.

'Please, God, stop Mummy shouting,' was his prayer tonight.

'Don't!' came his muffled protest from under the duvet when you tried to tickle him into giggles, to kiss away all your guilt, but he recoiled as if your touch would scald him which only made you want to caress him, cuddle him, envelop him all the more.

Susan is prattling on, she wants you to do the coffee before the class assembly on Monday and didn't catch you today. She is president of the P.T.A., you are a class rep, this is the new world you have thrown yourself into with the zeal you once reserved for law. You're deeply embedded in this intense little microcosm, yet feel sick every day now as you approach the gates for pick up. Wear a mask of joy – you have perfected it but if only they knew of your relief when for some reason, too rarely, you don't have to be there. It's your twice daily torture and you feel ill, sometimes, as you near the school gates. You wait in the car so you're not standing there early, having to talk. Filling up afternoons with play dates for the boys so they're not missing out and filling up your own evenings with drinks and dinners with your mummy friends for the same reason and you need the solace and release of using your brain, somehow. You've been with some of these women for over five years now. And their flaws are getting worse as they age – as are yours; it feels like you are all hardening into your weaknesses and you've got years of this school run ahead of you. The competitiveness, petty power games, boasting, one-upmanship; sometimes you feel like you're ten again, back in the school yard. It's stealing who you really are, who you became, once.

Lesson 12

Beware the outside friend who only rubs against one's angles

Your shout book.

What Mothers Do (or, The Tyranny of the School Gate)

* Ignore requests for play dates, just don't return emails, or constantly say their child can't do it. Or get their P.A. to decline on their behalf.

* Invite every child in the class to their son's party but yours.

* Talk and talk about their own child and never ask a single question about your own.

* At every mention of a problem your child has – e.g. crooked front teeth/can't do the maths/is having difficulties with friends – comes back with, 'Johnnie's teeth are beautifully straight, thank God, Johnnie's always been good at maths, he gets on with everyone,' etc. Whether you believe it or not.

* Drop their child off to your son's birthday party without a present, pick up their child with no mention of a present, happily take a party bag, say an extravagant thank you but never give a birthday present in return or mention the situation again, as if challenging you. Of course you say nothing.

* Never reciprocate with lifts to or from school, as if it just hasn't crossed their mind to do so.

* Like a butterfly buzz from school gate flower to flower, alighting on the freshest and most beautiful – the newest mum, the next best friend – before flitting off to someone else. Dropping you, just like that, into a cold, cold place. Phone calls are suddenly unanswered, coffee requests met with, 'So busy, another time'. Felling you with silence. Because someone else is filling up their lives now, whereas once you were the loveliest and most intriguing mum in the school; fresh from London, foreign, marked by difference. Long ago. The technique is stunning: how to bring a strong woman down, torment them with bewilderment, force them to ask the question, again and again, 'What's wrong with me?'

Sometimes you just want to scream at these women, at the height of all the pettiness (usually towards the end of term when everyone's frazzled). *Can't we all just value each other? Please?* It's hard, for every one of us, you're sure of that.

And then, specifically, there's Queen Susan:

* Using the royal 'we' when talking about the school because as P.T.A. president she has a sense of entitlement and ownership over the institution – and access to the headmaster – that no other parent has.

* Likes to slip in to conversations, often, her privileged position. For example, parking is difficult around the school

and everyone wings it, including you, with illegal, jittery, hovery pulling up at pick up and drop off. Except Susan. 'I'm president, I just can't,' she likes to remind everyone, often, with a rueful smile. 'I'm president, my boy has to do his homework ... I'm president, I can't be late for pick up.' If the job came with a badge she'd wear it.

* Always includes a link to her own website at the bottom of her weekly school newsletter, as if to rub it in that she has a life beyond all this, she has managed to be one of those ones who does it all, effortlessly (she runs a website selling bespoke wooden kitchenware along with her school duties).

If you were content, none of this would infect you; it would just roll away like water off a duck's back. But one woman, this woman, has become a focus for all your frustration and you know it's unfair and paranoid and ridiculous, she's a good person, you're just jealous of her position and the way she's worked out her life and it's eating you up, can't escape it. But you'd be happy to never see her again. Would never have befriended a Susan in your former existence, are not uplifted by her in any way; your heart doesn't skip with happiness to see her and you need heart-lifters around you now, more than ever – it feels like you're becoming more thin-skinned and vulnerable as you age. How can that be? That the great, raw wounds inflicted by others in the distant past are sharpening now, in middle age. You can't gouge them out and you have no idea why; have lost your voice, your strength.

Lesson 13

Friendship — a bond, not of nature but of choice,
it should be maintained, calm, free, and clear,
having neither rights nor jealousies, at once
the firmest and most independent of all human ties

_____

Your hand is straying into your pants, thinking of other things entirely, school dads, their spark. How one in particular, Ari, would spring you alive, back to the woman you once were. Ari, yes, he'd have the knowledge, the instinct; but you'd never do it. God no, the mess of it. Susan is still in your ear, telling you that Basti is just about to pass his first flute exam, can pick up any piece of music and just play it, he amazes her. (Rexi, God love him, is on page six of his guitar book and unlikely to progress.) And the coffee morning, 'Can you run it, babes?' Of course, yes. Susan will bake some muffins for you: 'I know you're not good at that bit.'

She is constantly baking, her house a show place, her children spotless – yours are the ones who sometimes wear grubby t-shirts you've flipped inside out, have cereal for dinner and Coca-Cola as a treat. In Susan's kitchen is a huge notice board in an ornate frame crammed with certificates of achievement and baby photos and colourful kids' drawings. The occasional certificates your own children get are lost in piles, somewhere, along with school reports and photos and Santa lists and they will all be sorted, sometime. Long ago, you were in control of your career, your friends, your life; you never feel in control within motherhood. The guilt at so much.

The time you folded up the push chair and placed it in the boot, only to hear a squeak – baby Pip still in it.

The time Jack rolled off the bed as you were changing his nappy and ended up with a dint in his skull.

The birthday cakes from Tesco, year after year.

The computer games that keep them all riveted, baby included.

The occasional McDonald's, three quarters of an hour's drive away on a Sunday night.

Basti, of course, has never had it in his life. He tells you this when he comes to your house. He has inherited his mother's heightened sense of censorious rightness, about everything in his life, and you fear for what's ahead of him, how the wider world will chip away at that. Meanwhile Susan bustles about in her flurry of energy, a tiny, dark sparrow of efficiency with an enormous, puffed chest, making you feel deficient in response, that you're always running and never quite catching up. Have had no role model in life for this. The best mothers are those who had bad mothers, you think, because they know what not to do – but what if you never had a mother? If she died before she was lodged in memory.

Susan's voice veers you back.

'Wasn't that homework hard today? Basti got it, eventually.'

'Rexi took a while. I had to snap off the TV just to get him to the table …'

'We don't miss ours. The kids never ask for it.'

A pause. 'Lucky you.'

Television, of course, is babysitting for you, your guilty secret. And you didn't notice exactly what Rexi was doing in his maths book.

'Just checking you're still on for Basti this Thursday?'

You're always scrupulously generous with play dates; it's why the routine works.

'Of course … can't wait.'

'Did you get the notice about nits? I know you never check their schoolbags, just reminding you. Basti's never had them. I don't know who it is …'

You shut your eyes, your knuckles little snow-capped mountains around the phone. Because of bath time, several hours earlier – all the boys, even Pip – and dragging out the lice with all their tiny, frantic legs. And Jack has a pathological aversion to nits, almost vomits with the horror of them, yells like you're scalping him. Then the pleas, the threats, to finish the homework due tomorrow, to stop the Wii, get to bed. Rexi storming off in frustration, his arms over his head. You feel, sometimes, he's a great open wound that you're pouring your love and puzzlement into. What's going on in there? Does it ever even out? He's only nine. His teacher says it's something to do with boys about this age, from seven onwards, their teeth coming through; there's a huge psychological change in them, hormones swirling. Does he mellow with age, does he strengthen? Is he too much like you, too emotional? You are fascinated and fearful at the depth of his feelings.

You are not responsible for your child's happiness, Rexi's teacher in her fifties told you gently the other day.

'All you're responsible for is what is said and done to them, as a parent. That's all. Nothing else.' You must remember that.

Lesson 14

Herein the patient must minister to herself

Nine-thirty. You step outside. Lock the door.

Now you are in control. You inhale a breath of steely night air; the cold never ceases to shock in this place, after all these years, still. The children are all asleep, you know they will not wake, know them well enough. You stood in the quietness of their rooms and breathed them in deep and felt a vast peace flood through you, whispering a soothing through your veins. Everyone down, your day done.

But now.

Walking fast through a stillness that is holding its breath. Feeling an old you coming back. The stone walls, the close woods, the bridge over the stream are all coated in a thick frost that has not broken for several days and it is ravishingly beautiful, all of it, but it will never hold your heart. Because it is not home.

It is flinchingly cold, you are not dressed for it, have not thought, just needed to walk, get away, out. Hugh has a work dinner, he'll be home in a couple of hours, you'll be back for him, of course. It is suddenly overwhelming you as you walk, the tears are coming now. You dream of being unlocked. By spareness. Simplicity. Light, screaming hurting light. Dream of tall skies, endless space, of being nourished within the sunlight, of never coming back. The tears are streaming now, great gulps, your mouth is webbed by wet. You are not strong here.

You are on the road now, not properly dressed, cannot go back, cannot face any of it. A car flashes by, swerves, beeps in annoyance. There are no footpaths, only grass verges, the lanes are too narrow, built for carts centuries ago, you shouldn't be walking in this place. You freeze in terror like a rabbit, can't go forward, can't go back. You hold your arms around you and weep, and weep, vined by circumstance – you are no longer you. Lost.

Lesson 15

We are able to pass out of our own small daily sphere

More headlights. A van.

Slowing, stopping. You shiver, your heart beats fast.

'Hello, stranger.'

It is Mel. Another school mum. The one who is different, who never quite belongs. Who breezes in and out of the school like she couldn't care less, who is … *unbound*. Who says fuck the quiz night, fuck the summer party, fuck the lot of it: *I've got better things to do with my life*. What, God knows.

She wears real, cool, vintage fur: *I don't do fake anything – coats, fingernails, orgasms.*

Everyone suspects she's been given the school fees for free, the charitable slot. She's a single mum with a son in Jack's class. You envy the every-second-weekend-off-from-motherhood that she gets – to sleep in, stay in bed all day, go dancing, potter, drink; to do nothing and everything for once. She runs an antique shop on the High Street – erratic opening hours, bric-a-brac from French flea markets – things you love that Hugh bats away as junk.

Mel picked up her boy, Otis, from a play date once, late. She'd come straight from her pole-dancing class and until that moment you'd had no idea such a thing existed in this place.

Mel would have been the girl who wore her school skirt too short and had her dad's ciggies in her pocket and smuggled dope into the dormitory; it's all in her face. Appetite and passion and life's hard knocks and a big open heart no matter how many times she's pounded upon the rocks. An aura of a woman who revels in life. Who has sex a lot.

Mel always lingers after the boys' occasional play dates. There's often been some strange pull, in the silence, you don't know why; you just want to lean across, it's ridiculous, she's not your type, your style. She wears skinny jeans, sometimes Uggs; your palette is the colour of reticence, careful camel or sand or chalk with a dash of black. She's a woman for God's sake.

Lesson 16

She hath done what she could

'Hey,' Mel says soft, frowning, with infinite understanding. 'Get in.'

You gulp your tears; the car is warm, the heating on.

'I don't know what's wrong –' you rush out, your voice veering high, off course.

'Sssh …'

'The boys, the school gate, Hugh –'

'I know, I know.'

Mel has pulled over, down a lane, she is not taking you back, thank God she is not taking you back. You barely register what she is doing: she is listening, that's all, she wants to know. Her hand is on your knee, just that.

'Sssh,' and now the tears are coming again, soft, in the stillness, the quiet; cracked by kindness. You begin to talk, in a way you haven't for so long.

'But you're so lucky.' Quiet, at the end of it. 'Don't you see that? You have so much.'

You look at her. Yes, you nod, yes, you know; yet it has all, bafflingly, come to this.

Mel leans across, holds your chin, and says your name, softly, gently. You smile; no one has spoken to you like that for so long, a cadence of … *caring*. She kisses you on the cheek, softly, affectionately, in comfort.

It strays.

The tenderness of it, you pull back – but the tenderness, it holds you, draws you.

Something is coming alive within you, after so long, so many years. You go to speak. 'Sssh,' Mel soothes, kissing you, kissing you. There is a stirring, like an anemone swaying into life under the water's caress; your belly is flipping and you remember long ago, the surrendering, opening out, when you had never felt more alive … once, long ago, for six transforming weeks, another place, life. Something long dormant is awakening within you.

Lesson 17

If we do not advance, we retrograde
_____

What you learn, in that tiny lane, in that van, in the darkness seared with light: that feeling, memory, sensation, vividness, can come flooding back. All it takes is the tenderness in a touch. After so long.

You pull away at the shock. Mel laughs softly.

'You know, sleeping with a woman can be like discovering sex all over again' – a fingertip slips gently down your cheek, your neck – 'because we know what works' – the finger teases – 'and where.'

You pause. So vulnerable now to touch, kindness, attention of any sort. You shake your head, reach for the door handle, breathe your thanks – the kids, you have to get back. You stumble out.

'See you at the quiz night.' Mel smiles a secret smile, starting the van. 'Or maybe not.'

Striding back, wondrous, tall, through the glittering alive achingly beautiful frost.

Like discovering sex all over again …

It has been so long. So many years, lives, places ago. So many harangued nights of sleeplessness and collapsings into beds without even saying good night to your husband because you're too tired and too annoyed by some minor irritation like his flossing and his pyjamas pulled up high and his noisy blowing of his nose and anyway he's already on the way to falling asleep on the couch, in front of the telly, because that is what he always does now, in the shrouded rhythm of your married life.

Lesson 18

Upon which he kisses his little wife, and grows mild

―――――――――

Hugh is home just after 10 p.m., just as he said.

'He won't notice, he won't notice,' you say to yourself, at the kitchen table, a glass of wine before you.

'Hiya,' he yells.

He does not come to you, he never does. Now he is throwing down his keys, his wallet, his change. Now he is removing his coat and tie, littering them around the lounge room, balustrades, bedroom; black crows you call them, black crows roosting all over your life.

'Hiya,' he calls again, enquiringly.

'Hi.'

He does not come to you, he does not see you. At the kitchen table, sitting there, cracked. Like you were once, long ago; that he has never witnessed, that he would not understand.

A woman, now, your mind is churning with it, the one thing you never tried.

But everything else …

'Thank God that pile of clothes has finally disappeared,' Hugh yells from the bedroom.

You shut your eyes and throw your head back and smile.

Blazing light, blazing life.

II

'My words roar, and my salvation is afar'

Psalm 22

Lesson 19

Truly, in this hard world, we should be accustomed to this law of love – love paramount and never ceasing

_____

You are eleven. It is your birthday. He takes you out to dinner. He tells you he has a surprise. You wonder what: a horse of your own perhaps, a trail bike. Your father takes you to a restaurant in town, you have never been to one like it, it has cloth napkins and waiters in uniform. Your father doesn't belong in this place. He has a face like a fist – fleshy, knobbly, rough.

There is a woman at your table. She is called Anne. Your father tells you they are getting married. As he speaks it is a father you have never seen before. His soft, surrendering eyes that look at her and not you; his glow.

Your world stops.

Your father tells you you will be a bridesmaid, with a beautiful dress. Anne will help you choose it. Your father tells you there will be proper food, finally, in your home, fresh sheets and a stocked fridge and even – wait for it – an ironed school uniform every Sunday night. The only concession either of you has ever made to the classroom is him brushing your long hair – his hand gently and firmly holding your crown so as not to hurt – at the start of every school week.

You take a deep breath. You nod. Your life, until this point, has been unfettered. You have been marinated by the bush that surrounds you. You are often barefoot, grubby and wild, answerable to no one; your father and yourself a tight buddy-unit. You have soil packed under your fingernails in tiny crescent moons and coal dust ingrained in fine lines along your knees and no one ever worries about that. You cannot do blanket stitch, crochet or knit, but you can change a tyre and suck poison out of a snake bite and shrivel a leech on your skin with salt.

This has been your world, since your mother died of breast cancer when you were a young child.

But now. A new life. Your father's sparkling eyes and the pretty, mascaraed eyes of the woman opposite. Their shine. And in between them, an aching enormous eleven-year-old heart churning with fear and excitement, and readiness. Because there is so much love in you. To pour out, to swamp, to receive.

Dad loves Anne. So you love Anne. So Anne loves you.

It is as simple as that. Isn't it?

Lesson 20

Utterly ignorant of the framework on which society moves,
she is perpetually straining at gnats and swallowing camels,
both in manners and morals

_____

You are eleven, you feel too much. You are an open wound that
can only be sutured by that simplest of balms: attention. Love
as a necessary verb – to rescue, plume, bloom, cradle, encircle,
uplift. Protect.

Beyond your father's flinty, sloppy love there is no rescue in
your world. It is a surprise of four little houses huddled amid
a great loom of trees. A scrap of a hamlet that barely deserves
a name, too small for its own postcode, with just a mine
manager's house, an under manager's, an electrical engineer's
and a mechanical engineer's. All servicing a tiny seam of coal
called Beddington Number Two, a tiny pebble of a mine in a
valley north of Sydney.

On the high hills of this place you feel as if you are standing
on the roof of the world, that you could reach up and touch the
very cheek of God – the breeze slippery with sun and the great
expanse of sky unspooling above you and around you to the very
corners of the earth but it is only the ground, of course, that is
valued in this place. This glorious land on the roof of the world

is scurried by towers and conveyor belts and trucks heaped high with their sooty spilling black, and wire fences keeping everyone but miners out. Above ground: the domain of the dispossessed. Convict ghosts, sandstone ruins, abandoned plots, Aboriginal paintings in under-hangings, families sickened by generations of coal dust. Below ground: energy, productivity, work. There is the smell of greed to extract in the very air of this place.

To get to your father's weatherboard house with its faded red tin roof you drive down obscure dirt roads that threaten to exhaust themselves, wither and fade and stop, claimed by virulent bush. Then the Beddy road narrows, in the very heart of the valley, and you wonder where you are going; to what dangerous, hidden place. A murderer's road, this – for dumping bodies, baggage, secrets, lives.

Not a woman's world.

'For God's sake, make something of yourself,' your father often tells you and by this he means: don't be useless, don't hang about like a bad smell. He's taught you to survive a bush fire, find water, read a motorbike manual, mend a chook house and a fence; all his knowledge imparted as you traverse the bush roads in his ute – as if driving, concentrating on something else, is the only time he can properly converse. Your whole discourse, it feels, takes place within cars or when he's poking in bonnets or tinkering, flat on his back, underneath; he's always got several old bombs lying about, gutted or up on bricks. Avoiding the slap of face to face, of what he will see in it, who. But with a car, yarning, when you do not have to look at each other's eyes, there is intimacy.

It is the only intimacy you get.

Your toughened, dusty, bare feet are always leaning on the dashboard or the windscreen; the dirty imprints of your toes forever in front of the passenger seat like a dog at its post leaving its mark. You're continually kicking off your shoes, never wanting that feeling of being confined, restrained, bound by anything. Your father's always letting you, rarely saying no to his wild, sweet, bush scrap of a kid, who knows nothing of the world beyond this place.

He tells you on the way home from your birthday dinner that Anne will help you with women ... stuff, you know, like what he can't. Anymore.

'Like what?'

'Just ... stuff. She'll be good for you. Yeah.'

His voice trails off.

In the vivid silence beyond you wonder what he means. He says all this haltingly, awkwardly; and all you really understand is that it's important. Whatever it is. You take your feet off the dash and look at your father coolly and there is the first sliver of an adult knowing in that look – that your father is just no good with talk, with anything that's not about spanners and carburettors and saddles and swags. He's like one of those icebergs with the huge unknown mass of him underneath.

What you also understand from that night: a new world awaits.

Lesson 21

Elegant infamy

There is only one word for your naivety then. Magnificent. You have learnt no defences for the wiliness of grown-ups, their sophisticated ways, have never had to. You have lived your whole life in a bell jar of isolation.

Learning how to fashion a bridle out of a piece of rope and splint a broken bone when you're stuck out bush, learning when to sense a coming rain; how to read a kookaburra's laugh. Your tiny house is bereft of pictures on the wall, ornaments or books. A Bible on a side table is the only tome – unread – and the television is on every evening but it's never the ABC with those posh, city voices. A *Sydney Morning Herald* has never crossed its threshold; classical music has never wafted out, it's all Johnny Cash and Elvis, talkback and the *Daily Telegraph*. Your father is deeply suspicious of the world of the Big Smoke, of the well-born and the educated he rarely encounters, their social and intellectual confidence. The *ease* of them. It is only physically that the likes of him can ever compete, not that he wants to. His world is this valley.

Not a doll is in the house, not a frill or scrap of pink. Your treasured possessions are your Snoopy diary and your bike,

Peddly, which becomes your horse as soon as you sit on its saddle, winging you every day to other worlds than this.

Your school, at Beddy Number One, is a single classroom. Twelve kids, aged five to eleven. Your teacher is like many of the women of the valley, soft-fleshed and ambitionless beyond snaring a husband and a motherly life; soon to be married and she'll then leave teaching, which she has never liked, to devote herself to the job of wife. Her job is limbo land, the dead zone until something else.

'Why do you want to do that, Miss? Wouldn't you prefer to be with us?' you ask, cheekily. 'He's a right old bush turkey the bloke you're marrying, that's what my daddy says. Beyond his use-by date.'

'Get out.'

Which is what you want, of course. Almost every day you are released from the tiny classroom. She has given up on you, doesn't know what to make of your blunt voice, your absence of understanding what's wrong and right, your wildness and your wilfulness, your constant gazing out the window, champing at the bit.

Wanting out. Licked by sun and wind. Now. Not a part of this. Every day.

She doesn't see your knottedness, your enormous heart, primed for love – to give and receive it. Doesn't know what to make of your vast alone that she senses has no desire for her world, for everything she represents. Because you perceive in her, even then, some kind of an erasure, that there is no audacious sense of who she really is. She wants to disappear into someone else's life; she desires it more than anything else. That, to you, is bizarre. The one message your teacher imparts to you, upon the dewy, blinkered brink of her shiny new existence, is that women who are thinkers do not get married.

Then there's Anne. Waiting in the wings to take over your life.

Lesson 22

Matrimony in the abstract; not *the* man, but any man — any person who will snatch her out of the dullness of her life

_____

'In order to be irreplaceable one must be different.'

A quote from Coco Chanel, from a page of the *Women's Weekly* all twelve of you have been tearing up to make collages like Roman mosaics.

You are intrigued by the statement. Slip the cutting into the pocket of your overalls. You are a thinker despite what your teacher puts on your report and you love new words like *irreplaceable* and you are gleaning, slowly, that in this place it takes a mighty courage to be different, to want to be something beyond your world. In this fragile, uncertain time before your father's marriage is a tiny seed of a thought, to one day write; to be a watcher, an observer, apart. Because of the shiver of a truth: that the women of this world would only enfold you if everything that was unique about you, everything vivid and sure and free and strong, was gone. And the alternative, here — aching, yowling loneliness.

You fly home on Peddly that afternoon with the scrap of words in your pocket and sense that one day you will be saved by a world very different from this, saved by everything this world is not. You have no idea what that existence will be or how you will get to it but even then, so young, you have a raging will for a life that is not theirs.

Lesson 23

This law of love – love that tries to be always as just as it is
tender, and never exercises one of its own rights
for its own pleasure and good, but for the child's

The wedding. The house of Colin, your father's best mate, his
only school friend who escaped the pit. Chosen because it has
a swimming pool and a cabana, the poshest thing possible in
your lives, and because the little wife can do prawn cocktails
for you, mate.

Eleven p.m. The latest you have been up in your life.

Colin lolls up to you, beer glass in hand, in the saggy,
stretched time after the main meal.

He cups your chin and gazes into your fierce little face, at
the long golden hair your father brushed last night – for the
last time, you suspect – and he murmurs, 'Your mother was
so beautiful.' Stretching out the 'so' with a secret smile, gazing
at you like no one has before, as if he sees something of your
mother in there, some whisper of potential, suddenly, to mirror
her. You jerk back like a spooked pony, afraid of that, in a way
you don't quite understand, afraid your father will reject you
because of it.

But more importantly, that someone else will.

You glance across at your newly minted stepmother, at her bouffant of a bridal gown and extravagantly thrown back veil, at her crazed untouchable radiance and you know in that moment your past life is gone. That this triumphant young woman in her gown of a first wife not a second will do her best to erase your father's previous existence, stamp on any whiff of your mother being the love of his life, without even realising, perhaps, what damage she is doing.

You start to cry. The last crying of childhood. You weep, and weep, cannot stop.

You have never done anything like this before. You can pull apart two bush dogs in a fight and shoot a rabbit and crack a whip but cannot explain why you are doing this; it just feels like a giant hand is dragging a piece of jagged, broken glass down the underbelly of your life, splitting you open and all the tears, of all the years, are finally out. Everyone comes up to you: your father, your brand-new stepmother, your grandmother. But the floodgates are opened and cannot be shut. You sense this is horribly unfair on Anne and are ashamed of it but can't stop.

Because your father is lost to you from this point.

And you know that no matter how much she tries, your stepmother politely tolerates you and nothing else; she doesn't want any of your enormous swamping ready love, actually; she doesn't want the encumbrance of it in her life. Your stepmother, who over the years will perfect the art of emotional terrorism; an adult upon a child. Who despatches you, from the age of eleven, into an affronted loneliness within the new family she creates. A loneliness vast and raw, horizonless.

The obscenity of that.

Lesson 24

The house-mother! What a beautiful, comprehensive word it is. How suggestive of all that is wise and kindly, comfortable and good.

You learn to live warily under the same roof. You learn that your presence is a source of distress to your stepmother – she is a good Catholic girl and is ashamed her new husband is not a cleanskin, wants to pretend to the world her husband is not twenty years older than her and never had a former life. She gave up her job in a petrol station at twenty, at the first whiff of matrimony and never worked again. Gave it all up to enter the longed-for world of vibrant tranquillity and status called marriage – and no grubby, gobby child is going to mar that. She is a typical valley girl – early school-leaver, thick set, the expectation that soon they'll be with child – married or not. The much-anticipated baby doesn't come, doesn't come, even though the readiness for motherhood is oozing from her and your father grunts at one point, from under the F.J., to stop asking about it, it'll happen in good time, 'zip it'.

Your father is now called Ted, not his nickname – Eddie – that everyone has always called him; his colleagues, his mates, your mother, even you. She insists. Everything from his past is gradually turfed out, the carpet your mum chose, wallpaper, crockery. Photos disappear into obscure drawers, not only of your mum but of you and him together until suddenly, you notice, there are none in the house.

'Don't you dare take her for a drive, Ted. It's *my* time, not hers.'

Yet it is only when you are alone with your father, in the car, that his fingertips find your earlobe and his voice softens and he whispers, 'You're still my China, aren't you?' as if it is the last time he will be able to tell you this and gravely you must hold it in your heart, you must never forget it; he has stolen this chance and it may not happen again. In the car, just the two of you, with his secret voice he never dares give you the gift of when his new wife is present. His life is now held hostage by her and it is only when he is away, in the car, that he is free – his old self.

You can taste your stepmother's spirit and are disheartened by it. She has the focus and insecurity and determination of the second wife, to make this marriage work. She crashes into your equilibrium. Living with her is like being trapped in sleeplessness; she sucks the oxygen from your world.

She never teaches you what your father wanted, all that woman stuff he could not articulate. Your father never asks. He assumes everything is alright. You do not tell him. Your whole relationship is built on inarticulacy, it would not feel right to suddenly blurt. You are learning silence and watchfulness and the solace of a pen that speaks when you cannot, as an explosive combination is being brewed: frustration, anger, boundless curiosity – and enormous innocence.

Lesson 25

When I go from home to home and see the sort of rule
or misrule there, the countless evil influences, physical and
spiritual, against which children have to struggle, I declare
I often have to wonder that in the rising generation
there should be any good men and women

Your bedroom is now the verandah at the back of the house
with a roll-down canvas flap at night. It is not far away enough.
You are no longer a part of the main house. It has not been
done by pushing you out, it has been done by removal, by
erasing everything that was secure and known in your past
life. All the roaring absences now; the hidden photographs, the
taken-down curtains, the painted-over marks of your mother's
on the kitchen door, as you stood up, grew tall, and then
they stopped. Aged three years and eight months. The whole
interior has become a ghost house to you; holding its breath for
someone who will never come back. You still see it – searingly
– as what it was. Not what it is now.

When it thunders in your back room you drop to the
ground with your belly to the floorboards and hear the house
talk through the rumbling in your skin. You smell the earth

opening out to the rain, opening wide, drinking it up, wider and wider the ground opens out, every pore of it, and you smile and breathe it in deep.

No respite, but the bush.

Lesson 26

Every family is a little kingdom in itself: the members and followers of which are often as hard to manage as any of the turbulent governments whose discords convulse our world

---

By a shaded cleft of a creek you make a bush hut out of broken branches – widow makers, they're known as locally – and great brooms of leaves; your home away from home, just for you. You love the cool smell of the water on the rock, the rich rust of the wet stone, the startling green of the ferns sucking from the restless stream. You love the clutter of vibrant life drawn to this secret tranquillity, the frogs, lizards, birds, wallabies if you're very still. The land beyond it is bleached pale, the colour of the sheep that feed from it, but you'd never know within this.

You stay out later and later in your sanctuary. Are intrigued the first time you come home – after dinner, but before your father has returned from his shift – to see the worry lines creasing your stepmother's face. It is the first time you have seen concern on her, with anything to do with you.

You learn, in that instant, the authority of removal.

You stay away longer and longer.

Then one day, after a big rain, the mosquitoes come. You need something to keep them away. There is only one thing in your world that is a length of fine netting, and you know exactly what room to find it in.

Lesson 27

Never expect in the child a degree of perfection
which one rarely finds even in a grown person

You never enter your father's bedroom anymore. He no longer
brushes your hair on a Sunday night, no one does. And the room
is not his now, in any way; it's been prettied up. It feels alien,
forbidden, scrubbed; sanctified by something unknowable. But
in it, now, is the only thing of hers you will ever want.

She is away, visiting her mother. When she is gone it is as if
the house breathes out, with a sigh – your whole world unfurls
and you can move freely in it. You won't have long. You scrabble
through her cupboard and rigidly ordered drawers; God, an
entire life spent making things neat, what a waste. You find
what you're looking for in a leather suitcase under the bed.

A carefully folded veil, under a circle of dried roses.

Your mosquito net lasts through storms and winds and possums
rampaging and the time you jumped away from a red-bellied
black snake and crashed through it; lasts through days of you
returning later and later until finally, one morning, she follows
you; to work out where you are disappearing to all these God
forsaken days, to work out what on earth is going on. And

with a scream of rage she flurries upon your hidden place and drags down her precious veil, now ingrained with grubbiness and torn beyond repair.

She gets you home by the hair, your long golden hair, and knees you in the back and now finally you see the strength of this hefty country lass, and you're so slight; she knees you like she would a calf and grabs your mother's old dressmaking scissors and hacks off all your hair, in great ragged clumps – as if this will be the only veil you will ever have in your life and she will destroy it, oh yes, and may it never grow back. So much hate in her, so much frustration at this stain in her life. Then she gets a bottle of black ink that your father uses for writing cheques and she tips it over your head so it runs down your face like black blood in huge streaks and screams, 'Get out, get out, get out of my life,' her voice naked, now, finally, with the one thing she has wanted ever since she came into this place.

That night, you gallop your hurt and your howl into your Snoopy diary, the only voice you have. Because you are becoming a woman in this claustrophobic place – you are learning not to let slip the roar of your true self, and your father, of course, will not be told any of this, what goes on between his two women. You are learning how it is to be female in this life.

Lesson 28

Follow openly and fearlessly that same law which makes
spring pass into summer, summer into autumn,
and autumn into winter

Suddenly, boarding school. Just like that.

Cast adrift. Unwanted. Emotionally whipped.

But curious. About a new life, a new chance.

Curious as to how to expose your aching, open wound to
the light; the wound that can only be sutured by one thing,
the simplest thing of all. Love. The necessary verb: to rescue,
bloom, protect. Aching for something, anything, to heal you
and perhaps here in this new life you will find it.

Your convent school is in the city's centre, its honey sandstone
shadowed by buildings taller than it. Your father's lucrative
night shifts are paying for it – eleven and three-quarter hours,
from 8 p.m., triple time. In the Big Smoke you're still the kid
from the bush, like a horse in a box kicking out, strong, if you
are too long in it. City-logged. Every so often you can smell
the bush when the breeze blows in from the south and you
hold your head high to it. Above the pollution and the cram of
the noise and the crush of the people you want to feel the dirt

between your toes and in your hair, you want to be strong with your land again, want silence and spareness, a place for your eyes to rest.

Want your father. The one person who gave you the gift of attention, once.

The one person who gave you the gift of touch, once.

Touch is taboo in this place. You are young ladies, at all times, no matter what. Eating a banana in public is sexually suggestive and will not be tolerated from girls of this establishment; school shoes must not be polished too highly lest the reflection of bright white cottontails be glimpsed too readily; surfaces of bath water must be encrusted with talcum powder so a glimpse of flesh is never caught under the cloudy surface. The only man you are allowed to adore is God. *The Thorn Birds* is eagerly, grubbily, passed around the class; Judith Krantz, Jackie Collins. You are growing up. Everywhere flesh, touch, skin, bodies changing, worlds expanding, nights churning.

You become best friends with Lune, the daughter of the French ambassador, the only one in the class whose parents are divorced. Lune loves her motherless little bush girl who knows nothing of this world – an outsider like herself. She teaches you about razors and tanning and tampons, French kisses and cigarettes, silk knickers and suspender belts. European-knowing, she teaches you about the power in a dirty smile, and the allure of confidence.

Lesson 29

Have the moral courage to assert your dignity
against the sneers of society

———————

You have been shut away within high convent walls to address
the wildness from the bush; to quieten you, dampen you,
smooth you down. You are too large-spirited, singular, raw.
You have become an embarrassment.

And yet, and yet, you are not convinced these women
who rule over you are so disapproving. The nuns sense your
difference, you are sure, that you will never be one of those
ranks of girls they brisk out year after year armed with Daddy's
gold credit card and a D.J.'s account. There is something …
carnal … about you. Non-conformist, untamed. *Hungry*. But
for what, no one knows, including yourself. You're like the
parched earth in a drought waiting, waiting, for nourishment
of some sort.

You see something in these nuns, the few of them left, that is
strong, lit. They are an intriguing new breed of female in your
life. They are doing exactly what they want to and have a great
calmness because of it. Precious few women you know have that
– certainly not any married ones, the mothers of school friends,
the valley women you come across. There is something so

courageous about the nuns' strength in swimming against the stream. You think of your stepmother, riddled with jealousy and insecurity, threatened by a slip of a girl half her size, made sour with it. These women at your school, in their resolutely interior world, are free of the world of men by choice and glow with it.

Can a married woman radiate serenity? You've never seen it in the wives of Beddy, in the brittle women you occasionally glimpse in *The Young and the Restless* and the harassed mothers at the school gate. Your Mother Superior is fifty-five years old and has a face unburdened by wrinkles and worries, kids and mortgages and debt. There is never make-up, never shadow; it is as if she has washed her face in the softness of a creek's water her entire life. Washed it with grace.

The serenity of choice, and you are intrigued by it. The courage to be different.

Lesson 30

To feel that you can or might be something,
is often the first step towards becoming it

_____

Your mother's old boss, from her restaurant management days, invites you for tea. He is the only person you know in the Big Smoke outside of school. He grew up in the bush, like your mother did, and found a way out. He's now mysteriously wealthy, has a sunken conversation pit and a Porsche.

In his high glass box hovering above the harbour he lifts up your hair – now grown back – and says wondrously that it is just like your mother's, how about that. He likes to talk about her, was fond of her, always teasing, asking her to marry him. He says he always likes a woman with narrow shoulders and runs his fingers along your collarbone, to see if you'll do, appraising you like a horse.

At his touch, your stomach feels as if it is being steamrollered.

You catch your breath. You step back.

He laughs.

You are not allowed to know, understand, exactly what this man now does; no one will tell you. All you perceive is that you are not like one of those women he employs and never will be; you will always be apart, removed, from that world.

He says with a smile that you're like a little bush filly he had as he was growing up, with some thoroughbred mixed in there somewhere, wild and sweet and strong and untamed inside that ridiculous school uniform with its skirt too long and its Peter Pan collar and then he looks at you gravely and says he doesn't want to see the wildness broken, ever, any of it, as he runs his fingers along your collarbone again; as your stomach churns again.

He makes you vividly aware of your teenage body.

Ripening.

The power of it.

Lesson 31

The only way to make people good is to make them happy

_____

A weekend at home. Your father picks you up from the train station, a legitimate drive that your stepmother has to allow. His fingertips stray absently to your earlobe, the old caress, and you shut your lids and feel the coming wet prickling in your eyes at the tenderness, so rare in your life, so ached for. Kindness will always crack you now, it is the legacy of your emotionally blunted childhood.

He doesn't say he loves you. He just gives you his snippet of a touch. It is all you need, it is enough.

Your father's philosophy of parenting has become: if you want a child to do well you ignore them, so the child will always be striving for attention. It is the rhythm of your boarding life.

'Look at me. Say something. Notice. *Respond!*'

You have been screaming it to him silently your entire time away; it is why you do so well in your new school, determined, focused, competitive. It's the only area of your life you can achieve in. Get right. You've always been a thinker, have always devoured anything you could get your hands on to read, being starved of words has worked. Your father doesn't engage in any of it. Doesn't read, doesn't write. The few times you have caught him at it – writing a cheque or a shopping list – he takes careful pleasure in the beauty of the letters, each one strikingly formed, every stroke a pattern, which betrays that he is still a relative beginner; he doesn't do it much.

And now, in the car, on the way home, his touch. You lean into it. Then as soon as you arrive with a screech of the handbrake and walk into the house he clamps down, no longer shows you the vivid pulse of this love. Is formal, distant, uninterested; veering into coldness, a different person entirely. What is he afraid to show her? What has she threatened?

You're his *daughter*.

When you're at school, in his few, precious phone calls to you – from the mine crib room, never at home – he almost pleads, *don't forget the old man loves ya*, and it's like a momentary weakness, a slip. What bewitchment has she woven around him? What weakness in him lets her? A grown man. So inarticulate, so cowed.

An earlobe caressed; a moment snatched, in secret, too brief. The only warmth you will ever get in this place now.

You will find something else.

Lesson 32

We have only to deal with facts — perhaps incapable of
remedy, but by no means incapable of amelioration

It is decided. At fourteen.

You will be an archivist, a collector. Of love and everything
that comes with it. You will learn how it happens, where it comes
from, how it's snared. For good. Your grand and meticulous
experiment. You are aching to begin but do not know how. You
must go beyond the four houses huddling under their looming
trees, beyond the high convent walls; you just long for touch,
warmth. A proper, sustained caress.

You feel so vividly. All your nerve endings are raw, opening
out. You are poised, on the brink. Of something, God knows
what.

It begins with water.

The house of your grandparents. Whom you cherish but
see all too rarely; they've retired further north up the coast, six
hours' drive away, and it's not often that they make it to the
Big Smoke to retrieve you.

Inside the house, your nanna communicates all her
strength through food — veggies are made lurid with bicarb

soda, there's an endless supply of apple and gramma pies, of custard and porridge, sugary tea and tarts. Her domain is a resolutely interior world. But outside, she has no idea what her little granddaughter's getting up to, never enquires about her becoming a woman, except to ask once if her 'friends' have visited yet.

'What?'

'You know, your *friends*. Your monthlies.'

'Oh,' and you're laughing. 'Oh yes, just.'

But outside, in your grandparents' back yard, your new world. Swimming to the pebble dash side of the pool, to the filter hole the size of a fifty-cent coin, to the water coming out at high pressure. Hooking your legs over the edge and holding your hands firm and then the deliciousness coming and you're stretching back, delirious, buoyed and grinning under your wide blue sky then floating your arms wide and arching your back. And inside the house your grandparents are going about their business, completely oblivious to your jet-pressure secret; your nanna who told you once she always hated sex and your pop doing his crosswords then heading off to the club for a game of bowls.

But you, outside, on your back.

Seared by wonder, made silly by it.

Lesson 33

You cannot dawdle away a whole forenoon

You are achingly alone, no anchor, no sense of belonging, of who you really are. But alone, you are learning what you can do with your body, your instrument, coaxing it into technicolour life.

Lune has stolen two *Penthouses* from the pile under her brother's bed; she slips you one.

Lune has bribed her older sister with a year's worth of pedicures and manicures; she buys you each a vibrator.

You squirrel your booty home.

Your hot breathlessness as you open the magazine, as you stare at the pictures. As you devour the letters to the editor at the front, the stories that transform you into something else. In the bathroom, while your stepmother is on her weekly supermarket shop, you slip out the vibrator and turn it over and over and wonder where to begin. Turn it on, turn it off, again, and hold it close, spread-eagled on the cold tiles, terrified she'll come back.

You work out an orgasm for yourself. You're confused by the female physiology. It doesn't make sense, all the nerve endings are on the outside and not the inside where they should be, shouldn't they, what's going on? You wonder if it's just you; if you're built wrong.

But the clit.

The power lying dormant in it. What it can transform you into. The first time where you have completely, utterly let go. Jolted into life. Combusted, with light.

Lesson 34

One may see many a young woman who has, outwardly
speaking, 'everything she can possibly want', absolutely
withering in the atmosphere of a loveless home

In school holidays, at home, your days are spent as far as
possible from your stepmother. She has won, there is nothing
left of your mother or yourself; she completely, triumphantly
owns her tiny life. A baby still hasn't come and you had hoped,
once, that would make her soften towards her stepdaughter,
but it only seems to harden the pushing away: you the constant
reminder of your mother's victory over her.

But beyond Anne, in the bush – your world – it doesn't
matter; you don't need any of it.

You stride with relief through the dry flick of grasshoppers
in long grass bristling with sound, through congregations of
cockatoos snowing the paddocks and watch them lifting like
clouds from the trees and you are strong in it, so strong, vividly
alone and filled up with air and light; your hair matted, your
soles permanently toughened.

Remembering the child you once were. Marinated by light.

At school, among the other girls, you are riddled with
awkwardness. At having to join them, be one of them, and you

will never belong, they all know that but here you are different, you are your true self. Balloon girl, zippy with happiness, flying on your Peddly, firm, confident; it is your default mode whenever you are back in your world.

At sunset the golden light washes like a mist over the land and then the sun dips behind a hill and the glow is snuffed out, so sudden, and the night chill is there; you gaze from your verandah at the spill of stars and the watching moon and the sky running away and then move to your bed and your hand slips between your legs and the vividness begins, in your head, the technicolour movies, every night, to lull you to sleep: people watching you – fresh, prized, *wanted*; an entirely different world to this; a house of beauty and abundance, of books and talk and laughter and warmth; men, many of them; your legs parted, on your back, your fast breathing, your hot wet.

All that you have, the only power that you have, lies in your body. You are fourteen, you have no other power in your life.

At night, alone, in command, confident; the open wound of your life forgotten, the rawness that can only be sutured by love, the necessary verb.

To rescue.

To *combust*.

III

'In this one small thing at least it seems
I am wiser – that I do not think I know what
I do not know'

Socrates

In this one small thing, at least, it seems

that I am not what I once was. What

I do not know

Lesson 35

Tenderly reared young ladies

The art room.

A new teacher. Mr Cooper.

A man.

Extremely rare in this place. He is one of a series where visiting artists run workshops in the school, explaining what they do; he is collected by the parents of Sophia Smegg, the richest girl in the class. He is young. A painter, apparently, a good one – his work has already been hung in the Archibald Prize.

His trousers have worn, grubby knees and paint splatters; a red sock peeps from the toe of a sneaker. He has made no concession to being in this place of constraint.

You are riveted. You are not the only one. You can taste the alertness in the air. And as the entire class of fourteen year olds gaze at this new specimen in their midst, something happens to his trousers. They grow. They stick out. At the crotch. It is excruciating, it is fascinating, it is appalling. Every girl in the class knows what it is. Every girl in the class cannot take their eyes from it. The entire phalanx of girls is silent, spellbound. Mr Cooper's face reddens, he has barely begun his talk. He falls silent.

He excuses himself.

Mr Cooper does not come back.

He has left the school, it is understood.

The next artist is a porcelain painter, a woman of seventy-six.

None of you know what happened after Mr Cooper left the room. You suspect he exited so rapidly because of deep embarrassment; couldn't face any of you again and you are intrigued by that, the blushing, mortification, vulnerability.

So. Mr Cooper. Gone from your life. And you will never forget. The power in you, in all of you. That collectively you could do this to him.

You feel too much, think too much; the intensity of the fantasies, every night before sleep. The *Penthouses*, at home on weekends, for when you are alone, vividly alone; you cannot look too much, it is unbearable, the intensity. And it is not the pictures of the men that excite you, intrigue you, it is the women; the men look terrifying, you cannot deal with that bit, but at night, every night, to lull you into sleep, the movie begins in your head. You are fourteen, you are not meant to know any of this. You are intrigued by your body, the concentration of what's between your legs, the potency of it, the way it changes its viscosity, its dynamism – what is it for? Your hand, in wonder, exploring.

Your life hasn't begun yet. When will it? You are aching for it to start.

Lesson 36

Would it raise the value of men's labour to depreciate ours?
Or advantage them to keep us, forcibly, in idleness, ignorance,
and incapacity? I trow not.

You have a fascination with artists, creators, thinkers; people
who express and reveal and articulate. Because you come
from a world that resolutely does not and as you get older
the exclusion from family and home and hearth – the lack of
explanation, the silence – only gets worse.

Your father walks into your verandah room one Saturday and
almost steps on a canvas flung across the room, a self-portrait
screaming its paint, and murmurs, 'Sometimes I wonder what
I've raised.' Serious, befuddled, fearful. Of the female with a
voice in his midst.

In your early twenties you will say to him, 'You know, Dad,
some time I'd like to write a book.' And he will respond, swiftly,
'Waste of time, that,' and never sway from his thinking and the
distance will grow even wider between you. The two Chinas
joined at the hip, once, bush mates – and that chasm will only
be broached when you become a parent yourself; put in your
proper place. Normalised. To your father, come good at last.
And by then the writing dream will have long gone because

you have always taken heed of what your father says; he is that ingrained in you, you have wanted to please him that much.

But at fourteen, you crave difference. So, the obsession with artists, creators, thinkers, the opposite of anything you have known in your life. All that: an escape. A world where people communicate honestly and openly; touch, laugh, cherish, seize life, sizzling like luminous fireflies in the dark; feel deeply and passionately, yes, yes, all that.

Lesson 37

Whatsoever ye do, do it heartily

_____

Friday afternoon. Central Station. You have just bought your train ticket to get you home for the weekend; you are walking across the concourse.

Ahead. Mr Cooper.

You, in your school uniform.

He glances at you, blushes. You are one of those girls he never wants to see again in his life; the whole school is laughing about it, at him. It is a split second, a moment. You could walk straight past him, not look.

You walk up to him.

'Are you OK?' Not knowing why that comes out, all you can think of is his reddening face, the vulnerability, the sweetness in it. It makes him oddly approachable.

'Yes,' he stammers, bewildered. 'Were you … ?'

'Do you live near here?' Blurting it out, covering up his awkwardness.

'Yes, my studio's across the road.'

'A real, live studio?' Your eyes sparkle. 'Wow.'

'Yes,' he laughs. 'It's disgustingly messy, I'm sure it'd disappoint you.'

'No!' In the presence of a man you are blushing, changing, becoming something else. Losing the sharp flint; have you ever been like this?

'Come and have a look.'

You nod, barely knowing why or what you are getting yourself into, words won't come, you've lost your voice, your heart is thumping, you walk beside him, your insides flipping. If only the other girls in your class could see you now. Something, someone, has taken over your body, your talk. Your curiosity has emboldened you; yes, the experiment will start here, now. You have to do this, you need to know.

'You don't have somewhere to go, do you?' he says at the entrance of his scruffy building.

'My train's delayed. Trackwork. I've got an hour to kill.'

The lie slips out, it surprises you, the ease of it. And the impertinence of your voice, your boldness – the collector, the archivist, with a task to complete.

'My parents don't like me hanging around Central alone.' A pause. 'I don't like it.'

Your desire for friendship, companionship, someone, anyone, is insatiable; your desire, too, to have something, one thing, over all those girls in your class, over their ease and smoothness and confidence, their sense of entitlement. You can't wait to tell Lune. She'll be so proud of you. An artist, the coolness of that. *The* artist. Yours.

It is beginning.

*

And you are following this man from the railway concourse because of something else that has recently crept into your life. The possibility of aloneness, all through your days. You feel you could be very good at being alone and it frightens you; needs arresting.

Lesson 38

Easy, pleasant and beautiful as it is to obey,
development of character is not complete
when the person is fitted only to obey

_____

His studio is in a warehouse, a proper one, whose second floor is reached by a scuffed and clanking goods lift. You say nothing as you are lifted high, high, but you are breathing tremulous, fast, clutching the straps of your backpack. Not looking, biting your lip, scarcely believing you are doing this. Trying not to show him anything of the great churning within you. He is wearing jeans and t-shirt, he looks different, a student himself. He shares the space with three other people, it is a hot Friday afternoon, they are out.

He gives you some lemonade. Lemonade! You are not allowed it at home.

You sit at the table, he accidently brushes your leg as he sits, you pretend not to notice, breathe shallow. You look around. Tacked on the wall are various postcards from galleries, and photographs, black and white and colour. Your eye rests on a print of a painting, a woman naked, the artist looking straight up her legs.

The meticulous detail.

He catches you looking.

'Courbet. *The Origin of the World*.'

A prickly silence. You don't want to look away, in shock, don't want to give him that; can feel a familiar tingling, in your belly, between your legs.

'Incredibly bold for way back then.' A pause. 'And now.'

You nod. Blush. The good student, taking in your lesson.

He stands in front of you. The bulge between his legs has grown again, he is right in front of you.

'Do you want to sit for me?' he breathes.

You try to still your breath.

So, this is it. You close your eyes, nod, can't speak. Finally you will learn how love happens, touching and cherishing and nourishing and wanting, *you*, just you; you will learn where love comes from, how it's snared, yes, this is the beginning of everything.

You stand, your finger finds the back of the chair, you don't know what to do next.

He strokes your cheek. It slips down. Over your neck, chest, breast. Something is taking you over, a vast yes. You are angling up your arms and awkwardly unzipping your school uniform, and now he is helping you, he is undressing you, leading you; reaching behind your back, as if this moment will disappear if he doesn't hurry, stumbling with the clasp and finally slipping off your small, pale bra then kneeling and holding his face to your skin, your quivering skin and with a great sigh burying himself in you, breathing you in. And staying there, staying.

Then his fingers. Slowly, slowly, like a daddy longlegs. Working their way into your white cotton panties.

Spidering inside, to your core, your great warmth; slowly prising your legs apart. You watch him watching, his mouth parted, his breathing. You are intrigued – his face, that you can do this to another person.

Transform them.

The power in that, and you have never felt such power in your life as he undresses you until there is nothing left.

So wet you feel you could crumble with it, now, buckle with his touch. You clutch his hair. Your legs collapse under you. He catches you and lays you on a worn Persian rug on the floor. Stands over you, smiles, assesses. Whips off his t-shirt.

Picks up a paintbrush.

Lesson 39

Would that, instead of educating our young girls with the
notion that they are to be wives, or nothing — we could instil
into them the principle that, above and before all,
they are to be women

You feel suddenly, brutally, exposed.

'Uh uh,' he admonishes, as your legs instinctively entwine,
shutting you away.

The rug is threadbare, thin, you can feel the sharpness of the
floorboards underneath.

He unzips his trousers, fast, and you are astonished at the
length of his penis, the size of it, it looks so big, it could never
fit.

'Are you a virgin?' he asks.

Yes, you nod, breathe, biting your lip, can scarcely talk.

'How old are you?'

'Fourteen.'

'*No one* must know we're doing this.' No talk in his voice,
just breath.

'Yes.' Your face turns away, to the Courbet, so this is what
women do, all women, you will learn, it is time.

'I don't know if I –' you suddenly blurt, the voice of a child.

'Sssh,' he says.

You glance across at his canvases, stacked against walls and on easels, the paint is viscous, tumultuous, raw; among the portraits are some other ones, secret ones, bodies, just bits, never a face; men and women, their genitals in stark, cold, medical close-up. You look and look at those ones and then something cold touches you, playfully, and you start; the paintbrush, it parts your lips, you yelp in shock, it brushes your clit, plays with the entrance of your secret interior, then slithers across your mouth and your taste the tang of it, of you. And he dips the brush inside, gentle but insistent and you gag and he stops, it goes back to your clit and your stomach flips and despite yourself you're suddenly opening your legs wider, wider, surrendering, arching your back and gasping, suddenly, and there is a great warmth, a tingling, something is taking over you, you are becoming someone else.

Who opens herself. Who is turned over. Who lifts her buttocks out, high to the sky, wanting, waiting, for God knows what, as the tip of the brush plays, explores. Teases and you wince and flop – no, this is going too fast, it's too unknown. All of it. You twist onto your back, legs clamped.

'You're beautiful,' he says, matter-of-fact, smiling, placing the paintbrush back in a crammed jar. You look at him, no one has ever said you are beautiful before. A blush roars through your body.

'I really want to paint you.'

You nod, the good girl, still biting your lip.

'Now,' he whispers.

But the spell is broken, you should be getting back, the golden light of late afternoon is slanting too obliquely through the tall, dusty windows and you must hurry to catch the next train, you'll be just in time for Dad to not be worried if you go now, quick.

'Next Friday,' you manage to stumble out. 'Same time.' Don't know what you're saying.

His fingertip draws a line across the top of your pubis, then slowly, slowly – as your belly rolls under him – his touch, teasing in the crevices and you rise to it you meet it then his finger darts inside, once, with a swift, hard jerk; he hooks you; you tense in shock. The tone, in an instant, has shifted into something else.

'Our secret, remember. No one must ever, ever know about this.'

You are too young for this, you are not sure, you shouldn't; you are the good girl. You nod, next Friday, yes.

Desperate to begin.

Living. Loving. Life.

You need this.

You are on a path now, you cannot turn back.

Lesson 40

Let us turn from the dreary, colourless lives
of the women who have nothing to do

_____

The thirstlands.

All through that week and if anyone touches you, brushes by you – near your midriff, belly, chest – you will implode. All nerve endings raw and clenched at the thought of him, and pants damp, soaked with want. Lune gives you a secret smile whenever she catches your eye; you're a woman now, more woman than her and you both know it. For the first time in your life you have something over her, over all of them, and it makes you walk tall, bold, right down the centre of the convent corridors with their polished parquet floors – you are becoming someone else. No more hugging the walls in this place, you are embarking on a new life.

Before you catch the bus that will take you to Central Station you change out of your school uniform, preparing for him, making sure you have more time this visit.

The force of the anticipation, as if a great hand has brushed a sheen of varnish over the tepidness of your life.

*

He smiles a triumphant smile as you step from the lift.

'Well well, I wasn't sure you'd come back.'

He is not wearing trousers, just a t-shirt. He is ready.

You hesitate, not sure why; roaming the kitchen, looking at anything but him as he gazes at you like a quarry caught, smiling his smile while he retrieves a lemonade for his guest and a beer for himself, opening it with one finger and still looking. Undressing you, with his eyes, as your fingers scurry to the buckles of your braces in self-consciousness.

There is a photograph on the battered fridge of three women, one of them is heavily pregnant, they are wearing bikinis on some deserted beach. 'My flatmate. The middle one,' he says. CWA is emblazoned in red lipstick across each of their tummies.

'C.W.A.?'

'Cunts With Attitude,' he laughs. 'I've painted the lot of them.'

Women who seem a world apart from you with their brazenness, bluntness. As does that word and the way they have colonised it; you've never heard it spoken aloud, thought it was only used by men who don't like women very much.

'Come on. Let's get going.'

A new briskness in his voice.

'We don't have much time.'

You turn. Take a deep breath. So, this is it. A fresh canvas waits in readiness. The Courbet print is high in its corner with a slice of masking tape. He comes up to you with his knowing smile and unclips you, bold, just like that he draws off your t-shirt and whips off your bra; impatience in his fingers now.

You step back.

He grabs your hips, rubs, close. Cups your buttocks under your underpants, draws you into him.

Right, it must be done, now, this is what you have always wanted, dreamt of – a painter, an artist, you are complicit in this; there will be your triumph over the other schoolgirls, your difference, you cannot go back.

He spits on his fingers. Gosh, so that is what men must do. A wet finger slips inside you. Another.

Feel him, exploring. Your eyes blink, smart.

Lesson 41

No power on earth can give you back that jewel of glory
and strength — your innocence

———————

Urgent now. Propelling you onto a well-worn fifties couch.
Whipping off your undies. Snatching up a paintbrush, clamping
it between his teeth. Standing over you, cocking his head, nudging
your legs apart. Lifting one knee casually into a crook, with his
foot; placing your own foot wider on the couch, wider, it hurts.

'Touch yourself,' he murmurs.

You frown, what? But you know, you have seen it in Lune's
magazines, you know instinctively. Your fingers stray, he is
holding his penis.

'Slip inside,' he breathes, directing, as his fingers move slowly,
up, down, and you touch yourself, obey, the good girl. Is this
right, asks your frown, your concentrating face. He nods.

'Yes, yes, keep going.' You close your eyes, try to lose yourself,
touch yourself like you do at night, every night, when the wet
comes, the flooding.

'That's it. Perfect.'

So.

The learning has begun, the collating of experience; you
must do as you are told, it all begins from here.

You widen your legs further, further, splaying your fingers and surrendering to the moment, closing your eyes, arching your back, catching your breath. You open your eyes, watch him watching you. The power in it, the spell that your body can cast. Then suddenly, urgently, need something inside, anything, need to be filled up. You gasp, he groans, holding his firm penis then coming close, whispering the paintbrush across your clit, your lips, your secret mouth. 'Deeper,' you whisper, you don't know why, needing it, something, anything, opening your legs wider.

'Good girl,' he whispers back chuffed, then to himself, 'my obedient little schoolgirl,' and you stop, frown, suddenly don't like it.

The tone.

You shut your legs. He's having none of it. He kisses you hard, suddenly, on the lips, a knee rough between your legs, and squeezes your chin firm, twisting your skin, pushing in the intrusion of his tongue and sweeping your mouth like a mine sweeper, kissing you hard as if his lips are wooden. You don't like it anymore, it hurts. He jiggles your breasts, scrunches them up. Flips you over, smartly, like a piece of meat; you're now kneeling with your belly over the couch and you cry out in shock, it's too rough, changed, insistent.

'Wait,' you gasp but he's not listening anymore, now something is between your legs nudging, pushing, bullying; it's too fast, there's no tenderness.

You pull away before it's too late.

'*Stop!*'

Lesson 42

Her poor little bones were crunched between his
dazzling jaws

Stumbling, reeling from his warehouse saturated in its golden light with your legs slightly apart and the ache, in all of you – at your tender parts so sullied, violated. But that is nothing compared to the enormous, flinched hurt of your heart. Where was the mystery, the grace, the empowerment?

There was no you.

In any of it.

From that moment he kissed.

It was wrong, just that.

And you knew in that instant something you will now know for the rest of your life, at the first touch of a man's lips: if it is wrong at that moment then what hope has the relationship got, can it ever endure?

It's all in the kiss.

You recall the lack of tenderness most of all. The violence of that. And the way he spat, sharp, on his fingertips – the cheapness of that gesture. And the sound. Like a fork in fettucini as he worked his way in. Hooked you, hard. In ownership. He had no right.

My good, obedient, little schoolgirl.

The chuff in his new voice. The ugliness. Taken over by someone else, a man you didn't recognise anymore. With … what was it, distance? Yes that, in his tone; you could have been anyone. In an instant he was changed – stripped – his true self and you didn't like it one bit.

Only one thing is certain now: they will never know how much you are watching them.

The way he clumsily jiggled your breasts as if he'd read how to do it in a manual, that this is what turning on a girl was all about. Not *feeling* it. And you, staring at him in shock, at everything he was suddenly doing. Not participating. You have no idea if this is what is meant to happen but it just felt wrong, mechanical, bleak; it was not the sex of your imagination, your mind defrauded you. Or he did.

He didn't *like* women, that was the most shocking lesson from it.

The affronted, luminous pain of the experience is like a bell of sadness inside you, pushing against your skin, as you stumble, dazed, into the late afternoon.

No idea where to go from it.

Lune will know none of it. You shut down, shamed, will never talk of it.

And the knowing, now, one other thing: you are too clever to love anything like that.

Furiously you wipe away the tears, lift your face high to a ravishing sunset. You've got a train to catch.

Lesson 43

The free, happy ignorance of maidenhood is gone forever

In your diary, late that raw, ranging night, you come across a scrap of something from Gabriel Garcia Marquez describing the loss of his virginity as a teenager – how it triggered a vital force within him.

The sense of celebration, the boldness, intrigues and angers you. You wonder if this feeling of empowerment is a particularly male phenomenon. *What* vital force? You've been shocked into silence; in the addled aftermath of this episode you're experiencing a catastrophic loss of spark, of certainty. You can barely record the episode in your diary – the sheer, puny grubbiness of it. Once you felt so cheeky and curious, bold and sure; now, suddenly, you're faltering. What happened back there? As soon as a man put his arm around you something was rubbed out; some inner certainty. Why the leakage of confidence, the capitulation, as you entered the realm of the sexual? Why did you nod and gush so pathetically, saying 'yes please, a studio, wow,' on that concourse?

Your bewilderment, over the lot of it.

You suspect a terrifying secret: that virginity and chastity by choice are the magic elixirs that can make a woman calm, audacious, strong. You will have to find out. You don't know how. The experiment feels almost derailed from the start. Love must be tracked, studied, dissected, yes of course, but you must never allow it to snap you in its strong jaws like a steel trap. No, the jagged pain of your father's withholding has taught you the folly of that.

Lesson 44

Nature's law undoubtedly is that our nearest ties
should be those of blood

Several days with your grandmother.

You need her right now, the certainty of her powdery
smell and flannelette sheets, her unconditional warmth.
You've begged your father and he's complied with phone calls
arranging pick ups and train tickets; as if he senses something
rattling within you that is beyond him and he's more than
happy to palm it off. Women's business, all that emotional
stuff – his mother will sort it out.

You have not told her anything. Does she sense … something?
A changing, a turning.

Over her meat-and-three-veg dinner you talk school and
careers and marriage and life, she asks if you've got a boyfriend
and you shake your head and laugh and she nods – plenty of
time, love, plenty of time – and tells you how good she was,
once, at so much: maths and English, geography and athletics,
but then as soon as a boy put his arms around her she was gone.

'Just like that.'

She married young.

'It was all I wanted, and it killed my ambition, every single scrap of it. And my energy,' she cackles. 'Which was just bursting from me, once.'

You smile, wondering what she sees in you that has changed and why she is saying all this.

Later, as she's tucking you into your bed with its electric blanket on and smoothing down the hair on your forehead, she adds, 'There's a strength about us women that scares men, I think. You keep your chin up, love. Get a degree; be a doctor or a lawyer. Make me proud. Your father too. You could be the first in the family to finish school, let alone university. Your dad left at fourteen to go down the pit, I left to go into service. Do it for us.'

You will not tell her what has happened, will never tell her, it would break her heart.

Lesson 45

To young people, the world is always a paradise

_____

No idea where to go from it.

You shut down. For a couple of years. A spring coiled tight.

Waiting, for God knows what.

Lost.

IV

'I could fancy a love for life here almost
possible …'

Emily Bronte, *Wuthering Heights*

Lesson 46

When it comes to 'each for herself' – when Miss This cannot be asked to a party for fear of meeting Madame That, or if they do meet, through all their smiling civility you perceive their backs are up, like two strange cats meeting at a parlour door – I say, this is the most lamentable of all results which the world effects on women

———

Summer holidays. Eight weeks ahead of thick heat, cicadas, bush-fire alerts.

Your stepmother is ignoring you. It is her one weapon, her only way to have power over you. With silence.

You are too different. You have city-awareness now. You will never lose yourself like she has done, and no matter how much she thinks she has won – when your father doesn't show up to your speech days, when he never talks with the parents of your new friends, when he neglects to set foot in your world – you would never, ever want your stepmother's life. The sourness of it, her closed heart. It is the one power you have over her.

The energy between you is wrong. You could never be her, she could never be you. It is never discussed, but you both know it.

Today she has designated a cleaning day, is buried in a flurry of activity. Sorting through her Tupperware boxes, rinsing and airing – she takes them to gatherings to scoop up leftover food. You can't bear the bustling little world of domesticity she creates around her, crowding out any trace of your mother in this scrap of a house that was renovated by your parents long ago – working side by side, he told you once. And now, an obsessive accumulation of new and shiny possessions from daytime ads on the telly cluttering it up – newfangled mosquito zappers, wall-mounted can-openers, sewing tables, kitchen knife sets.

You have few possessions. Like it that way. Like to see the bones of these old valley houses and their heart, running hands along the old plaster walls like horses' flanks, marvelling at the carpentry in dinky corner cabinets and the bread tins filled with concrete holding up porch roofs and the mouldings of pressed-tin ceilings and the beauty in deco bush flowers scattered in old bathroom tiles, like your own. Tiles now obscured by a stick-on plastic railing and a matching avocado towel set that you know you must keep straight.

So. Cleaning day. And you're jumping on Peddly to get away from it all and smiling at the familiarity of that hard, worn saddle. Feel young again, out, shedding your city skin. You're flinging your bike aside and walking thigh-deep in bleached grass, catching grasshoppers and feeling the dry flick of them inside the bauble of your palm before you free them to leap in a great springing arc of release, laughing, away from your stepmother's narrow, silent, affronted little world.

Go. GO!

*

At three o'clock you return.

You hear her footsteps thudding through the house towards you. Furious. You shut your eyes. What have you done now? There's always something to vex her and usually she doesn't say, it's just in the thud of her step, her contained fury when you're in her space.

She has found your diary.

Which was under your bed, still in your school bag. She has gone into your bedroom, your private place, and dug it out. And read it of course, you know instantly. It's on her face. You have never seen her so incensed, tight, repulsed.

'Get out, you … *thing* … you. I don't want you here. Your words, your filth, in my house.'

'It's *my* place as much as yours. I lived here long before *you*.'

You try snatching the book back but the sturdy girl with her big country thighs has it firm.

'Give it back,' you scream – because it's your words, your truth, everything that has happened in your life. 'You spoil *everything*.' Clawing your hair in frustration, can't make this right, win, can't think fast enough. Your tears in that moment are from years of competitiveness and exhaustion and bafflement – you're his *daughter*, you were a child, you do not understand the jealousy; what you have with your father is a blood tie, a given, a totally different relationship to hers. But you can't speak properly, can't get it out, are clotted before her, as clotted as your father. The only place you can talk is in your diary.

Which she's got.

With everything recorded in it.

That she has done.

The relationship between the three of you is all about the gift of attention, and your father cannot bestow it upon two women at once. And she will win, always. She is an adult and you are not, she knows how to do it; to demand and punish. To withhold what he wants.

You both know that when your father comes back the two of you will be quiet and he will know none of this, the explosive fury between females. That is the code of you both, the only common code you adhere to; this is women's business.

She spits on your diary in contempt. Has no intention of giving it back. Stomps inside with a slap of the screen door. You hear your words being flung across the room in disgust.

And then quiet.

The only power in her life. A withholding.

Lesson 47

Only be honest. No falsehoods,
no concealments of any kind.

But something new.

What honesty can do. The power of it.

She has opened your words and she has read them. All the little incidents over the years, all the hurts, cruelties, vulnerabilities; all the disobedience and confusion and longing and touch. The truth has been forensically trapped. Your meticulous record. And she has been incensed by it.

You smile.

Lesson 48

The most of women are, in their youth at least, decidedly 'adjective'. Few of them have had the chance of becoming a 'noun substantive' — they have been accustomed all their lives to be governed, if not guarded; protected

---

You run far from her world of Tupperware boxes and spotless surfaces, run and run in your bib-and-brace overalls cut off at the knees and your flannelette shirt; dirt girl, sun girl, strong in it. You find your old bush shelter, still there, just, and curl into it.

Stilled by the bubble of the creek. Its insistent coolness. You shut your eyes as the talking water soothes you down; you'll get your book back, you'll find it, she's not so smart.

You jerk up.

Smoke. On the breeze.

Fire.

With a pounding heart you rush back.

She has stoked up the incinerator in its rusty metal drum, is ripping apart your diary's spine and feeding great chunks of it to the flames as methodically as she feeds clothes to the washing machine.

Nooooooooooooo!

Too late. She flings the last chunk of your words into the furnace and turns, and looks at you, saying nothing but everything in her face. She has won. She is burning them because she never wants your father to find the meticulous chronicle of her unkindness. And you know that if you tell him about her cruelty, she will tell him about Central Station.

So. Caught.

Magnificently.

You leap on Peddly, barefoot, the sharp ridges on the pedals press hard into your bare feet but you need that, need the pain to blot everything else out and you spin and ride away from her, faster and faster, away from the claustrophobia; the enormous swamping of hate.

You won't be hurrying back. Teaching them, teaching *her*.

Forcing them to care. To notice. Finally, please.

By absence. *Your* withholding.

Lesson 49

Does ever any man or woman remember the feeling of being 'whipped' — as a child — the fierce anger, the insupportable ignominy, the longing for revenge?

_____

Gulping your shock, pushing your bike down dirt roads, further and further away from her, down fire trails scarcely used and barely noticing what you're doing, where you're going. Wiping away furious tears as you pedal by a tall wire fence you've barely noticed in the past, an anonymous, official-looking barrier hiding away some old mine you've never given a second thought to; but stopping, this time, skidding in the dirt.

Its double gate is open. The sturdy chain always locking it hangs limp.

'B.M.C.' declares a sign on the gate: the Something Mining Company. Of course. So what.

'No Trespassers. No Shooters.'

Right. But you're not a trespasser, you're an observer; you're not going to steal or destroy anything. It's just that in all your life this gate has never been ajar and you can't *not* do this. You feel the old sizzle of curiosity revving up. A mine of your own, an enormous playground to colonise, hide away in, to fall down a shaft and be rescued by your father, after several days in an agony of unknowing; his arms in a furious embrace of relief and love and torment.

Imagine her face at that.

Maybe there's a rusty tower you can climb, a queen surveying the roof of her world; maybe a metal cage that sinks to the hot, drippy bowels of the earth; an abandoned office with a typewriter and forgotten safe. Mine records in meticulous ink, faded photographs, mysterious pulleys and rail tracks. Who knows what's in there. A washroom containing lockers with forgotten treasures – penknives and hard hats, tin cribs and cap lamps. You once snuck near the washroom of your father's mine and caught the men with their shirts hanging off their waists as they prepared to slough away the black dust from the bowels of the earth; the torsos and taut flesh, so different to the men of the city, so different to Mr Cooper with his softness, round shoulders, paleness, city sweat. You are addicted to the unknown, love not knowing what to expect.

No Trespassers. No Shooters.

You are neither. You are a lookaholic.

You push your bike through the gate.

Lesson 50

The wicked world without

A narrow dirt road. Forbidding trees. Trunks leaning from high banks. Not a mine road, you know that almost instantly, and not a welcome place. You do not turn back. Glints of light flash through the trees. You feel your back prickling up: *go away* it all seems to be saying as you climb higher, higher, and start to pant, standing up on the pedals of your bike and pushing hard as the spikes dig spitefully into your feet. The twisted bark of the trees spirals as if a furious wind has whipped it but then at the top it all clears, magically, into an exhilarating table top and you smile in wonder: a cap of cleared land awaits.

But not a mine at all.

A house.

A colonial mansion. Honey sandstone. You never knew it existed; that your dusty, blackened valley could conceal something so beautiful. Two storeyed, a verandah like a collar around it. Tall windows are blank or shut off by corrugated iron like a blindfold over a face, daylight floods from the front door to the back.

You fling your bike down a ditch. Creep forward on high alert; someone might be in it, might react. No shooters, but they could have a gun themselves, you never know in these parts. As you approach, the thick shrill of cicadas – their deafening chorus – abruptly stops, as crisp as an orchestra. It's as if the whole world is watching, listening, waiting. A trickle of sweat rolls down your stomach. The tin roof cracks in the heat, from somewhere a door bangs shut, you jump; the breeze, just that. By the front door is a brass nameplate mottled by age and neglect. *Woondala*.

The far left corner, ground level: a shadow of movement through shredded lace curtains.

Someone inside. Right. You lick your lips. Catch sight of an old car parked to the side of the house. A Volvo, playful and low and nothing like the boxy ones now, corroding with rust and as faded as the building. You can't go back. You have to investigate. You hope the old wooden floorboards on the verandah won't creak and with a pounding heart inch to the window as silently as an Aboriginal tracker. The lace of the curtains is fragile, feminine, blackened and hanging in strips.

A man.

His back to you.

He seems to be working but you can't make it out. Leaning over a bench that runs almost the length of the room, an industrial high table. On it, resting against the wall, is a line of objects with the precision of a museum arrangement: shells as big as fans, plaster cornices, photos in tarnished silver frames, dried seed pods, teapot fragments, old plates as wide as clocks. You look and look. You have blundered into a secret place. A magpie's lair of loveliness.

You cannot move, transfixed.

The man is bending over his bench with the concentration of a monk at an illuminated manuscript. He is left-handed. You always notice this and trust it; you also are left-handed, close friends always seem to be. His hand curves awkwardly around a pen with such complete absorption that to disturb it would feel like violence; it curves just as yours does, as if you've never properly learnt how to do it. He is dressed like no man you have ever seen, there is something English about it, careful, a traveller perhaps, a collector of some sort. You have no idea what he is doing except that it is something completely consuming and a great warmth spreads through you, a dipping in your belly: you want all of it, all – his desk, house, stillness, car, work, this entire secret place. So close! A world utterly alien in terms of everything in your life. And you were expecting corrugated sheds and conveyor belts; coarse language, heavy work boots.

There is a great silence – the silence of creativity, of being lost in a world that's not physically around you. He never looks up. He wiggles his finger in his ear, runs his hand through a flop of fringe, hitches up his belt; trying to make something work and frustrated with it but not giving up. He never looks around, trusts this place. No one will disturb it. You bet he has no idea his gate is open, it's an oversight that won't be repeated, you'll never get inside here again and don't know what to do with the gift of it. All you can see is his back, the grace in it, and all you can feel is something unfurling within you as you look, and look.

You have fallen for a flop of hair and the curve of a back.

How can that be? So fast, just a back, a hand through a fringe, irrational and senseless but you're always doing this; with boys on a bus or behind the counter of a milk bar or in a school art room. All it takes is the nape of a neck, the shyness in a glance, a curve in a lip and you're gone, instantly. The mere idea of them.

And now this.

You turn away, your back against the wall, the man inside oblivious. So, one of the ones you've fallen for and they're always the men you can never talk smoothly to, of course. You could never approach him now; your voice would be stopped up and your face held hostage by a furious blush and a tongue like felt in your mouth. You should go. You should leave this place and never come back.

Can't.

Lesson 51

It is the women who poke about with undefended farthing
candles in the choke-damp passages of this dangerous world

He walks to the window – you flick away. Fingers curl around
the sill; he's gazing out. Clean nails, blunt, not the hands of
this land.

His difference.

Your back pressing into the sandstone next to him, your
roaring heart.

You glance down in panic at your dirt-laden overalls and
grubby shirt; you look like a gypsy child, a bush scamp. His
footsteps walk away, returning to his bench. You exhale. You
must go now, quick, but there's too much to absorb, work out.
And there's stubbornness here too, a need to stay out until
the worry's well and truly festering back home. Something
dangerous and wilful is colouring this: the desire to alarm.
You run across the yard and climb a tree that shelters you in its
crook like a great, curving hand, and wait.

For goodness knows what.

Reading his land. The fallen branches bleached to the colour
of bone in the paddocks. The barely there circular driveway – a
past pretension. Fences drooping like a Dali painting, keeping

nothing out. Or in. The scrub winning as it encroaches; the greedy lantana, the bush tomatoes. This place hasn't hosted humans for a very long time. He doesn't understand it, what will happen soon, the triumphant erasure of all of it. He's not a bushy, it's in everything about him – the curve of his hand around his pen and the sound of his footsteps and his clothes – he wouldn't be able to read this place and protect it. Like you can.

He comes out. Walking differently to any man you've ever known, not quite right, as if his hips are too swivelly and his feet are compensating, especially the right. It doesn't detract, it intrigues; you want to help him. God knows what's next. This afternoon already feels tattooed upon your life.

He holds a mug of something hot. Runs his hand through his hair; he's buggered, deserves this break. He sits on the top verandah step cradling his mug in both hands, squinting at … what? The stretch of sky, a kookaburra staring straight at him, the land. He's completely relaxed in it; the chuff of ownership. A dog pads out and shakes its head as if it has just emerged from sleep. A golden retriever but the colour of amber. It settles close. The man's hand reaches out without looking and plays with its ear with the absent-minded fondness your dad used to have with your own earlobe, long ago, as he was driving. The dog shuffles closer and rests its nose on his thigh in perfect peace. The man leans his head against the verandah post and shuts his eyes, basking in the repairing light.

Then glances at his watch. Stands abruptly. Flings away the remains of his tea in a whip of gold. Strides inside.

You start. He might be driving off, locking the gate. You can't be trapped overnight – can't get over that fence and God knows how many days, weeks, months he'll be gone from this place. Before you're out of the suddenly difficult tree he's slamming down his study window and hurrying from the house with his dog at his heels and jumping in the car and driving off, fast.

You slice your leg as you slither down the bark, feel the hot wet of blood, barely notice. You have to get out of here. You grab your bike and streak after him, pedalling furiously, stumbling over rocks. Damn. A puncture. Fling Peddly aside, and sprint.

He's gone by the time you get to the entrance. The thick chain is now padlocking the double gate. A gap of just ten centimetres. You can't, can't squeeze through. And mean little triangles of wire are too tiny to get your bare feet into, they slice into your soles, it's impossible. The fence is three times your height.

You're stuck.

The only one here.

No one knows where you are.

Trapped with a broken bike and a house full of ghosts.

For goodness knows how long.

You dive into the fence in frustration with your hands clenched, it catches your weight and mocks you with its bounce. It's new wire, it's not letting you out.

Lesson 52

We *must* help ourselves

The late-afternoon air is keen with coming rain. Lost people die in this valley. You will have to find shelter, water, warmth.

You return to Woondala, your best bet. A huge, spreading pine grows to the side of it and the wind whistles strangely through its needles as if it is telling you to be gone, this place is not for humans, the rest have been pushed out in the dropping light. The house is neglected except for the corner you found him in: he's obviously working his way through the rooms, waking it up, but it's an enormous task.

The kitchen has been fixed to a serviceable level. Just. A kettle on a portable gas hob rests by a wide, whitewashed, colonial hearth. A bathroom has rusty-coloured water from its tap – water, thank God – and a toilet that flushes when a broken chain is yanked. A box of tissues is beside it. A bedroom has a mattress on the floor and a single pillow with the indent of a head in it and not much else. His workroom is locked, the battered iron knob of its door won't budge.

The only thing locked in this place.

You thread through other rooms, the thick stone outer walls like a blanket around you. The house has the feeling of being abandoned in great haste, as if news of a coming pestilence has forced everyone to flee in a single afternoon. There are scatterings of past lives, generations of them – convicts, fragrant mistresses, Edwardian children, Aboriginal cooks, ghosts.

Various walls are covered with newspapers from the last century and pages from the *Bulletin* magazine, and in one room sheets of old bush poetry, at head height by a bed: Percy Russell, Henry Lawson, Banjo Paterson, Dora Wilcox. Thick wide plates crazed with age from some grandness long ago line the pantry, spotted silver spoons and forks in rusty old billy cans are collected on a bench along with encrusted black cooking pots. A tarnished silver candelabra is lonely in the grate of a fireplace. A grand piano awaits in what looks like the remains of a drawing room; keys are missing and possum droppings are scattered on its lid and a stool is drawn and quartered with its horsehair matting tumbling out. A line of five attached theatre chairs watch – God knows what – in an incongruous row. A hessian chaise longue broods in a corner, pining for another chance. Leather-bound books are stacked upstairs by the frames of iron bed heads. Dropped cigars, whisky bottles, stirrups, buttons, empty cotton reels, mustard jars, coins – they all litter rooms gloomed down by corrugated-iron sheets over windows, the insistent light of afternoon straining through in precise pinpoints.

That light feels like it will eventually triumph in this house, it will one day reach into every window and corner and through the roof until only the strong outer walls will be left. Some rooms, on the top floor, already ring with air and emptiness.

And waiting.

You could do so much with this place. With all your bush knowledge, all the watching over the years, everything your father has taught. You spin – a smile filling you up – imagining where you'd start.

Lesson 53

A solid, useful, available happiness

Now you're standing tall in the attic with its windows punched out to the sky, surveying the vastness around you. This is big sky land. What a find, what a jewel, secure in its corporate disguise as a disused mine. Clever, that. Beside the house is a small, muddy dam the colour of milky tea that looks perfect for a dip on a stinker of a day and rocks like sentinels litter the hills and you stare at the stately migration of clouds across this tall ceiling of blue and the hum of the wind crawls into your skin and always, somewhere, are birds, their sound cramming the air – bellbirds, whip birds, currawongs, kookaburras.

Kookaburras!

Which means that somewhere, soon, is rain. You look to the south, a chill is already staining the sky. A southerly buster is hurrying upon you, ready to crack the back of the heat. You wrap your arms around your thinness and retreat, alone and not welcome in this place.

Need distraction. Something that eats up the wait. You return to a room upstairs of stacked books, flick through them. Old farming manuals, geology guides, a book of sheep breeding, a volume of Shakespeare, *For the Term of His Natural Life* and some type of manual for women, *A Woman's Thoughts About Women*.

The thick card cover falls away in your hand and you yelp – you've broken it. *1858, London*, it says on the brittle first page that is spotted with the circular droppings of insects. *Hurst and Blackett, Great Marlborough Street, London*.

Great. Impossible to replace, and probably worth buckets.

You begin to read. The reassuring voice hooks you like a hand around your neck, drawing you in. You smile and settle on your belly, caught.

Tell the truth and don't be afraid of it.

Yes of course. It's the only power you've got, the only way to be noticed in this life.

In this book many women will find simply the expression of what they have themselves, consciously or unconsciously, often times thought; and the more deeply, perhaps, because it has never come to the surface in words or writing.

Who was this woman? You flick through the book, the front, the back. It doesn't say. Anywhere. All you've got to go on is the warm, knowing tone of her voice. It feels like she's been married for decades and had a dozen kids; there's a richness of living in her words; a certainty you've rarely known.

This book has been planned and completed, honestly, carefully, solemnly, even fearfully, with a keen sense of all it might do.

You stand, pocketing the little tome.

Lesson 54

Courage inexhaustible! Sustain it under difficulties,
misfortunes and rebuffs of every conceivable kind

Now you're wandering his house, agitated, the air laden with
its coming storm. The stillness is banking up at the windows,
pushing at the walls, wanting in before the rain comes and
hammers the valley in great sheets; you can read this sky. His
sky. Yours. You are nervy, skittery, you take off your flannelette
shirt and wipe your brow with it; bathing your skin in coolness,
God knows when you'll get rescued from this place. You return
to the bedroom and lie like a Goldilocks on the mattress, your
head in the hollow of the pillow. It smells adult – hair oil, male
sweat, ingrained sleeps.

Time slips by. The storm threatens, all talk no substance.
Your cheeky little Victorian manual is your only comfort in
the fading light.

*My young lady friend, your time, and the use of it, is as
essential to you as to any father or brother of you all.*

*A lady of my acquaintance has as her sine qua non of
domestic felicity, that the 'men of the family' should
always be absent at least six hours in the day.*

In this much-suffering world, a woman who can take care of herself can always take care of other people.

Far safer to call crime by its right name – treating it even as The Ragged Schools did the young vagabonds of our streets.

You wonder what a ragged school was, smiling as you curl on the bed, devouring the tiny print. The sky is still pregnant with rain yet it doesn't fall, everything is waiting, poised: the world outside softens as night comes stealing in, dusk is like a thin film of milk washing over the land. You read on, fast, before you lose the light; there are candles but no matches in this place. The night pushes up the band of sunset in the sky and finally you close your book, defeated by the gloom. The distant thunder rumbles in the floorboards, far away, moving on to somewhere else and you can feel the house talk, willing you out, leaving it to its darkness. If you don't return to Beddy soon it will mean search parties – your father will be home shortly from his afternoon shift, wondering where you are. It will mean helicopters and sniffer dogs and you stand, in panic; don't want anyone to find this, your fragile discovery, don't want anything from your real world crashing in on it.

Taking it from you.

Your hidden place, that you will find a way back to.

To help. To mend. To patch up. To watch his hands as he works, as he caresses his dog. If he is like that with animals what must he be like with people? A tenderness you have never seen in a man before, a grace, and you just want to watch, nothing else. You have not grown up with the expectation that someone will look after you and it's not what you want from this world – it's the promise it holds. Of a different life, a different way, an escape. You just want to watch and learn and be nourished by it. So much enchantment in this place.

But first you have to get home.

To keep it safe.

Lesson 55

If there is no joy like the rapture of a first love,
God's great mercy has also granted that there is no anguish
like youth's pain

A car. Its sound as it climbs, carefully, the rough winding road. You leap to a window. Can see the search of its headlights threading through the dust. Rescue. You shut your eyes in relief.

The old Volvo. Back, thank God, back. You are safe, this world is safe, no one will find it; you can go home now. A screech of the handbrake and a slam of the car door and then he is here, the great loom of him striding in strong and you are rushing out with his dog jumping about you in a mad flurrying cacophony of barks. The dog grabs your wrist in its jaws and has you tight by its gums and its owner is exclaiming in shock and stepping back, as if he's seen a ghost, dropping his groceries and a bottle of wine is smashing and a thread of red shoots out fast across the floor.

'What –' In absolute bewilderment.

'I'm sorry, I'm sorry,' as you try to bend down and clean up but the dog has you firm.

He can't comprehend, someone here, in his space, *now*. How? He sees the book you're still holding.

'Is that – ?'

Your face reddens. 'I wasn't stealing.'

You hand it back with the quickness of guilt. He looks at the the title, the cover falls off. Frowns as if he didn't realise he had it. Is it his, is it yours, did he break it, did you?

'Any tips?' he murmurs.

You don't know what to say, whether to laugh or explain or run. Totally stumped. By this man, six foot tall with his vigorous strap of black hair over his high forehead, and green eyes, curiously pale, a paleness that doesn't match the vigour of everything else about him, that feels all of the mind, seems so wrong in this house. Physically, he is not of this valley world. The dog still has your wrist in its gums, you try to extricate yourself. He suddenly realises.

'Bec, down!'

Free.

'I – I got stuck. By mistake.'

'What?' As if it's impossible that anyone but him could be in this place, could have stumbled across it let alone got into it.

'The gate was open. By accident. You drove away and locked me in. I want to go home.'

'But no one lives around here. Where on earth did you come from?'

'B–Beddy,' you stumble out.

He looks at you as if he has no idea what language you're speaking; sideways, as if he can't make head nor tail of it. Looks at the book – nope – it's not going to yield a clue.

'*Beddington.*'

Your head indicates, frustrated, over the ridge.

It dawns – obviously not from these parts. He nods. Right. One of *them*, now he has you placed. He looks you up and down and you see, suddenly, what he is seeing – the horror of your clothes, wild hair, general grubbiness – a bush scrap of a thing. Everything that you are, that you represent. He looks at your pockets as if he suddenly expects them to be bulging; at the book as if he can't believe someone from there would be reading it. Would be reading full stop. Flips it open like he's expecting stolen sheets of gold to fall from it. Snaps it shut, pockets it in ownership.

'Can you leave now, please. I have work to do.'

You stare at him, rooted to the spot.

'Shall I involve the police?'

As if you are about to bring an entire mining community of thieves and claimants crowding into his place.

Too much gap.

Not *seeing* you. Who you are, who you're not.

Just wanting you gone and his world back.

The piracy of indifference; and your hackles rise at it.

Lesson 56

Some instinct warns you that you are making yourself
ridiculous

Anger unlocks you. You'd never be able to talk to him but for
this.

'I'm stuck. I need to get home but the gate was locked.'
Indignant, slow; as if it's him, now, who doesn't understand.
'I'm not *staying*.'

'Well off you go then.' He scoops up his groceries. 'I left
the gate open *again*, I've just realised,' he mutters absently,
furiously. 'And yes, it's the last time that'll be happening.'

As if he suddenly can't bear to have you here, in his secret
place; an uninvited encroachment from the surrounding world
– he's been found out and he's consumingly distracted by the
thought of that. As he lifts up his groceries they tumble out
of a slit in the plastic: tin cans and sausages, bread, chocolate
biscuits.

'Blast.'

He has to bend to scoop them up, awkwardly, with those
gammy hips. It makes him curiously vulnerable and it spines
you up.

'I need a pump.'

You're reaching down to help; he's snatching things up, doesn't want you or need you – scat!

'*What?*' Incomprehension. 'Could you go now, please, or I will call the police.' And he bundles away his groceries, awkwardly cradling them in his arms and they're tumbling to the floor but he doesn't pick them up, he's in too much of a hurry to get away, to his study, to get you out.

'Wait.' You stride after him but he shuts the workroom door, leaving the dog and you looking at each other in perplexed solidarity. The dog whines, you rap loudly. Silence. Almost laugh, 'Haven't you got the wrong room there for the shopping?'

No laughter in response.

Right.

'Um, my bike has a puncture. I need a pump. That's all. To get home.' And never come back, you almost add.

'I am not a cyclist.'

Quick as a flash: 'What about that shed? Out the back.'

You had a look earlier. Behind a dusty window was a stack of cobwebby bikes.

'So what else have you sized up?'

Silence. Your hot cheeks.

'Help yourself to a pump – if there is one – then go, immediately. Thank you.' You're a pest, nothing else. 'And don't even think about the bikes.'

Yep, you know exactly what he thinks of those Beddy people.

'Or the books.'

I bet he never even knew he *had* bikes until this moment. The anger rises in you, magnificent.

'I wasn't taking your book, I was *reading* it.'

God this would never work. You want to throttle him.

'And don't worry, I wouldn't dream of coming back,' you throw at him in parting, in the voice of a kid with their tongue stuck out.

Lesson 57

If you want a thing done, go yourself

There *is* a pump, of course; you know bike sheds. You find it in the fumbly gloom, dragging cobwebs furiously from your face. Fill the tyre outside, fast, the light is now rapidly fading. He's watching from his kitchen window; watching like you're going to curl up in that shed and make a right home of it or grab for the taking a different bike.

You fling his pump back inside the shed. An almighty clatter. Don't care. Ride off without looking back. Cycling fast, swerving wildly at a twisted bit of muffler rearing up like a petrified snake and righting yourself hurtling on but in less than three minutes the tyre is flat, again; now you're speeding on the rim and feeling every jeering bump. You fling the bike down in disgust, it's not going to work. Turn back to the window. Yep, still watching. Of course. The little girl inside you screams. You sweep your hands out theatrically before the carcass of your useless bike: behold. You're going to have to go back, whether he likes it or not.

A loud rap on his workroom door.
    'I'm stuck.'
    'So I see.'

'You'll have to drive me home or I'm here all night. And you've got a lot of books.'

Despite himself, the snort of a laugh.

The door snaps open. Car keys are in his hand. The voice is low, warning, but there's just a hint of a smile.

'Never, ever mention that you've found this place.'

'What'll you give me?' You grin, can't help it, naughtied up. 'My uncle knows the inside of every house in this valley … except this one.'

The shudder is almost visible. You eye the book in his pocket. He clamps his hand protectively to the little Victorian volume and turns on his heel, to the car.

'Your reward is a lift home which I've really got no time for because I've got a hell of a lot of work to finish. Tonight.'

He pats his pocket, his back to you.

'And besides, she may have something to teach me. Thanks for that.'

Lesson 58

They who are little spoken of in the world at large
_____

You've overtaken him, leaping into the passenger seat before he's near his car. Bec is flurrying all over you with snuffles and licks, all the unconditional love which you return, laughing in relief; at least someone appreciates you in this place.

'You're very ... *alive* ... aren't you?' the man says in bemused distaste, as he starts the ignition.

'And you're not?'

Annoyance is smoothing your self-consciousness, and being in a car, and with a dog; if you were in any other situation you'd never be able to talk like this. Just the careful way he's dressed would usually stumble your talk – all he'd need is a Gauloises to complete the image and Lune has told you, wild-eyed, about the men who smoke them. He takes a deep breath.

'I'll drop you on the outskirts of Beddington. And remember, you'll never be able to come back here, I'll see to that. Don't even think about it.'

Intrigued. By all of it. Too much you don't know and it's right at your doorstep and you've got weeks of holidays ahead of you and a home you need to escape and he's reeling you in and has no idea of it.

His voice is smooth and sure, a hidden creek overarched by the bush, strong and cool and self-sufficient. You, on the other hand, are a desert before him: wide open, ready, aching for nourishment. And he smiled, he laughed – was it once, twice – you got him to do it, just.

The car roars through a cathedral of trees, you've never driven so fast.

'Whoo hooooo!' You're suddenly laughing, winding down your window and butting the wind with your face.

'Get your head in,' he snaps, 'or you'll lose it.'

Silence, glary, as he flies down the axle-breaking road. Trees lean in close, branches slap against the car and your hand sneaks back outside: trying to grab the night's coolness with your palm.

'Get *in*!'

You withdraw your hand from the slap of the air but put your bare feet on the dashboard, as you always do.

Violent braking.

You jerk forward.

The car's clicking stillness.

He looks at you in that stopping as if he's never come across anything like you: half wild, half human, utterly incomprehensible, impossible to contain.

You spurt a laugh, in nervousness as much as anything. 'What?' You shrug, perplexed. Your feet remain on the dash.

He revs and shoots forward, your feet can't grip, they drop.

'Good one, mate,' you giggle and raise your thumb.

He chuckles, shaking his head; he's given up. For a moment there's a slipping into something else.

His hand. On the leather gearstick. The fingers you've never seen before. Not worker's fingers. No coarseness, no calluses, no grubby black collecting in crevices. You want to lick them, like an animal; learn them. Hold each tip still and savouring in the cave of your mouth. You lift up both your own blunt hands in front of your face and turn them around in wonder, as if you've never seen the like of them before; staring at the dirt compacted in crescent moons under the nails and the river map of lines in the cracks of your palms and not just your hands, of course, but your bare feet, too; you sit cross-legged on the seat and drag them up – yep, filthy black, as they always are, with the skin ridged up the sides in deep fissured cracks; and then your knees, you're curving right over now and examining the coal dust permanently tattooed across them in thin leeches and you lick them and of course the black doesn't come off and how bizarre you must seem to someone like him and it is as if you have awareness of your bush self, for the first time in your life – all the raggedness, the loudness, the rawness in this place – the vast affront of who you are and what you represent. To someone like him.

You stare across, at his eyes, resolutely not engaging with you.

With everything he is not.

Lesson 59

The age of chivalry, with all its benefits and harmfulness,
is gone by for us women

———————

The gate to his property.

Locked.

You burst out laughing. Despite himself, he does too.

'Yes, I *am* going mad. Alright. You win. Don't ask. Too much in my head.' He shakes it as he stops the car, as if trying to clear it out, takes the keys from the ignition and hands them across. Looks at you. Cocks his head.

'It's the small silver one.'

Well, that's one rule of the bush he's absorbed. You jump out grinning and swing the two halves wide. Glad to help, mister, glad to help. He drives through and stops abrupt.

'Padlock it.'

'Aren't you coming back?'

'You might get back before me.' He raises his eyes to the heavens. 'I wouldn't be surprised.'

You fiddle with the lock, standing with the sole of one foot resting on your knee, as you always do; it takes a while, you can't make the loop click. He toots in exasperation.

'Come on. Your dinner's getting cold.'

'But it's not fair, I want to come back,' you tease, standing tall at the front of his car, your feet on his bumper and balancing with your hands on the bonnet, the ten year old wheedling to her dad. 'Pleeeeeeeeease.'

Something shuts down his face like a roller door on a shop. In an instant his mood has changed. You've gone too far. He gets out of the car.

'I have *work* to do. Alright? And you're not welcome in this place.' He grips your shoulders hard and lifts you out of the way and propels you towards the passenger seat. You rub your collarbone and examine the affronted skin on your upper arms, the bruises like pale yellow petals already rushing onto it.

A clotted silence.

That you're wrong in some way. That you have no idea.

A silence you have faced for much of your life.

Lesson 60

It is in transactions between women and women
that the difficulty lies

No more talk, no more teasing, as you bullet south to
Beddington. Dust hangs among the trees like smoke. You drink
in the watchfulness of the moon, it's following the Volvo like a
hovering mother on the edges of a first date. Dusty old cassettes
under his car radio have Ephemera 1, 2 and 3 written on them.
You'd love to know what's on them, would love to know what
Ephemera means. You run your fingertip along a spine, tracing
the distinctive boldness of the handwriting. Someone who is very
sure of themselves, oh yes. Glance across to a stony concentration
on the road. You retreat. Drum your hand on the car roof.

The lights of Beddy. Not long now.

Your heart accelerates. You don't want to go back, it's too
soon after the diary incident; you have an instinctive wariness
at the thought of home, it's no longer a sanctuary in any way.
You gaze at this new specimen in your life, so rarely get someone
new in it. There's a halo of aloneness around him, a pushing
away that's flinty in him. And wounded, somehow. There's
something about it that you want to enfold. You haven't caught
nearly enough of him, time is running out.

'What's your name?'

His look says you don't need to know. 'There's no point. We're not seeing each other again, remember?'

What you're not telling him is that you left your bike behind. It gives you a purchase on his world. You will be back. Somehow. Because you are a work in progress and he can teach you.

What, you've got no idea.

Lesson 61

Small minds expend themselves in meddling, gossip
and scandal-mongering

He drops you on a ridge overlooking your home. You must walk
in from the high road. You understand that there is something
adult about this; that he will not come near your world, your
family, he would never do that. Because of misunderstandings.
A grown-up world, all that; an unbreachable gulf.

He hands across the little Victorian volume.

'Not a whisper,' he grins. 'Alright?'

Doesn't say another word, doesn't say goodbye, just turns
the car around and drives off.

An enormous smile plumes through as you look at the book;
you're like a goddamn firefly blazing in that dark.

You'll find a way back. He said the author might be able to
teach him something – he'll need this returned.

Tell the truth and don't be afraid of it.

Lesson 62

A torment from which there is no escape but death

That night the memory of him, all of it, soaked through you, like smoke; in your hair, your clothes, in the pores of your skin. The memory of his fingers, his desk, his dog, his hand on the gearstick, his waiting house.

The sky has released its payload at last. Rain pummels the tin roof. You open the canvas flaps, fling them up and breathe in the earth as you lie on your stomach on the pillow, and watch.

Your sky, his sky.

The only thing you have in common, and you are caught.

Lesson 63

One only 'right' we have to assert in common with
mankind — the right of something to do

_____

You cannot stay away. He is a brake on your life, stopping everything else.

It takes an hour and a half to walk back. You are wearing your denim overalls cut off at the knees and a Bonds singlet; the book with its cover cellotaped back on, and a screwdriver and hammer and new inner tube of a bicycle in your pockets: an excuse. You do not know what to expect when you get to the fence, you will walk the perimeter if you have to, to glean some way in; to firm everything about yesterday, that it was real.

The gate is ajar. Well, well. His head _is_ in another place. You slip through, kicking a stone in a wide arc in triumph. Weren't expecting this.

A second car is beside the Volvo. A Mustang, as decrepit as his. So, a friend. You slip off your Blunnies and sneak onto the verandah, heart thudding — please not a woman, you're not ready for it.

A man.

Through the window of the drawing room. Much older, of no interest. Curly hair, already greying. Tall, a wide, round face. The two of them are playing cards, half-heartedly; the vigour is in their conversation which you can't quite catch. They have glasses of red wine and bread and cheese on a plank of plywood and thick weekend papers, unread, and a scattering of books. It looks like they've been there for some time, rabbiting on, mates.

Your bike is not where you flung it. Odd. As odd as a gate still unlocked. As if you're being enticed further into this. No, surely? You feel a prickle of a something as you watch, and watch.

You slip through the gap of a front door soundlessly. Hesitate, then knock softly, apologetically, on the doorpost.

The door into your new life.

His friend jumps as if he's seen a ghost.

Your man from last night does not.

As if he was expecting this. As if you had misread him entirely. You look at him and he stares back but his face says nothing. He stares with the detachment of an anthropologist, waiting to see what will come next.

A blush.

Vining your face, neck, body. Saying more than words ever could, of course; and how you hate that.

Lesson 64

In moral and mental growth it is impossible to remain
stationary

'Who is –?' sputters the friend. 'Hello? Can we help you?'

'Hello indeed,' your man replies coolly without taking his
eyes from you, which only pushes the blushing deeper.

'You never said anyone else was in on this,' the friend says
indignantly.

'They aren't.'

Your hands ball at your hips: excuse me. The friend is
confused.

'But you seem to know each other …'

'Oh no. This is some wild thing from Beddington that the
bush keeps coughing up. That keeps coming back – no matter
how many times they're told they can't.' As if you're not quite
there.

You point your hammer at him – the gate, mate, the gate.
He smiles, distracted, looking at your bare feet; can't make
head nor tail of how you'd get here like that.

'Your bike's in the shed. For safekeeping. I had no idea when
you'd be back.' He raises an eyebrow. 'Today. Yes. Of course.'

'You left the gate *open*,' you blurt indignantly.

'Oh. Right. Yes.'

'No distraction, mister,' the friend warns, waggling his finger.

'I know.' The snap back.

'You told me you'd sworn off the entire world and universe until everything was done.'

'I'm here to work.'

'Swore off wine –' he looks down at his glass, shrugs, there goes that one – 'bars, all night benders, parties, mothers, travels, women …'

'It's not a woman.'

'Excuse me!' you yelp.

The friend steps back, examining, his eyes resting on your hammer gripped tight. 'Weeeell … what is it then?'

'An annoyance.'

'That wants her bike back,' you retort. 'You can't go stealing it, you know.'

Your man smiles a ragged smile, despite himself. Touché.

His friend winces in exaggerated disgust. 'I do apologise. He's beyond repair.'

'He was *so* rude to me!'

'He always is. Especially when he's got a project to finish … and will not.' The friend gulps the last of his wine and wipes the rim of his glass unceremoniously on his shirt. 'Would you like some?' he asks absently, as if he does this automatically to anyone who crosses his orbit. 'Sorry I can't offer you another glass. He's only got two. He lives rough out bush. Disgustingly.'

You look at him dubiously. 'That's a goblet you're holding. It's not a Vegemite jar.'

The friend holds the glass at a distance and looks at it theatrically, as if he's seeing it for the first time. 'Oh? Really?'

Your man snatches it away. 'No.'

You redden again. Have never drunk before, your father doesn't allow it in his house. But here, now, there is an inkling of a want, to crash catastrophe into your life; in some way, to allow it. God knows what. Before everything vanishes, before your proper life comes scuttling back.

'As I explained before, your bike's waiting for you. In the shed,' your man from last night says brusquely, standing up and brushing himself off. 'I've got work to do. And I might as well do it.'

He turns on his heel and stalks off to his study without looking back, everything in retreat.

The two of you stare after him.

Gone, just like that.

Lesson 65

A human being should be improving with every day
of a lifetime

So. Alone. With this new person. In a room vibrating with the charged absence of someone else. The atmosphere as swiftly altered as a power cut in a night club.

'I should be going.'

'Do you have to?' His eyes are resting again on your hammer. 'It looks like you could be of some use. What's Mr Grumpy roped you in for? Is he paying you? What does he want from you? This place needs all the help it can get.'

You step back, your arm slipping across your waist, don't know why all of a sudden, what's changed.

'I'm a good ... girl,' you trail out, don't know what you're saying anymore, it's all wrong, you just feel intensely awkward and out of your depth. You pick up a book and flick through it, reading nothing, as if it's a text you're studying and your lesson's about to commence. 'I'm learning,' you mumble, embarrassed, turning away; speaking without thinking, mortified.

The man chuckles, astounded, at the thought of it.

'About *what*? Him in there –' he shakes his head with the

sheer hopelessness of it all – '*I* haven't been able to get a single thing out of him for an entire year ... more.'

'I – I ... want to know things.'

The conversation has run away from you, you're not in control, don't know where it's going anymore. This new man looks at you sideways, your cheeks are burning, you feel so young, redundant, foolish; want out.

He plucks the book from your hands: '*Sheep Husbandry of the Highlands*,' he reads. Great. Trust it to be that one. 'Um, lessons about ... *what*?'

You just look at him, stricken. How can you explain? That you want lessons in how to talk, to be, to act, not from people who covet gold American Express cards and Porsches but from those who read books and who've been to university and watch the ABC and read Tolstoy and Proust. Who drink wine and coffee, say supper instead of tea and eat at ten o'clock instead of five and go to Italy and France instead of Jindabyne and the Gold Coast. People who fall asleep at 3 a.m. and wake at ten in the morning and read half an hour of poetry, every morning, before getting up to drink absinthe or whatever they do and, and – all that. Men who *live*, seize life in the way that you want, who talk. Not shut themselves down from being eager beaver, sparky little lads, only to enter a world of muted inarticulacy, dampened down by adulthood, their conversation slipping into grunts and put-downs and awkwardness. No, these ones are different. And you want to be a part of it.

But of course you can't say any of this.

'I … I like it here.' Looking around, at your hammer, their newspapers, books, rubbing your head like it hurts. 'It's different. A different … class …' you stumble, barely a whisper.

But he caught it. He is stepping back, squinting as he's looking at you, smiling; as if you're the most peculiar mix he's ever come across. You feel stripped.

'There's no class in this country,' he says gently.

'*You* say that. Your lot always say that.' You hold your head high, cheeks flaming. '*I* don't.'

The man looks at you and looks, and then nods.

With new, what?

Respect.

Yes, that.

Lesson 66

Such a life is not to be pitied

'Tell me about your yourself. Who do you belong to?'

'Nobody,' you protest.

'But where's your family? What does your father do? Beddington, eh. So, a miner? A tradie?' He smiles, warming you up. 'A dole bludger?'

You giggle. 'You don't need to know. You'll never be meeting him, believe me. He'd take one look at you and it'd all be in his face – pah, couldn't change a tyre, or fix a radiator, or spark a plug. That's what he'd be like. Horribly rude and terrible to you, like you're not worth the effort.'

'And he'd be absolutely right. I can't do a bit of it.'

You both burst out laughing.

'Well *I* can.'

'I bet you can.' The man picks up his friend's leftover glass of wine and raises it in a toast. 'And hooray to that. I'm so glad you've found us in Woondala. I think you're a breath of fresh air. Just what the doctor ordered.'

'What's his name?' Your head flicks to the study door. 'He never told me. Is this his house? How long has he been here?'

'That man who stormed out on us both is extremely rude,' he says loudly, 'and there is no point in learning anything from him for he has nothing useful to impart and too much work to do for anyone – or anything – else.' His voice drops. 'But if you must know – and I think you do – his name is Tolly.'

You blink. 'Tol …' The word fills up your mouth.

'He *hates* it. You must call him it instantly.'

You chuckle. 'Maybe he'll be nice to me then.'

'Oh, don't count on it. He's not good at noticing *anyone* at the moment. Including me, his oldest friend.'

'Really? I notice everyone.'

'I know you do. I can tell. No, young Tolly in there is quite impossible. A man full of secrets. An exile, by nature, an exile from life; but I am *extremely* fond of him – when he's not driving me around the bend. Admire him, to be honest. And don't I hate saying that.'

'Why?'

'Because he does what so many of us dream of doing and never, actually, manage.'

'What's that?'

'He's always been very good at constructing precisely the life that he wants. With no compromises. And crucially, sticking to it.' He sighs. 'And few of us have the courage to do that.'

'So who are *you*, by the way?'

'Julian.'

'Julian! What kind of poncy name is that? You'd never get a Julian in Beddington.'

He roars with laughter and polishes off his glass.

'But that's why I'm staying in here, cowering behind the big fence.'

Lesson 67

The illiterate village lass,
who thinks it's so grand to be made a lady of

Your fingers run the length of a wallpaper strip that's falling away to reveal its horsehair and plaster underneath. You could fix it in ten minutes, you tell Julian. Tell him that Tolly touches everything so lightly in this place. That if it was yours you'd be cherishing it quick smart before it's completely beyond repair – which is not far off. Can't he see it?

'Is this *all* his?'

'Yes,' Julian grimaces, in pity for the house. 'His grandmother left it to him – much to the annoyance of the rest of the family – and he hasn't done a thing with it since. The lazy bugger. Well, he's working through it, apparently, but it'll never get done at this rate. It's a poisoned chalice to be honest; too big a task. Arsenic was used in the original paint. The roof's falling in, window frames are falling out, ants are starting to investigate and the bush is taking over the paddocks. There are convict nails in the joins and they're not holding anything, anymore – everything is full of rust. Their revenge, I think. The walls need stripping. The wallpaper was made using child labour way back in England; it's all very Dickensian, in a most horrible way. It's cotton flocking, which gave all the little Oliver Twists a life expectancy of about seven years. Buggered their lungs. This place has many ghosts.'

'It needs a lot of love.'

'Tolly's also — extremely — protective of it,' Julian says carefully. 'It's his sanctuary. No one comes to it, except me. Or so I thought.' He sighs. 'And now, of course, we have you. The, what was it? Annoyance.' He chuckles warmly.

'I can help here.' You spin around, assessing bowed ceilings and peeling paint and wall cracks. Julian smiles as if he knows exactly what you need right now. His finger swirls around the empty glass and is popped in his mouth.

'Come on,' he says conspiratorially.

You are grabbed by the hand, you are led out.

The flutter of your belly.

Lesson 68

The notion of keeping a balance sheet with
heaven for work done to our fellow creatures

You are led to the door of the workroom.

Julian raps smartly with the back of his knuckles.

'Hey, you. A handyman awaits. Sorry, *woman*.'

'What's my payment?' you whisper, giggly. 'I'm not doing
this for free you know.'

Julian narrows his eyes and surveys, turning you slightly
this way and that, as if he is setting a prized piece of porcelain
on the mantelpiece to catch the best view from the door. He
holds your chin, puts his palm flat on your back to stand you
up straight, tilts your shoulders, correcting.

'Payment. Better posture. A new life. Lots of new words.
New experiences. And, er, numerous lessons about livestock
husbandry.'

'Cheeky!'

From the locked room, silence.

'She might be good for you,' Julian teases to the firmly shut
door. 'Get you working again, along with the house. Yes? Any
takers?'

From the room, silence.

'Come on, mate. Do us all a favour.' Julian winks at you with an enormous grin.

A fist thumps onto a surface, probably the work bench.

'Something's got to change, Tol.' Deadly serious.

'I have work to do. This is a *child*.' The voice dismissive.

'Really?' Julian puts on his glasses and examines you close, up and down, as if it's the first time he's properly noticed you.

'From the valley,' the voice adds. Pointed, as if that explains it all and concludes it all.

'I bet she'd scrub up beautifully. Why don't you take her on? Make it your project. Have a bit of fun. Get things moving again.'

'What needs to get moving?' you ask.

'See? Enthusiasm! And we could *all* do with a bit more of that,' Julian laughs.

'The bike is in the shed.'

'Hey, wait,' you wail, not wanting this to stop just yet.

'Let her help around the house. She's up for anything.' Julian lifts out your arms as if sculpting you for a dance then spins you around.

'What's going on here?' you ask, stepping back, it's a game veering too far.

'It's a most frightful situation,' Julian explains, putting his arm around you and shaking his head sorrowfully. 'My poor young friend has become quite the recluse up here. You see, his heart was broken most cruelly some time ago and since then he's just shut himself away, hiding from all the world –' his tone darkens dramatically – 'not being productive in *any* way.

It's utterly crushed him. He's never recovered. We all despair. His mother most of all.'

'Julian …' The growl is furious from the other side.

'The situation is completely hopeless,' he sighs in mock despair.

'The shed. *Now*.' The voice roars. You jump. Julian ushers you hurriedly away.

'Well, it was worth a try.'

He shakes your hand firmly in farewell, and winks.

'Good luck … Annoyance.'

Lesson 69

That cleanness of soul which is not afraid of anything
in earth or heaven

The joy roguish through you as you retrieve your bike, slip out
the new tube from your pocket, fix the tyre and leave the old
inner tube looped jauntily over the handle of the shed door and
ride off tall, knowing they're both watching; zinging with life,
and power, and light.

Your *difference*.

You'll be back. Oh yes.

V

'... [Eros] made Helen's heart fly like a wing in her chest and she went out of her mind for a Trojan man and followed him over the sea ...'

Alkaios

Lesson 70

Well, the man may come, or he may not

_____

Just as you know that you would never be attracted to a Julian, you also know that Tol has snared you and the trap is now binding your heart. And a flicker of something from him, too, in response; yes, no, surely? It is how he looked at you when you came back – how he didn't look – how he talked to you and how he couldn't. You are sure. You have no idea.

How he left the gate open when he said he would not.

Everything a sign, everything a signal and you fever it all in your head, over and over, trying to make sense of it.

Only one way to find out.

You return two days later. Around your waist is a leather tool belt worn to the softness of pelt. It is from your father's shed, with its precise walls of sized screwdrivers and spanners, the most ordered pocket of his life. A skewer has worked through another hole in the belt so it sits perfectly across your hips.

The gate is ajar.

As you knew it would be.

You walk your bike up Tol's driveway. He is sitting on the verandah with his dog beside him; running his hands through the fur and looking for ticks. He glances up. He blushes, in annoyance or shock or something else, you can't read it. He is looking at your tool belt. You come right up to him. He doesn't say anything. He stands.

He does not say to go away.

Everything a sign, everything a signal.

The heat of that afternoon weighted with it. As you stand, face to face.

Lesson 71

The heaven-given honour of being the workers of the world

_____

'I'm going to help you.'

Because you can. Because you are better at this than him. Because he has no idea, he's never been taught, it's all in his hands.

'I don't need help.'

'You so do.'

He still doesn't say to go. He walks inside. You don't know what it means. You brush past him to thin carpet half-heartedly lifted in the hallway, it is curled over, abandoned, ripe for a tripping. With one vigorous rip you lift away the tiny studs holding it down.

'Stop,' he barks.

It needs to be done, says your determined face as you turn and stare in response. You know how to do this, you have watched your father your entire life, his energy is yours: the worker who will die working and who gets affirmation from it. You have watched your father smooth cement in great fans the length of his arm and slice away fillings from bricks like icing from a cake, his eye, always, on the taut string; you have watched him rip away wallpaper like a sheet from a lover and plug pipes whose water threatens to crash through a bowed ceiling. And now, in this waiting house, you use your blunt, bush hands and work with vigour and expertise and grace, and Tol no longer tells you to stop.

Assaulted by his stare.

Suddenly, within it all, he is beside you. Your sweat, and soon his – the smell of work rising off your bodies. The clumsy, awkward city hands with their too-clean nails and pale wrists. You are ripping up the carpet in strips, shoulder to shoulder; you are ripping away sheets of tin from great windows and flooding stale rooms with dust-crammed air, anointing them with light.

Saying nothing. Saying everything. In the shining silence.

As his hand brushes yours, a crisis of touch.

You are sure.

Lesson 72

We are actually 'possessed'; cease almost to be accountable beings, and are fitter for the lunatic asylum than for the home circle

---

No staying away now.

Love has made you hopeless.

It is as if a great fist has wrenched the heart from your chest and the sense from your head.

The gate is still unlocked. Every day, and every day you expect the opposite.

Everything a sign, everything a signal.

Several days into the rhythm of this new life he corrects the fallen brace of your overalls as you drill a hole for a mirror. You are using your grandfather's ancient, manual drill with its pleasing mechanics, intrigued by the precise, clockwork beauty of how the cogs work. He flits by and corrects that fallen brace with the lightest of touches. Flipping the strap up and you barely grunt your thanks. Without looking at him, without talk.

The simplest of gestures, the simplest of responses.

But your skin. Alive with possibility.

Lesson 73

Beautiful is youth's enthusiasm

You are arriving earlier, leaving later. In command, working strong, this is your domain in terms of skill and he is allowing it – it is as if your whole life with your father has been in preparation for this task. Everything you have gleaned over the years; you feel you know nothing about anything else. You caress the bones of this beautiful Woondala – built by convicts in 1842 with Georgian economy – marvelling at its simplicity and its strength. These valley houses are deep in your bones, the familiar sandstone and flagstone and timber and tin. You recognise this wood crying out for moisture, its groan and creak at the valley's high winds; the persistent soundtrack of your childhood has been a tin roof, just like this one, warping and cracking in the heat. And then the release of nourishing, thundering, dancing rain.

Barely able to look at him as you bury yourself in the work, the only way you are comfortable, no eye contact. It is like your father in the car – with distraction you can connect. If you were forced to talk to Tol over a dinner table, in formal dress, you would be blunted by awkwardness as if your mouth was broken. But painting and sawing and ripping and tacking you are strong – teaching this man your energy, to work farmers' hours, first light to last, hauling him into your rhythms. If your father stops working he will die, he's always saying that and you want to impart something of that to Tol, the energy of it.

The future has been wiped, the past has been wiped; there is only now, in this place, the vivid present. You steal glances that tremor you as you bury yourself in work, not knowing what's next, planning nothing beyond this. And then at the end of each day with barely a word passed between you, you leave without a word; you put away your tools and jump on your bike and ride off.

Knowing now the gate will always be open for you. The firming of that over the week here.

It is the only conversation between you.

Lesson 74

'Young ladies', who have never been brought up to do
anything

A painting in the piano room now dominates the space.
A portrait of a woman with an impossible waist and dancing
eyes – as if she's secretly laughing at life – that until now has
had its back to the room. But she needs to be shown. You
had whooped with delight when you first peeked behind the
loosened canvas.

'Well, well, *you*, madam, need to come out!' And you had
flipped her around and dusted her down.

Now it is late, hot, you are tired, you wipe the sweat from
your eyes. It is Friday afternoon, you are not concentrating.
The flap of your checked shirt gets caught up in the drill and
before you know it the cogs have eaten the bottom corner of
the fabric; it will not unwind.

'Shoot,' you murmur under your breath.

The more you try to disentangle it the more it bunches into
the cogs; grease now blackening it in tiny tractor treads. You
groan in frustration, it's your favourite shirt. Tol raises his
finger, signalling to wait. The woman's eyes look straight at
you, and laugh.

He leaves the room. You wait. He returns with a pair of scissors.

'Hold still.'

'I love this shirt.'

'There's no other way to do it.'

He kneels, his face to your stomach, and cuts – so close you can feel his breath on your bare skin underneath and at one stage his hand brushes your belly and springs back like he has touched something hot and the electricity is shooting through you and you step back, need this to stop.

'What?' He looks up and laughs.

Nothing, you shake your head. He pulls you forward by your shirt.

'Uh uh. Get back here. I haven't finished.'

The steel blade. The shock of its cold against your skin. You gasp and hold his hair for a moment – 'It tickles!' – and he laughs again.

You hold your breath. Looking down at him. His half-closed eyes, his concentration. His fingers that brush your belly again, which ripples in response. He *must* have felt it; he says nothing.

His face so close, his skin to yours, his breath on your belly, you bite your lip. He looks up when he is done as though he is looking for approval and his lashes are so dark and you can see the little boy, suddenly, the child he would have been, the vulnerability he rarely shows; that you want to hold in the cup of your hands, here, now; that you want to bow down to and murmur on with your lips.

In gratitude.

The rescued cloth in his hand. That you do not ask for. That he does not give back.

Everything a sign, everything a signal.

And in the golden light of that late afternoon you fly home on your bike, standing tall on the pedals, laughing out loud, laughing at life. Because something between you is cracked.

Lesson 75

She alone can be a law unto herself

A whole weekend away. Your stomach trembles at every thought of going back, you can feel it in your groin, a sharp intake of want. He has taken over your body – he has taken over your thoughts, your serenity and your life. He has shut up your future, locked it away in a box that only he has the key to.

You retrieve an old apothecary bottle that has always lived on the window ledge of your father's shed, sure his eye has stopped noticing it long ago. It is a tiny bottle of the deepest, richest, ocean blue. For Tol's desk of mysterious objects. That you saw once through the window of that room always locked.

He holds the bottle high to the sun, chuffed at its marine depths. 'You don't want it?'

You do. You shake your head.

'You could turn out to be useful, you know,' he teases, pocketing it with a smile. 'Thank you. I'll put it in my study.'

As you knew he would.

'Where's Bec?' His dog who's never far from him.

'She's Julian's, actually. She's gone home. Julian was kicked out by his girlfriend and was homeless for a while and I was just minding her. But Julian's found a place now, with a big back yard.'

'Oh.'

You shiver in that moment, don't know why. So. Utterly alone with Tol, now – not even a licky, laughy dog to flurry all over you anymore. You look about. It feels like you are suddenly in a bell jar of mysteriousness, a dome of seclusion here with just this stranger and the heat and the deafening cicadas, and your father and your stepmother and your school and your life are on the outside and you are completely alone with this man and no one knows it, not a single soul, you don't know what you're getting yourself into, what's next. It's a new week, you don't know him well enough.

'So what's in that room of yours?' you ask as you follow him into the kitchen. He is making a cup of tea for you, weak and milky and sweet, just as your grandmother does; it's how you always begin a day's work. 'What do you do?'

He doesn't answer. He dumps the dregs of the tea leaves out a glassless kitchen window, lost in thought.

'I want to know.' You persist.

'I *hate* talking about work.'

'I *love* it.'

He sighs, wearily, and his face says it all: I know you do.

'What do you think I do?'

'I dunno.' You're examining a porcelain plate, a silver salt shaker, an ivory-handled bread knife; picking them all up and running your fingers over them, looking at anything but him. He's uncomfortable suddenly and you have no idea why.

'Drug dealer,' you blurt, not sure where that came from.

He looks up, abrupt.

'Sorry,' you giggle. 'It's the car. And the location. The cops'd never find you. It's perfect.'

He raises an eyebrow.

'Oh I dunno.' You roll your eyes. 'Mad scientist. Smuggler. Pirate. Stolen goods. Museum stuff. Dole bludger.' He shoots out a laugh. 'Photographer,' you prattle on, emboldened. 'Yeah. That's it. You shoot schoolgirls in swimming costumes, it's highly controversial, creates the hugest stink –' You can't control your talk, it's suddenly all zooming out wrong, just like before, with the teacher – someone else is taking over and pushing the real you out. You redden.

He pokes his head into your space, forces you to look at him. His dancing eyes.

'Hey. Hey.' Forcing you to concentrate. 'You are so, completely, wrong. About everything. Come on. Come and have a look.'

He takes you by the hand, he leads you from the kitchen to his study, his secret space.

Your stomach, steamrollered.

The sharp intake, the little pull.

Of want. Purely that.

Lesson 76

Our natural and happiest life is when we lose ourselves
in the exquisite absorption of home

In.

At last.

Industry, order, light. Mouth opened in wonder, you are
gulping the space, roaming it as you would a museum in
miniature, this pale box of loveliness. Photos cram an entire
wall on a corkboard painted white; there are typed quotes,
postcards, feathers and leaves and seed pods from the bush,
watercolour scraps. Paint samples, scribbles of words, sketchy
diagrams of – what? Narrative arcs for some kind of article or
movie script or story; yes, that. Photos of people in magazines
he's scrawled names across and circled fragile eyes, a clenched
hand, a woman's ready lips. Along one wall are bowed stacks of
shelves on bricks reaching to the ceiling, then more books on
the floor in high stacks. Your eyes assess with the thoroughness
of a forensic detective. Trying to unlock it all, trying to guess.

He leans against the doorpost, watching the looking,
amused. You roll your eyes at him, once, as if 'God knows',
and get back to your examination. A collection of antique ink
wells that appear to have been dug up from the nearby earth

are lined up along a windowsill. Filthy fountain pens cram a ceramic jar – *James Keiller & Sons, Dundee, 1862*, reads its beautiful type. The scrap of your work shirt lies on the desk. An old black typewriter is dead centre. A blank sheet is poised. The scrap of your shirt. The scrap of your shirt. You finger it, prickle up, step back.

'So?' He throws across.

You dangle the piece of cloth in front of him and with laughing eyes dip a fountain pen in waiting ink and write *yes* across his empty sheet in scratchy blobs of messiness.

'A writer.'

He pings a rolled up piece of paper at you in affirmation. You laugh and catch it in an overhand snatch, just like your dad taught you, and flick it back hard with a boyish twist of your wrist.

Of course a writer. The pale hands that just failed to catch your paper ball, the hopelessness with life, the face that feels too much. The thick black glasses, the hair never brushed. Now the room is unlocked, now you see him; of course.

Lesson 77

Such a life will not have been lived in vain

You jiggle the scrap of your cloth in front of his eyes.

'This one's off limits, mate.'

'But I've never met anything like her,' he teases. 'She's a fascinating specimen.'

'No. Way.'

You waggle your finger at him in warning and he nods, concurs. Satisfied, you gleefully spin on his factory stool and play the typewriter keys like a piano, with pretend expertise, your back secretarial straight. Your fingers hover above all the waiting letter circles, almost touching but not quite.

'You still use one of these things?'

'Yep. It means I have to consider every single word. Make everything count. It also means I take a very, *very* long time. To Julian's despair.'

'What's he got to do with all this?'

'He's my agent. And I'm extremely behind on a manuscript that he managed to get a lot of money for, which is driving him absolutely bananas. I might have to give the money back. He's furious –'

'I don't blame him.'

You look at Tol with an eyebrow raised, the mother with

their child over the latest homework excuse. Back to the typewriter.

'I've never met one of you before.' Staring at everything, gulping it up; the working mind laid out before you. So, this is him, finally, his core, his life.

A sigh. 'We're terrible people, the worst type. You should leave immediately.'

'Why?'

'Because we're deeply competitive and insecure and our work is never good enough – which we know, despairingly, and just hope that no one else ever finds out. And because everything is fuel for our fiction, which is why no one should come too close. Everyone is a possible subject.' He glances at the scrap of cloth back in its place; you snatch it up and point your finger, again, in playful warning.

'Don't worry, I promise.' Hands high, all innocence. 'But believe me, it's wise not to get too close. We're full of frustration – for our publishers for not pushing us enough, for our critics for not getting it, our families for giving us a rotten childhood and our kids for exhausting us. We're wary of every other writer, never want them to succeed. Friends clutter up our time. We need someone to do everything for us because we're completely hopeless at life, yet crave being alone more than anything else. We will do anything not to work. Make a cup of tea, go for a walk.' He looks around, shaking his head and laughing. 'Strip a house. Believe me, writing is the hardest thing I've ever done. And it only gets harder. I don't know why I persist. I've only published one book –' His eyes wince as if he really can't bear it.

'Don't ask, I hate talking about it – and am appallingly stuck with this next one. It makes me tremendously grumpy and it's why I'm exiled in this place. Why *Julian* has exiled me …' A deep breath, a hopeless sigh. 'Your father wouldn't think much of me, I'm afraid.'

'Why?' Knowing he's right.

'There was this Sydney writer called Michael Dransfield, who said that to be a poet in Australia was the ultimate commitment.' He shakes his head as if he's just about given up. 'All I can say is, I know *exactly* where he's coming from.'

You step away from his typewriter. Swirl around slowly, breathing his world in. Knowing now what you want more than anything else.

This life. Him. All of it.

The ultimate commitment.

Lesson 78

Daughters should be early taught to check every tendency towards 'a romantic attachment' – the insane folly of loving a man for what he is, rather than for what he has got

---

There are no words but the Bible's in your own home. Your life with your father is all gristle; there is no meat in it, no juice. He left school at fourteen and never got around to proper punctuation and when he writes a letter it presses through several pages of his writing pad underneath, the words are so painstakingly formed. The amateur writer, still, like a schoolboy just learning; trying not to betray his ignorance.

He's only ever written you one letter in his life. He sent it to your boarding school the week you left home. No punctuation, of course.

Don't forget the old man loves you have to go now crib time don't forget all right.

It was preserved in the back of your diary.
Burnt, of course.

Lesson 79

If you waste time, you waste not only your substance
but your very soul – not that which is your own,
but your maker's

'Why does Julian stick you all the way out here?'

Because everything about them says they're city types.

'It's my choice. Sydney's too noisy to work in. Everything invades my life there too much. And … I'm a bit shy in it, to be honest. I feel stronger in this place.' He looks at you; you cock your head, believe him – he's stripping himself here and it's something new and you smile, slowly, at it and nod. You feel stronger too in the bush.

'It's like, when I'm not given the space to do what I really want to do I get agitated, I'm all at sea, lost.' He shrugs. 'I'm a nightmare to be around.'

'Mmmm.' You're smiling in vigorous agreement.

He chuckles; alright. Takes a tumbler from the book shelf and lifts a glass stopper from a crystal decanter and pours out a golden liquid, swirls it, and teases its tart earthiness under your nose. You jerk back like a spooked horse. He laughs, examining you afresh, and downs it.

'Not for you, eh?'

You sit again at his seat and arch your back with your hands stretching high above you, then flop them over your head and slowly spin, surveying his lovely cocoon of a world.

'I want to stay here forever,' you breathe deep. 'Dive, right into this life.'

He steps back. Holds up his hands as if everything's – suddenly – galloping ahead too fast.

'Oh no, no. Don't say that. This world would crush you in a week and you'd end up being anything but a writer. A banker, an accountant, anything. You'd be scarred for life.'

He raises his glass to you, it's not quite celebratory.

'You, young lady, have what Harper Lee calls "one's original promise". And believe me, it'd be lost around here quick smart.'

You screw up your face. 'What are you *on* about?'

'You're an appreciator,' he says. 'I am not. I'm far too cynical for the likes of you. You seize life, I watch it. The difference is too great.'

A prickly silence. He's right; he's a watcher, like a cat. You're a participator, every particle of your body is roaring to muck in, to grab and cherish and savour and possess.

The difference, yes, is too great. He said it. Something slinks away in you in that moment like a dog with its tail between its legs.

'I don't want any of me rubbing off on you,' he adds gently. 'Don't want you changing. You should go home immediately and never come back.'

He means it.

'Go on. Scat.'

You're standing, confused, stopped. Can't tell if he's joking or not, can't tell anything anymore. Everything a sign, everything a signal – or not – you're breathing fast, too young for this. You've entered a new phase of play in this room and cannot read it, it's so confusing, adult; he doesn't seem grumpy and cynical in any way in here, he's like a man supremely happy with this secret life that he has chiselled out for himself and he doesn't want anything to invade it.

Which you have, of course. Which you want.

This room, this house – they're all teaching you the importance of living a light life, of surrounding yourself with things that are beautiful but do not weigh you down and you are learning the great balm of simplicity here; a house that envelops you with reassurance and it's been so long since you've had that. You want it and he knows it and he's let you in too far. Yes, that's it.

The 'annoyance', he saw that from the start.

With a thudding heart you pick up the ocean-blue bottle from your father's shed. It's in front of a row of books, Patrick Whites, all covered in careful plastic. You place the beautiful little object squarely in front of his typewriter, right in his line of sight. As if in ownership. Then you slip out his little Victorian volume from your pocket – that always accompanies you now – and slide it in snugly next to the Patrick Whites.

You turn and look straight at him.

He does not move. He does not speak. But he is smiling, from the corner of his mouth, just. Intrigued, surprised; it's in his eyes, you note it. He looks at the book shelf and shakes his head – uh uh – something's wrong, it can't work like this. He plucks your little leather volume from his shelf and hands it back, insists. The tone has switched again.

So, an unspoken game, a gift for a gift.

You flip open a random page.

Close the eyes that no husband ever kissed.

You do, and your insides peel away as if he has slipped his fingers into a secret place and brushed a whisper of a touch. You smile, can't help it. At the book, at the blue bottle, at this speaking silence.

It has begun.

Whether he likes it or not.

Every time you come from now on – and you *will* come – a gift will accompany you.

That you will place.

Lesson 80

Close the eyes that no husband ever kissed

_____

Cycling to him the next day, faster than you've ever ridden, shackled now by want. A water bag is looped over your handlebars, 'Austral Canvas' stamped across its honeyed cloth.

The next gift. That would have been placed over a car's radiator once. You can barely think what will be yours in return.

Thunder threatens, the sky is bruised like a plum; you shouldn't go today, you must. You glance behind you at a curtain of grey falling across the land and pedal faster, flint in the air and you push yourself to stay ahead of it and then the first, fat splats come; the rain has beaten you. Do you turn back or do you get caught? No time. A flash of lightning. You jump, you hate lightning. Pedal more furiously. The rain catches you, grows heavier, pounds. Mud splashes into your face as you fly down the dirt roads, you are freezing, teeth chattering, your hair hangs in ratty rivulets, wet – it is spitting into your eyes, blurring your vision and you have to drag it off to see, make progress.

The gate, at last.

His road barely there in the driving rain, you can hardly make it out, the dirt flies up and the leaves whip across your face, you fall and get up, slimy now with mud and wet. Woondala is just ahead, finally, you are drenched. You see him waiting tall on the verandah and faster and faster you fly, grinning, waving; you only see at the last moment the pothole the rain has carved in the road, huge and filled with its needles of dancing rain. You swerve.

Too late.

You try to correct yourself; pitch over the handlebars.

And black.

Lesson 81

The boys may do a thousand things which are
'not proper for little girls'

Your earlobe, held in the hollow of a mouth. Hands, lips, the tip of a tongue, waking you up.

'You're my downfall.' The whisper of a breath. A mouth in the clavicle of your neck and the violin dip of your hip; against the vulnerability of your inner wrist and on your eyelids, just, trembling.

Or was that air? A cloud shift? A moth? What are you dreaming and what are you not?

Your eyelids so heavy, they roll back, again, into the dense lovely rain of deep sleep.

'I'm sorry,' he is breathing, apologetically, 'you're soaking wet.' As you are turned, as your clothes are slipped off. 'You'll get pneumonia if I don't.' Are you dreaming it, you cannot climb out; hands are hovering, fingertips, the softest of touches, learning you as if they have never learnt a woman in their life, as if you are lit. Eating the dirt and the mud from your skin, licking it off with a tongue-tip; a mouth finding yours, a soul in the lips, waking you up. You shoot up with a gasp.

You are on the hessian lounge in the piano room.

A blanket is over you.

Your clothes are dry.

You have no idea how long you have been here. The slant of the light tells you it is late afternoon; you have no idea how many minutes have passed, hours, days.

You are alone.

Lesson 82

Driven at last into open rupture

He is in the kitchen. His back to you, at the sink.

'I'm here.'

'Good.'

He does not look at you. He does not turn.

You are thrumming.

Unbearably close.

You know you should go now, you should turn around and walk from Woondala and never come back, you have to.

You walk up to him, to his back, and you stand on tiptoe and kiss him, a whisper of breath, on the back of his vulnerable neck.

'I'm here.'

Lesson 83

Whatever is worth doing at all is worth doing well

Done.

God in it.

At last.

A communication between you but more than that – a communion – that word of grace and connection; spiritually softened.

'You feel beautiful,' he says in the afterwards, a fingertip trailing from the dip of your neck to the top of your pubis. Your belly dips and you giggle, pushing him off.

'You're like a brand-new ballet slipper. Silky. Unscuffed.' He shakes his head in wonder; at what has just happened, how it has got to this, how on earth it all began, here, in this lone man's place.

'Yeah, a ballet slipper just waiting to be all grubbied up,' you tease. 'To be flung into a corner and tossed out.'

'Oh no,' he exclaims, wounded, 'no, not that. Never that.'

In the long golden stillness of late afternoon you lie in silence, Tol's arm a seatbelt across your waist, and listen to the sky outside slowing, fading, in perfect peace.

The rain has stopped. The world is clean. You lift his arm from your sticky belly and put on your clothes. Slip away without saying goodbye. Without looking back. Your bike is propped by the front door, still with its water bottle looped over the handlebars. You sling the canvas bag over the knocker by the front door, a lion with a ring in its mouth.

The second gift.

That you have placed.

Lesson 84

We begin to taste the full meaning of the world as a place
where 'we shall know even as we are known'

_____

Days stagger by. You do not go back. Cannot. Cannot bear to
return to find him gone, spooked, the gate padlocked; he didn't
want to do it, of course, his back was turned in the kitchen as if
in shame, he was resisting, it was a dream – was it a dream? –
he can't go on, you're a schoolgirl, you have exams to study for,
a proper life, your father must never find out.

Too much no in it.

But then one – enormous – yes.

That moment when he turned from the sink, and kissed
you.

When you forgot everything else.

Lesson 85

Those only can find true friends who have in themselves
the will and capacity to be such

Endlessly you flick through his little Victorian volume in your room on the back verandah. The brisk, sparky voice released by its anonymity, glowing with honesty and common sense. Then you come across it.

> *Let there be no hesitations, no regrets, no compromises —*
> *they are at once cowardly and vain.*

You snap the volume shut.
Jump on your bike.

Lesson 86

Love, also

_____

Because you are the collator, the collector. Because this is the next phase of the experiment begun at fourteen and abandoned for a couple of years and now re-awakened, you need to know what follows, you are learning, deepening, opening up. Because he has shown you another way and it cannot stop yet. Because he pressed his disbelief into you at one point – that you were both doing this, that it had gone this far – and you don't want that as an abiding memory for you both; a sense of wrongness, the stain of it.

Because you cannot stay away.

As simple as that.

Flying on your bike, arrowed to his north. Trembling between your legs, trembling in your chest. Your head telling you this is ridiculous, you have to stay away, he won't be there, the gate will be locked – you feel too much, have to turn back, you'll be hurt. You can't. You must.

You stop at a willow tree and plait two crowns. The third gift.

The gate is ajar.

As you knew it would be. Your belly is somersaulting, you are wet. He wants this; he cannot bring himself to say it because of the illicitness in it and you need to come back to show him it's alright, your choice, you are absolutely complicit in this. Flying down his driveway and he is there, on the verandah, waiting; he sees you and stands, comes striding down the drive, runs.

With relief.

With so much else.

You are standing there, strong, a vast smile shining you up; stripping off your singlet like a miner at the end of a shift, crossed hands pulling it over your head in a clean yank. He is reaching you, helping, saying nothing, laughing, falling on his knees as he pulls down your pants, you are almost fucking into the car, you fall to the ground, both, ramming, hard, giggling in the dirt. His finger is suddenly enquiring around your arse and you recoil. *Sssh*, he soothes, *sssh* – and you obey, give in, can't help it, want it, you spread your legs wider, you feel his two fingers between the thin membrane of skin, exploring, the extreme pleasure of it and you are giving yourself to him, you want to be swallowed up. You can't bear it, you come and come in great floods of wet and he holds your trembling, he clamps it still like you're an animal in its death throes caught in a trap and he's soothing you into a stopping, into quiet, *sssh*. The cheeks of both of you are sudden-soft together and you say nothing and neither does he and above you, around you, is the wheeling sky and then he moves in you slowly, so slowly and he comes, too, withdrawing with a jerk and the hot spumy wet spreads over your stomach and then he flops onto his back in the dust beside you, spent.

You muddle together back to Woondala, dirt encrusted,

sex encrusted; holding, pushing, basking, wondrous at this force between you, that has taken over you both. You place one willow crown on his head and the other on your own; straighten his, giggling at the ridiculousness of it, brimming with laughter and light, both of you, as you walk back to his house, talled up.

You have entered the realm of surrender.

Your summer holiday, now, an enormous cleared path.

To whatever he wants.

Lesson 87

A solitude so full of peace and hope that it is like Jacob's
sleep in the wilderness: 'all things are less dreadful
than they seem'

Cracked open into womanhood. Never to reclaim that little girl
you once were. An enormous rushing road of experience and
knowing and shock now carves you off from that schoolgirl
looking at you, from across the far pavement, the child you
once were, just several days previously. A lifetime ago.

You have become someone else.

You can never go back.

The learning has begun; the proper learning.

At last.

Lesson 88

Labour is worship

_____

You touch, palm to palm. He kisses each knuckle.

'You have such strong, old woman's hands,' he chuckles, flattening them out. 'I feel very safe with them.'

'Worker's hands, mate.'

He wants to watch you. Sawing, hammering, drilling. With concentration and ingenuity and skill; he wants to learn it all, wants you to teach him and to hear you talk. And then he comes at you. Drawing you to him. Drawing in your energy.

You feel entirely awake.

Cicadas all about you, in the solid heat; their wall of shrillness keeping the world at bay, drowning out the sounds coming from you that you have never heard before, from the base of your spine, your core. Joyous and animal and astonished, as loud as you want. Because no one can hear you but Tol, leaning back. Smiling. Observing.

At what he has cracked from you.

'My biggest turn-on is how much you're enjoying it,' he says at one point and you tuck it away, must remember it; so removed from a grubby little episode in a warehouse near a train station once.

Back home, in your real life, your glee is the only leakage from your secret world and it gives you resilience and it gives you strength. To make someone so happy, what a power in that! A supreme power, surely, in a woman's life. Your days have been shrouded in cloud for so long but suddenly the sun has burst through and you are unscowled; filled with light. Sailing through all the wounds and slights of your stepmother now, through all the silences of your father; everything slipping from you like rain from an oil cloth. Nothing can touch you, nothing. You were born in a happy hour, you remember that from your early childhood; how uncomplicated everything was then, in the cradling, shining happiness of being cherished.

Lesson 89

There is a certain amount of work to be done,
and somebody must do it
___

The next gift. A geometry set your grandfather gave you, from
his school days; the handmade wooden case a marvel of careful
trays and slots. Tol whistles at its ingenuity. Hastily screws a
pencil stub into the compass's rusty metal and draws circles, in
delight, on a paper scrap.

'One thing you always have to do, is tell me – precisely –
what you want.'

He hands across a sheet of perfect circles, so carefully done
you can't discern the joins.

'But I don't *know* what I want. It has to be taught, doesn't it?
Like the finger in … in …'

Can't bring yourself to say it, he whispers it close. The blush
burns through you.

'There's this Italian author called Italo Calvino, who said
something about how the pleasures of love, just like gluttony,
depend on absolute … utter … precision.' His tongue laps your
earlobe, once, quick. You shiver.

'But where do I begin? I don't know.'

Without a word he leads you to the couch. Unclips one brace then the other. Holds a fingertip to your lips when you try to talk, to find out what's coming next. Three seconds his finger clamps your lips, four, five, six. Silence, anticipation, exquisite wet. He unbuttons the sides of your overalls. Kneels. Breathing shallow, pulling down your underpants as if he can scarcely believe he is doing this.

'It starts … right … here.'

He parts your lips, he finds your bud.

His tongue upon it as precise as a droplet of mercury.

You gasp.

Lesson 90

This busy, bright, beautiful world

'I want to learn. Understand. Be good at it, like you. I did it once before — well, almost' — Tol's eyebrows raise, he pulls back — 'but it was *nothing* like this.'

Completely serious, baffled; that two experiences, two men, could be so different. The shock of that — that you could have easily gone through life only knowing the former, never the latter; a whole universe denied, that you never knew existed. One experience so reducing; the other so alive, invigorating.

The wonder of that.

'I need to know more.' You speak slowly, faltering. It's so important, this. 'I have to understand what I shouldn't allow. Stand for.' Your voice drops. 'Ever.' A pause. 'And so I can give something back, too.'

He laughs in bewilderment — his fingers running like a rake through his hair — the weight of the request, the responsibility.

You're revving up, thinking how it can work.

'Lessons. Yeah. And then from me, something in return.' Because there must be a sense of giving, generously, on both sides; it's the only way you'll be comfortable with it. Thinking, thinking. 'I can help, of course. Around the house. I'll be teaching you, too. There's so much to still do here.' You clasp his hands. 'And you must tell me what you want. From me. With everything.' Utterly sincere. 'Please, *please* say yes.'

Tol's chin disappears into his neck as he stares and stares, blinking. His face saying it all: he doesn't quite know *what* to make of you, this strange, complex, thinking creature with its tool belt and happily grubby bare feet, so suddenly and forcefully in his midst; so eager to gulp up life, question, dissect. He goes to say something, stops. Holds your shoulders. Screws up his face. Kisses you once, soft, in the valley at the base of your neck then speaks with gravity, straight at you.

'I could only do it ... on two conditions.'

You grin. Gotcha. 'Which are?'

'Everything has to be consensual. Always.'

'On both sides,' you fire back and he laughs.

'Of course. You must never do something you're uncomfortable with – and that goes for me too.' He winces with helplessness.

'Oooh, the things I'm going to get you to do,' you tease, rubbing your hands with glee.

'And ...' He bites his lip. 'I'd love to teach you one thing –' a pause – 'just one, that I don't come across, very much.'

Your eyes narrow. 'Which is?'

'The woman who makes love heroically.'

'*What?*'

'Just remember, a man's biggest thrill is that his partner is enjoying it. Well, *this* man at least.' He comes up close, his fingers trickling deftly down your arms. 'We have to begin with tenderness. Yes. Always. Because that's all, ultimately, that's needed. It comes from a cherishing.' His eyes shine as he looks at you, his funny little scrap of a bush thing; his voice cracks and veers into something else. 'From love. And with that comes the best kind of sex. Because it's tinged with a … a reverence. It's almost like a holiness fluttering in you both.'

You feel like a blinded pit pony surfacing, coming up, up, into the light.

'Now,' you breathe.

He chuckles softly. 'Hang on, I need to prepare. Think. If we're going to do this properly. And we must.' A smile. 'The Most Secret and Mysterious Woondala Love Academy. Good grief. Who'd have thought. *Me*.'

You laugh, rubbing your hands in glee.

'Now. We need something to write in. Notes. Observations. So you'll always have them. They might come in handy one day. I'm a great believer in it.' His face lights up. 'That little instruction manual.'

You shake your head – 'I couldn't' – it's too old, valuable.

'Come on. Cough it up. Writers are always scribbling in books. It's often the only paper we can find. It's got some blank pages up the back, I remember.'

You slip it out of your pocket. He seizes it, flips through it, lingering over a line here and there.

'She'll be pleased, the old fox, chuckling away at it all, willing you on. She's a joy-seeker, this one. Cheeky. I just know.' He kneels, his hands travelling down your body. 'Yes, yes,' he's whispering, his mind galloping ahead, kissing your scuffed knees with their runnels of black, the rim of ochre between your toes, your ankle bone. He stands and holds your arms, looks straight at you, smiles secrets.

'My hidden … lovely … fabulous … crazy … school.' As if he can't quite believe it.

You smile, complicit. '*Our* hidden school.'

He nods. 'God yes. I need to do it better.'

'What?'

'Oh, everything. Life. Houses. Love. The lot.'

Your fingertip presses his lips, *sssh*, he kisses your nail in obeyance. 'But who's going to be the teacher here,' he murmurs. 'I wonder, I wonder.'

'Sssh,' you whisper again, hurry in your fingers as you pull him outside, to the waiting dam, the allure of its silky softness and the shock of its coolness in the heat, the possibility within it. He has never walked into it, felt the ooze of the mud between his toes, you can tell.

'The first classroom,' you instruct, 'come on.' Dropping the notebook down into the dust and whipping off your top and kneeling and unbuckling his belt.

Holding, in laden water, feeling the drips of your sweat, feeling yourself turning to water beneath him as you wrap yourself around him, in tenderness, where it always must start – holding and holding in the stillness and feeling him firm; reaching down, guiding him in; need him, crave him; you are all fluid, all marine under the cavern of that sky, briny and tasty and trembling and rolling and now you are a skin-diver, drinking in his depths with your lips and your breath and the wetness of your cunt — letting his world, this world, wash over you, drown you.

Lesson 91

Total and sublime equality

That night, late, you open your notebook, the meticulous record from now on; your voice adding to the author's over the coming days and weeks, the accumulation of your knowing in all its pages at the back. Your hands sweep across their waiting emptiness in exquisite anticipation. All the riches ahead that will fill it.

You flick back through her musings. A phrase leaps out.

Total and sublime equality.

Yes, of course.

It's the only way it can work, can ever work. You dog-ear the bottom of its page, the paper so brittle with age it's almost severed.

An invisible thumbnail beside her command — your first, secret indent in his book.

VI

'You should flee Eros: empty effort!
How shall I elude on foot one who chases
me on wings?'

Archias

Lesson 92

You will recognise the presence of a happy woman the moment she crosses your path – by a sense of brightness and cheerfulness that enters with her

---

Love.

The sheer malevolent force of it.

Stealing your sleep, stripping the flesh from your bones, watering your bowels, scrambling your thoughts; maddened by it all, when you are away from him. Maddened by tremors deep in your belly and tiny jolts unfurling through your groin, those sweetest shudderings of all – for the promise that's in them.

'Wait, wait,' he laughs. 'We have to do this methodically.'

'I can't.' You haul him down, hungry, always hungry.

He is careful, he is always thinking. You have a rash between your legs from his stubble but around your lips he never leaves a visible mark, so as not to draw attention to any of this. You are young, from the valley – this is a fierce mountain place – you are surrounded by mining men and he is everything this world is not. They will never know that you are snared in the heady days of this secret, illicit, cicada-shrill summer and you cannot escape, all these days when you both burn burn burn like a raging fire across a dry grass plain, consuming everything in its path.

'I just want to drink you,' he whispers, 'to the limit.' A finger to your lips. 'But we must be patient, my love, we must take this slowly, only now and then, step by step.'

'How do you mean? I don't want to!'

'Discipline, waiting, holding back – all of those things can be incredibly … potent. Be patient.'

But you, a wild thing in his midst. A force of nature, rampaging through his work, house, life; champing at the bit.

Lesson 93

You must put into her poor sore heart, if you can,
a little more than peace — comfort

He has gone to Sydney. He needed the break for work, business in town.

Three days, three churning days. You, wild, with want. Pacing, daydreaming, clutching your stomach, laughing out loud and barely knowing you're doing it. You cannot say why, to anyone. You hate it, the apart — but know instinctively you must respect his work, give him his time. He needs his space or you will lose him. You can't bear it. You have to.

Now. Back. Finally. On the top step of his verandah is a flat black box tied with a wide satin ribbon of the deepest grey. Waiting.

You slip apart the bow.

Lift high in wonder a high-collared cheongsam. The freshest, palest spring print from Liberty of London. You've never seen anything like it. Can't imagine wearing it. It's for another world, another life.

'Specially made. Just for you.' He leans against the door, watching. 'I know your size.' He comes forward. 'I know your waist span' – he brushes your belly with a kiss – 'and your neck.' His hands slip around it and his lips whisper a kiss against the dip of your throat. 'I know everything.' He asks you soft to wear the dress for him one day – not now – when you're ready.

'And one day you will be. We're only just beginning with this …'

Wet, at the thought. At what on earth is ahead, and you cannot imagine.

'One day I will button those tiny little silken buds in a firm, taut line.' A thrill of a stroke across your breast. 'A uniform of constraint … and release.'

You blush, don't know why. He picks up your little book. Turns to the back, to the fly-spotted card behind the cover, and writes.

RESTRAINT

'Elegance is refusal, and refusal is seductive.'

Diana Vreeland

He snaps the volume shut. Lifts up your flannelette shirt. Kisses you, once, on your nakedness, kisses your rolling belly, and tells you that this is all for today, enough – you must remember this feeling, this desire for release, this sense of explosion on its cusp.

'It's not a punishment, this waiting; it's a pleasure. The sweetness of anticipation … and the aching pain of it.'

You go to say something, he shushes you. 'I have work to

do, I need to crack on. This drives me as crazy as you. There's a lesson in that.'

Your crestfallen face.

'Tomorrow. All afternoon. I promise.'

Leaving you craving. Of course.

Craving as you wheel your bike along the Woondala road, squinting high into the ringing light, feeling like you're gazing up, up, up into a dazzling universe of borealis like sheets flapping on an enormous clothesline, and paper lanterns sailing to the heavens and gold leaf and gargoyles and shooting stars and snow petrels and supersonic jets, a brave new world, crammed with all manner of loveliness – a world you can't quite reach, that you don't completely know about.

Yet.

Lesson 94

What women need to learn in their friendships is
the sanctity of silence

Rain thrums on the roof in mid afternoon and he is in you,
in silence, unbearably close. He treats lovemaking with such
a reverence, you think; as he moves in you, there is something
close to a holiness in it. You must remember this, jot it in your
book. *Reverence*. So different to Mr Cooper. The gift of it.

The shuddering, up to your chest; the fluttering, deep in
your thighs. And then you fall asleep, back to back, as the rain
drums on the tin and lessens and stops and you press close,
sleeping like Siamese twins feeding off each other. Keeping
each other warm, alive, repaired, whole; being here together,
in perfect peace. You have become mixed with him, someone
else. There are no edges in your love, his flesh is yours and
yours his.

Shaken gently awake. To a new entry in your book, open on
his pillow, a rusty horseshoe splaying the pages.

SLEEP

*'Love does not make itself felt in the desire for copulation
(a desire that extends to an infinite number of women)*

but in the desire for shared sleep (a desire limited to one woman).'

Milan Kundera

He only writes inside the back cover; scrupulously never ventures to any page before it. The trust unspoken between you – that he will not hurt you or exploit you, will not chip away or reduce you. The understanding is explicit: you can never take this to its natural fulfilment without it.

'I have a big responsibility here,' he has said, 'you so young, eager, fresh. I never want to plunder that. Never want to make you cynical or bitter. I don't get why sex always seems to … taint. It shouldn't be like that.'

You smile as you turn from him, the rain patting softer now on the tin roof. Plumed by love; it is stealing your body, stealing your life – your future, your plans, your resolve – growing you tall, smiling you up, singing you into wakefulness. Stealing up through your limbs, stealing every part of you until finally it has snared the last resistor, your head that says no, this can never work, your father would never walk you down an aisle to this man, it cannot be, stop.

Too late.

Lesson 95

Begin again

'Tell me about your mother.'

'Why?' Defensive. It's never discussed. Any questions over the years about her, from anyone, have been bluntly headed off. Only with your father have you ever wanted to talk. And he won't.

'I just want to know about her. Understand. *You*. What's really in here.' He taps your skull. 'Why did you say to Julian way back at the start that you came from "nobody"?'

'I don't know. I don't want to talk about it.'

'Hey. I'm interested. In *you*. A good relationship is all about listening. Understanding. No one ever listens enough. Especially me. I've been told I need to get better at it.'

'But where does love fit into all of this?'

'Ah. That's about trusting someone enough to show them your true self. Being so comfortable with them that you can relax, completely. Be unlocked.'

You look at him. Take a deep, wavering breath.

'I never knew her ... really.'

Slowly, you begin; slowly, it all comes out. A whole afternoon of talk, the pain like a balloon of sadness within you, pressing against your insides, until at one stage the hot tears sneak through and he enfolds you silently in his arms and just holds you and holds you as the tears come and come, until you are quiet.

A wind-tossed boat, come to rest in a harbour, at last.

Thank you, you croak your gratitude at the end of it; for it feels like the first time you have ever properly talked about your past.

Lesson 96

Make your daily round of life as
harmoniously methodical as possible

The two of you are lying side by side on a flat slab of rock,
reading, the heat trapped in the stone that's pressing into your
stomachs.

'Tell me what didn't work before.'

'Why?'

'We have to wipe the memory of it.'

'That could be difficult,' you grimace.

'No harm in trying,' he grins.

You place your little Victorian volume face down on the
stone and rest your head on folded arms, thinking of the
bleakest, loneliest hour you've ever had in your life.

'There wasn't any tenderness. Even his kiss. His lips were
like these blocks of wood. They didn't know how to do it, I
could just tell.'

'Ah ha!' He snatches up your book, scrabbling in his pocket
for a pen. 'I have just the remedy.'

THE KISS

'The moth's kiss, first!
Kiss me as if you made believe
You were not sure, this eve'

Robert Browning

He hands the book back to you with the solemnity of ceremony. Instructs you to turn over, to close your eyes. Leans over you, arms propped, blocking out the glare of the sun, and kisses you.

The softest tiptoe of a kiss.

Later, inside you, he murmurs, 'Close your eyes.' And he kisses your eyelids and whispers, close, 'Wearing away our lips, from kissing each other's souls.'

'Excuse me, I should write that down.'

'Mr Pablo Neruda, if you must.'

You pick up the notebook that's increasingly shop-worn and try scribbling but abandon it as he kisses you, kisses you, kisses you and you, devouring, surrender and kiss back.

In the shining malaise of afterwards you tell Tol that you don't get it, how a kiss can feel so much more intimate than actual sex, is that right, are you mad?

'Oh no. You can't fake it. Whereas you can with intercourse.'

'Have you ever felt really, really lonely when you make love?'

'Explain.'

'Sort of like, the loneliest you've ever felt in your life. That there's an absolute – shocking – lack of connection.'

'Ooooh yes.'

'Who with?'

'Imagine feeling that through a long-term relationship. A marriage. And people do. A loneliness slicing through you. The kiss can signal a level of commitment that intercourse never can. There's something about the most connected of them that points to the deepest, profoundest intimacy.'

'Who with?' you press.

He doesn't say. 'We have to wipe away all our memories of the past ...'

'Show me again.'

He smiles. He complies. 'It's like a communication between equals, isn't it?'

'Equals,' you savour, drawing him to you again.

As you both grow more passionate he suddenly pulls back.

'I have to be careful not to leave a single trace on your face.' A finger travels down your cheek. 'But the moth's first kiss, again. Always. That's *our* kiss, yes. Forever.'

'Yes. Come on. I need to get this right,' you giggle.

Racing home in a high wind through the rearing, leaning, talking trees it's as if the very bush has watching eyes and applauding hearts; that the whole world about you knows your rapturous secret but you don't care, this cannot be stopped, it will journey on and on, further, deeper. To God knows what. Forever, he said. Forever.

You suddenly realise that you've left your notebook behind. All your deepest vulnerabilities, the raw underbelly of your life, the truth; you couldn't bear for anyone to read it. You hesitate, should go back, no.

You trust him, you trust.

Lesson 97

Look as you will, you cannot see your girlhood face anymore

―――――――――

'Where were we again?' he teases next time, first thing. 'I need reminding.'

Without a word you hook your hand around his neck and draw him in strong, a shepherd with their steady crook.

The moth's first kiss.

You have mastered it.

Wiping away anyone else.

'A fabulous kiss can be as evocative as smell, I think,' he smiles afterwards, in appreciation. 'One whiff – or one kiss like it again – and whoosh, it can plunge you back to another time, another place. A brighter phase of love. There can be something so … restoring … about it.'

You wipe your lip and stop. He suddenly feels past tense whereas you – achingly, enormously – are present.

'A passionate kiss can arrest a relationship's slow, glacial slide towards indifference,' he's murmuring on, pottering about, forever thinking, teaching, musing. 'Can wake a couple up – remind them of what they were.' He turns back to you. 'Thank you for that.' Gravely, as if he's tucking it into his heart.

You frown, wonder what he's referring to. He has a whole

other life in Sydney, you must never forget that, you barely know who he is. His former life, his *current* life. Beyond this hidden place, this secret summer. And he never tells you too much – he has a flat in Rushcutters Bay and a mother he never sees enough and a girlfriend who's ex. You think.

Your hand is arrested at your mouth. He reads the confusion, the dawning. Retrieves your book and hands it across, instructing you to look at his page at the back – not now, but tonight.

Later, you read:

'Wearing away our lips/from kissing each other's souls.'

Pablo Neruda

In an instant, you are veered back. All complication wiped.

Lesson 98

Our value is – exactly what we choose to make it

Your gratitude, your guilt. That it's starting to feel selfish. From your side, too much. That he's giving giving giving and you're taking and now you need to give something back. Isn't that how the world works?

'But my pleasure is watching your pleasure. That I can do this to someone. Unlock them, open them up. To joy.' He smiles a dirty smile. 'And lead you into another, better place.'

'But what can I do for *you*? Tell me one thing you love.'

He pauses. Rolls in his lips. 'There *is* something. But a lot of women … don't like it. I haven't suggested it before because I didn't want to turn you off. I never want to do that. Some women are revolted.'

'Try me.'

He traces the outline of your mouth with a fingertip. 'You have blow-job lips,' he says soft.

'Urgh. Lune says blow jobs are just for prostitutes.'

He laughs. 'I'd like to meet this girl some day. Have you ever given one?'

'Nup.'

'Do you want to?'

You think of give and take, generosity and selfishness,

dispensing pleasure as well as receiving it. 'I don't know. Maybe I'll just … try. A little.'

Kneeling. Naked. He standing before you, holding his penis.

'Now close your eyes, and lick,' he instructs. 'Like you're licking an ice cream. Imagine a flavour you're unsure of, that you find, actually, you love. Can't get enough of. Imagine.'

You giggle, hesitate.

'Sssh, it'll help.' He firms your head, you lick the tip of his penis. A bead of clear liquid emerges, a single drop, you tremble it up with your tongue tip.

'Now suck,' he whispers, pushing the back of your head onto him, deep into your mouth, further, until you are gagging and he pulls back and you suck soft and then lick in sweeps and he groans and comes, too quick, in a great jerking spurt, it spills down your throat and over your mouth and breasts and you gag and cough the sourness up.

He loved it. You can tell.

You did not.

He catches your expression. 'I'll never get you to do that again. But thank you, thank you for trying it.'

'But there was absolutely nothing in it for me!' you muse in the quiet of afterwards, spooning side by side on his mattress.

'You think too much, my lovely. You have to, don't you,' he teases. 'Dissecting everything.'

'It just felt so mechanical. Bleak. I could have been anyone, it wouldn't have mattered. No eye contact, nothing. Yuck.'

'Well aren't you lucky I enjoy giving so much, then?'

'Yes.' You wrap his arms tighter around you. 'I know, I know.' The guilt, but you have to be blunt.

'Some women find it incredibly empowering to be giving their man so much pleasure. They love calling all the shots, so to speak.'

'But it just felt so selfish to me. On *your* part.' You turn and poke him playfully in the stomach. 'I'm sorry.' You blush. 'It's not fair, I know.'

He chuckles. Point taken. 'Well, you might just be on to something there. There's this government campaign right now to reduce the teenage pregnancy rate by encouraging oral sex. Fascinating, isn't it?'

'Yep, and I bet it's always meant to be girls doing it to boys, never the other way around. And I bet a roomful of blokes was behind it.'

He looks at you solemnly. 'I'll never force you into anything you don't like. It's never my intention. Everything has to come willingly from you. OK? With whatever happens beyond this.'

'What do you mean? What's beyond this?'

You're teasing, he's serious.

'The best sex is all about equality. Listening. You're never going to get a great experience by demanding or insisting or bullying – because the other person will only shut down. And we mustn't have that.' A kiss lingers on the top of your forehead. 'I know there's a lot going on in that pretty little head of yours. I just want to find out what. Play. But I will always give you the chance to opt out.'

'Of what? *Tell me.*'

'Wait.' His finger on your lips. 'Be patient. You, my love, have to lead me – as much as I lead you.'

'But I don't *know* what I want!'

'Oh you do,' he breathes deep, once, shutting his eyes, 'you're just not telling me.' He abruptly stands. 'I'll see you in two days. I've got work to do.'

Maddened. By all of it. An electric fence he has switched on – ever alert, waiting, poised; ever ready to crackle and fizz and jump.

For whatever he wants.

Lesson 99

All I desire is that you should love worthily
_____

That night, late, you write in your notebook something Tol said to you once, about his previous partner. 'Sex with a girlfriend always becomes routine. *Always*. No matter how much you love them. The trick is to arrest the sense of sameness – if you can. If she lets you. And you hope she does. I do, at least.'

Addled, by whatever is next. By how the lessons will be ratcheted up. How to detonate ennui with difference of some sort. The grand experiment. For both of you.

You suspect it has everything to do with honesty.

That's all he wants.

What's in your head, your deepest, hidden thoughts.

Lesson 100

What a reward there is in this — to a woman!

'I want to read. Learn. In the days in between. When you're working. Give me some books.'

'Hmm, let me think. Neruda, of course. And Sappho, lovely, sexy, stroppy Sappho. Nin. *The Story of O*. Oh yes.'

'But how do I get them? I can't just walk into a bookshop. Ask my father. Or stepmother.'

He laughs. 'Lie down on the couch, and wait.'

Slivers your big toe into the curl of his tongue. Pushes your index finger into your cleft. 'You have to learn to do all this for yourself, young lady. For those times when I'm not around.'

Your heart skips a beat. He reads it.

'Like when I'm in the next room, that's all. *You*. Stop thinking too much. Like when I'm choosing your latest textbook. That will give your stepmother a coronary, alright?'

'Oh!' A relieved laugh.

Lying on the couch, waiting, as languid as an abandoned scarf.

A battered paperback.

'Read it,' he instructs.

You do. Introducing yourself to a woman called O. A tingling washing through you as you are lost within her story, devouring her vulnerability, her need, her honesty, her appetite, forgetting he is watching until he is suddenly pulling away your panties – assisting, urgently – and you are pushing your fingers in further, then further, tickling, swirling, groaning; until he is taking over, with a rush dipping in with his tongue and his fingers and his lips and slurping you up until you slam the book down and arch your back and come and come, in great briny gushes, lost in the loveliness.

'Turn over,' he whispers.

'I can't,' you murmur. 'I have to be alone –' as the waves of lovely pulsing pain glare on, and on, and on.

'Trust me,' he whispers. And when you are still, when you are quiet, you do what he asks. Because you do.

Gently, so gently, he raises you on your haunches, on all fours. Tenderly he parts your cheeks. You feel the shiver of a shock of his tongue on your arse, around it; you gasp in surprise and after the initial clench you let go, you surrender and you are suddenly thrusting your buttocks out to him – needing it wanting it your back a straining saddle and then you come again, too quick. Lying curled on your side. Spent. Away from him. Away from the world.

Wondrous.

That your body is capable of so much. So much *pleasure*. Cracking you open, into someone else. Someone intensely alive, fully human; to the absolute limit of who you are. You lie back and laugh in astonishment.

He gathers you up, cocooning you in his arms like a caterpillar in a leaf.

'This is just the start, my love. And now you know the secret: that great sex can only happen when we completely, totally, let go. All our masks, all our inhibitions, gone. And if we surrender completely, like that good, brave O, then we show someone else our true selves, our very core. And that can be ... extraordinary. To do, and to witness.' He's quiet. 'Rare,' he whispers. 'Thank you for that.' A butterfly of breath flits by your ear.

You smile. At the power you have just wielded.

For he is speaking as if he has never before seen it.

Who is snaring who?

Live your life as bravely and generously as possible. Never forget that.

You find it that night, in the back of your notebook.

Lesson 101

Oh, if women did but know what comfort there is in a
cheerful spirit!

_____

It is written. What he loves:

> *A woman who looks like she knows what she is doing.*
> *Who laughs in bed. Who looks like she has sex every day,*
> *three times a day – whether she does or not.*

'It's that sense of carnality, shall we say. Even just a hint of
it drives me wild. I saw it in you right from the start, from the
moment my groceries were dropped. Did everything to resist.'
You poke out your tongue. 'Well I won, didn't I?'
'Maybe ...'

It is written. What you are learning:

> *The more sex I have the more I want. And the more*
> *extreme I want it.*

'You're like a baby Jane Birkin,' he laughs when you pounce
on him now, in greedy greeting, wrapping your legs around his

waist and trying to scrabble his clothes off; not a second of this precious time to waste – bugger the book! 'There's a gamine steel to you, isn't there?'

'Who are you talking about?'

He mock-groans, shakes his head.

'So much to learn, young miss.'

'Yep. Come on then, let's begin.' You rip two buttons off his shirt with sheer, brute, exuberant strength. 'The lesson for today is …'

Lesson 102

The principle cause of woman's downfall
is their being afraid of truth

But at night, late, the worry comes sneaking in, elbowing aside any sleep. Who was this old girlfriend who crushed him so cruelly, where is she, is she hovering, lingering, *how far did it go*? Why is he trying to do all this, with you – pushing boundaries, promising extremities until God knows what. What's his motive? Is it dark? Are you distraction? Some kind of experiment? Is she still there, somewhere; is he using you to work out what's best; how far he can take it? There's a triangle here, a mysterious absence, you just don't know enough. He won't tell you a lot yet is asking too much now for memories, desires, thoughts, truths, with the greed of a surgeon extracting organs for research.

'But what *happened*?'

A sigh. Always a sigh, when he wants your probing to stop. You're not letting up.

'Tell me, or I'm never coming back. She's like this great weight on me. And it's because I don't know – so can only guess. I'm going crazy with it. Julian seemed to think it was pretty huge. What did he say … that it's taken you *years* to get over it.'

An abrupt sigh. 'She's called Cecilia. I don't like talking about it.'

'Why?'

'For some people, fear ends up dictating all their choices in life.'

'Fear of *what*?'

'Oh, everything. Not pleasing, being judged, showing your true self et cetera.'

'Go on.'

'Well, if you must know, there's a school of thought that the whole point of sex is to destroy a person's sense of self-containment. To bring them closer to living, to life, if you like. In all its magic – and all its messiness.'

He unbuttons your overalls. Swiftly, as if he barely knows what he is doing. He folds down the flap. Undoes the shirt. His fingers hover over your bare breasts and your nipples slowly harden under his gaze but he does not touch, not touch, as if he can't, anymore, can't bear it, can't do it anymore; this has to stop.

You clamp his hands to you, hold them firm, you do not let up.

'She never had the courage to be known,' he whispers, 'truly, deeply. She never spoke her mind.' He looks up at you. 'Which meant I never knew what she was really thinking. And I *need* to know that.'

You step back. Why does he need to, so much? His hand brushes against the Victorian volume in your pocket, the secret rawness of all your thinking that no one will ever know; you couldn't bear it. He comes right up close, grips your upper arms and whispers that everyone is at their most vulnerable when it comes to sex; that it's the closest we ever get to revealing our true selves in all our banality and our beauty, our desperation and our foolishness, and it's beautiful, so beautiful – the complexity of it – the glittering, vulnerable, fascinating, greedy, ugly, intriguing truth.

'A lot of us can't face the thought of being seen as we really are, and we never get closer to the core of our deepest selves than with sex. I failed Cecilia. Failed *with* her. Never made her comfortable enough.'

'For what?'

'For opening up.'

He slips out your notebook and you exclaim, try to grab it back but he's got it, high, he swivels away and turns to the back page, his allotted space that only he ever goes to. Fumbles in his pocket for a pen, scribbles something. You snap up the buckles of your overalls. Want this to stop now. There's some kind of coldness operating here; some sense of excavation, gutting.

'I love you,' you say. He doesn't respond. Glances up with what, warmth, pity? You feel stripped.

'I don't feel like doing this anymore. Today,' you say.

He looks at you. Surprise. A new tone, for the first time in all this. He nods, OK, and without a word he hands your notebook back.

It is only outside, before you get on your bike, that you open the page he has written on.

CARNALITY

'How many splendid loves I have dreamt of.'

Rimbaud

It doesn't help. You snap the book shut.

Lesson 103

She should never lie down at night without counting up,
'How much have I done today?'

———————

Harangued by sleeplessness.

Learning from your stepmother. The power in withdrawal and in silence. You do not go back, the next day or the next, leaving no explanation; let him sweat.

Feverishly you are writing in your little book, gathering all your thoughts; every page but his filling up.

What you are learning about what men want. Your grand and meticulous experiment. You, too, can be the observer in all this.

Precision: Saying exactly what is required, and where.

A verbal response: 'Too many women believe sex is a spectator sport,' he has said. 'Silence is not always golden. Women want to feel loved, desired, attractive – well, we men do too, only we don't like to admit it. Verbal encouragement is the biggest turn on. It confirms desire. And we all want to see that.'

Enthusiasm: 'We don't want to feel a partner's just going through the motions. If you love someone, yet get the feeling during sex that they're just not that interested, it's such a turn off.' You can't ever imagine that, with him. 'If the man's always the one to propose sex eventually we feel like some small kid pestering Mum for sweets — unwanted, undesirable, a nuisance.'

Happiness: 'All I want is a woman who's happy.'
'Really?'
'It's all a man ever wants.'
'Why?'
'Because from that comes everything else.'

Imagination: It's not unusual, or wrong, or odd, to be thinking of another scenario entirely as you're being made love to; a scenario that has little to do with the person having sex with you. They may be just a trigger for the process, a trigger for the movie in your head. There shouldn't be any guilt about it; you have come to this conclusion yourself, haven't discussed it with him.

You slam down your pen, it's what he wants, of course: to chisel out your innermost thoughts. Jackhammering away at all the defences you put up, that anyone puts up. What is he writing himself? You wonder. Turn back to your book with a furious pen.

*HE WILL NEVER KNOW. THE CORE OF WHO I
AM. NO ONE WILL EVER KNOW THAT.*

He will not let you go until he knows, instinctively you
sense this. You are gaining knowledge, strength.

He will no longer write in your book. You will not give him
the chance.

The potency in withdrawal, in silence. The magnificent
coldness of the punishment.

Lesson 104

Contemn her not, for her state might not have always been thus; you know not the causes which produced it; and — stay till you see her end

---

But then you soften, can't do this; the cruelty of no explanation. Can't live with the sourness of your stepmother, it's not in your heart.

He has laid a claim over you. Over land, property, possessions, a body — the violence is the same; there is nothing economical or skimped about your obsession — it is fulsome, extravagant, wasteful. *Complete*.

On the outside Tol's everything your father couldn't bear, couldn't understand. But you have found who you should be with him. It feels like he is more you than you.

Your father will never understand.

I HAVE NO CHOICE.

You write jagged in your notebook.

Like a butterfly you are pinned, by desire.
So. Back. Of course. You will always go back.

Lesson 105

This, her life-chronicle, which, out of its very fullness,
has taught her that the more one does,
the more one finds to do

His smile on the verandah, as he waits, as you walk up the path, says he knows exactly where you've been and why you've done it.

'Your lesson today – a treat,' is all he says, leading you inside by the hand; just squeezing it tight, in thanks. 'If you're up for it.'

You squeeze your readiness back.

Leading you to a razor placed carefully on a folded linen napkin. Pleasingly weighty, silver. Waiting in readiness, by the chaise longue.

'Take off your clothes,' he breathes, 'and lie down. Now, think of O. Being readied …'

He retreats to the kitchen and returns with a bowl of soapy water.

'Trust me,' he whispers, tenderly parting your legs. 'This is not going to hurt. But tell me if you want to stop …'

You wince at the first stroke, the shock of the cold. He is removing the hair in long, practised strokes, gently guiding the instrument in all the dips and crevices.

Wetter, and wetter, and wetter, as he works.

'Women have been doing this for centuries,' he explains softly. 'They used tweezers in Roman times. South Sea Islanders did it and then tattooed the lovely, brave flesh. It's a tradition in Arabic cultures. It increases sensation, apparently. Just you wait.'

You can't. You come.

Feeling so raw, open, exposed. Can barely contain your coming, the spasms tripping over themselves. His head dips down, he is laughing in delight, he is lapping you up in eagerness. When you come again you almost break his neck – he is scissored between your legs, trapped, drenched, you have varnished his face. He laughs and you laugh and now you know why men perceive women in terms of the sea, water, fluids, and you have no idea what is next, how this ends, does it ever end? He is like dry ice on the tongue, you flinch in shock but you can't help tasting again and again, coming back for more, always more, in blind and furious want.

'It's so weird,' he murmurs in the solid quiet of afterwards, 'that what began as a trend purely for male fantasy – to maximise exposure, if you like, as in porn – has become this amazing symbol of sexual empowerment for women. Do you feel empowered? Does it really work like that?'

'Yes,' you whisper, 'yes.' Opening your raw lips for him with the V of your fingers, spreading yourself wide, in wonder, splitting yourself apart. 'Yes, yes. Come in. Now. *Please.*'

He is a drug. You are enslaved.

Back and back you will go, always back. You can't not.

Lesson 106

Maria and Bob used to go home laughing,
and thanking their stars that they *did*
live in that shocking place London

A constant state of readiness, now. Bare. Sublimely aware, and knowing you'll have this raging sense of illicitness later, and days later – every time you move, as you peel the potatoes, eat the Sunday roast, vacuum and sweep, clean out the chook house – all the time you'll be squeezing your legs together and thinking of *him*, what he has transformed you into; a woman bound. By want.

'It'll start to itch,' he's warned you, his fingers tracing his handiwork and bringing on the stirring all over again, the slightest touch triggering you off. 'I'm sorry.'

'Well, we'll just have to keep doing it. Maintenance. It's always important, that.'

Aware, as you walk inside your house with a childish slap of the screen door.

Aware, as you brush past your stepmother and put on your apron.

Aware, as you greet your dad from his shift and yarn over the bonnet of an old Ford Falcon up on bricks, yakking away about the heat, how it's bringing out the snakes, and the dams are dropping and church, on Sunday, you need to get back, yes Dad, yes.

Almost coming with it as you talk, squeezing your groin on it.

Do they see it in your face, your stroll, your stance? Your proud, walk tall love. Do they have any inkling, of any of it?

This threshold you have crossed.

You congratulate yourself on your cleverness. Squeezing your rawness, smiling, exquisitely calibrated.

Lesson 107

The wonderful law of sex exists spiritually
as well as materially

_____

He has taken to writing on sheets of paper, he has retreated
from your book but he will not give up.

THE KEY

One of the most transcendent joys available to women.

'And I'm so jealous of it.' He smiles a knowing smile as he
holds up the page. 'Ready?'

You nod. Bite your lip.

Delicately, he parts your lips. Licks, once; a shiver of tongue.
You exclaim as if you've been burnt.

'God has given women the most glorious gift imaginable.'

'Which is?' you groan, clutching his hair.

'The only organ on the human body – on either body – that's
devoted entirely to one thing. *Sensation*,' he chuckles, stroking,
teasing. 'Endless, lovely ... sensation. It is, of course, the clit.
Which has eight thousand nerve endings. Can you believe it?
Twice as many as the boring old penis. And you must never,
ever believe that the vagina is the explosive centre of female
pleasure. Alfred Kinsey found that its interior walls, deep

inside, actually have very few nerve endings, that they're real[ly]
quite enormously insensitive – compared to what's on top.' H[e]
smiles conspiratorially. 'But this is something, I think, that a[ny]
woman knows.'

He kisses your clit in reverence.

'This tiny, beautiful bud is the doorway to all the myster[y]
and power of making love; a woman's gateway to the divin[e.]
In Greek mythology, when Zeus and Hera visited th[e]
hermaphrodite Tiresias – trying to work out whether it wa[s]
men or women who experienced the more pleasure from sex [–]
Tiresias replied, "If the sum of love's pleasure adds up to te[n,]
nine parts go to women, only one to men." And it's all dow[n]
to this.' His tongue gently encircles your clit. 'The one thin[g]
guaranteed to lay a woman waste. If she'll let you near it.'

You push Tol's face onto you, into you, can hardly bear [it]
anymore; need all this talking to stop.

He bobs up, grins. 'I need to get your toes pointing. That[']s
my next task.'

'*What*? Just get on with it.'

'It's a sure sign of orgasm. And there's an awful lot of to[e]
pointing with cunnilingus. It's a much more certain way o[f]
bringing a woman to orgasm than vaginal sex ever is.'

Your toes as flexed as a ballerina's, again and again, tha[t]
afternoon. Until you have to push him from you, away, ge[t]
him off. Because your nerve endings are aching, exhauste[d,]
screaming for rest.

Lesson 108

We just plod on together, men and women alike,
on the same road

A grave instruction, the next time: you must always, *always* tell him if you don't orgasm, if what he is doing isn't working, you must never pretend; this whole process will grind to a halt if you do that.

'But wouldn't you know?'

'Sometimes, believe me, it's hard for us Neanderthals to work out.'

'I thought modern girls knew how to have orgasms like their mums knew how to cook Sunday roasts.'

He laughs. 'You'd be surprised. It's extremely easy for a woman to pretend. But if you do it means I've failed. I have married friends – women – who've never had an orgasm in their life. I need to know. So I can help. I need honesty, that's all, you know that.'

'Are you doing this for me, or for you?'

He rolls his eyes, he says nothing.

A chill, again, at why exactly he is doing this. You will never know him; you love him. The impossibility of that. You wonder if you love him because of the chip of ice within him

– that rangy, jittery distance you can't quite broach. He says he is obsessed, can't get enough of you and then he walks away, because of his work, apparently, shutting you out; he goes off to his room and locks the door and tells you to go away, time is up, he needs to be alone. For a day, two, sometimes three. And then he rushes to you when you walk your bicycle up his drive and you are so pathetically grateful; craven, greedy, lost. Ready. For anything. He knows it.

Resistance is sexy. He has mastered that. The tension in a stretched wire, singing with tautness.

You are writing all through the notebook now, cramming the margins of the author's written words, the bottom of her pages and the top of them.

The awful question, the perilous dynamism; a dynamism of absence and presence. If he wanted you completely and consumingly, if he conveyed that weakness – would *you* want him? Would serenity, stasis, knowing sink the boat? This love is a verb not a noun. It is galloping, withdrawing, retreating, surging – backwards, forwards – forever restless, refusing stillness and rest.

It is exhausting.

You are becoming thin with it, skin and bone. And it can only get worse.

You can't get it stopped.

You need to know what's next. Always what's next. It's how he has bound you to all this.

You are on a path.

And every morning now your little diary of observation is slipped into the pocket of your overalls, the new journal that your stepmother will never find because she would never think to glance at it; just another old book with a patched-up cover, from school no doubt. It is your explosive instruction manual for encroaching womanhood, the words you must never forget. *Your* words, now, more so than his; as you become more aware. As you step into being the woman he wants. And observe. Detach.

Lesson 109

In any profession, there is nothing which is so injurious,
so fatal, as mediocrity

Exploring what your body can do.

To the limit, he commands.

His project. That he will facilitate. That he will observe.
And take mental notes, you are sure; so keenly he watches.

He tells you he wants you to be in awe of what your body
can achieve, to learn it, revel in it, *unlock it*.

'Work out what's best; use me, come on. Position me. Find out
what you want. Every woman is different. Should I be behind
you, on top, underneath? Experiment. Live with audacity! Make
your man a better lover. Every man you have. *Teach* them. We
need to learn as much as you. Find the animal in you, the carnal,
what you feel not what you think. What *works*.'

You do. Working out the best ways to orgasm while he's
inside you; angling him with hands on slim hips. So he's
rubbing against your pelvic bone, so he's stimulating your clit;
guiding him, talking him through it, yes, over there, yes, more,
that's it!

'I'm learning *so* much,' he pants his gratitude, 'you're like
a blank slate, pure instinct, it's glorious.'

You giggle to hear it and then suddenly, without understanding, you are crying. He licks up your tears in one long salty sweep, one cheek, then the other.

'What's this?'

'I – I don't know.' Struggling to find words. 'It's just ... all of this, it feels like it's for ... I don't know, men, in the future, you said *every man you have* but I don't want anyone else – I – you're shaping me for ... what? Someone else. Some*thing* else. My future? Like you're not going to be in it? You want to create the perfect lover – but for who?' You thump his chest. '*Who?*'

He stares in surprise.

'I'm doing this for you.' Finally, matter-of-fact. 'Don't you get it?'

'No.'

'One day you will.' He rolls off you. 'And you'll be grateful. That you had all this at the start. Because believe me, most women don't have the luxury of it.'

You thump him hard in the chest with your fists.

'Ow!'

Lesson 110

I once asked a man — in his own house a father whose authority was unquestioned, his least word held in reverence, his smallest wish obeyed — 'How did you manage to bring up these children?' He said: 'By *love*.'

'Come on,' he soothes, 'let's have some fun. We both need it right now.' He raises an eyebrow. Goes to the kitchen. Returns with a bowl of ice cubes.

'Allow me to demonstrate.'

He parts your legs, pops in a cube, and leans down with the utmost tenderness.

Your back arched in a radiant flinch.

That afternoon, the shadow of a terrible truth. Whether you love Tol or hate him is indiscernible, not important anymore. You want him, just that. It is neither love nor hate but hunger: wolfish, rangy, focused.

Something entirely different.

Lesson 111

Put the whole past life aside as if it had never been

_____

Wiped clean by a new day, the anticipation over what's next.
A heading on his page, just that:

THE G SPOT

The rest of the paper blank.
'Where's the lesson?'
'This one, you have to work out for yourself.'
You snort a laugh.
'Some people think it doesn't exist in a woman,' he whispers,
a moth to your ear. 'But it does, oh it does.'
'Where?'
'You have to find it. I can't help. Much.'
A full-length mirror from his bedroom is placed in readiness
against a lounge room wall.
'In men the G spot's in their arse.' He chuckles as he guides
you before the mirror. 'But with you, well, let's just see if we
can locate it. Sit. Legs wide.'
You do.
'Wider.'
You laugh, you do.

'Now get your finger, your ring one, yep, and kind of hook it – on the front wall, so to speak. Tender. Slow. Yes. That's it. Forget about me, concentrate.' He says nothing more, he sits back on the couch, he watches, leaves you to it.

It takes a while, and then, and then, oh God, it is found.

Cracked. Blazing, with light. With life.

His hand is around his cock and you both come at the same time and through the haze of your exquisiteness, your body seized up, you see his semen spurting out; its beautiful blue white as shiny as varnish and he comes to you and gathers you up and holds you and holds you, dabbing it on your forehead and cheeks and lips, thanking you for the gift of it.

Anointing you, blooding you, binding you.

'I promise that I will never ask that vile little question, "how was it for you?"' he says later, helping you into your clothes.

'Don't all boys do that? Lune says they do.'

'Not this one.'

'And why would that be, mister?'

'Because I know.'

Lesson 112

Mature age – when the passions die out or are quieted down
_____

He is expecting guests, for three days, you'll have to stay away. He bats off all your questions, they're old acquaintances, too boring to talk about but they have to come – sigh – they must.

Your crestfallen face.

'Hey,' he soothes, 'none of that. Just remember one thing. A woman is sexy if she thinks she is. OK? And you *are*. Don't lose it. Neediness isn't sexy. Hold that thought.' His voice drops to a whisper. '*Believe* the power that you have. That will stay with me over the coming days, hours, minutes. Alright?'

He runs a fingertip down your belly and stops, shutting his eyes for a moment. Your fingers hover at the buckles of your overalls, he catches them up.

'Not yet. Wait. Imagine us as two dogs on heat, kept apart in their cages and then ... released. This is good, reviving. We need it. Constraint, and release – remember?'

Of course you return. The next day. You have your bush skills, can be as quiet as a tracker when you want.

The gate is locked.

You bang your fist into it. It rings with your fury.

Right.

Crazed, now, with suspicion.

Because of that comment about how sex with the same partner always becomes routine, no matter what; we all need variety he said and you still aren't quite sure what he meant; your heart pounds. *Who's in there?* You are his plaything, his construct; he is moulding you for something – someone – else. Who? What?

Love to hate, such a little step, and you can feel, even now, a whiff of its fetid breath. If he stops craving you then by God you will stop craving him; you feed off each other, it's the only way this can exist.

Thumping your fists into the fence. Again, and again, and again.

Lesson 113

Man and woman were made for, and not like, one another
_____

Three days later.

The gate is unlocked, of course, and you are rushing through it knowing it's pathetic but you can't not do this. Be this. He runs out to you, encircling you in his arms and mumbling something about how vile it all was, the guests, it didn't work, crashing into his life and his writing and his space; but he won't say who, what; claims he has no idea about a gate that was locked and you seize it and are assuaged, you have to be for this to work. Have to trust, yes. And you note as he speaks, as if for the first time, the something that's always so sad about his eyes. When he sees you, when he smiles, they detonate with warmth but when he's not aware you're looking – it's like a peek through a curtain at a secret you know nothing of and you wouldn't want to, no, you shouldn't delve, you won't like it, you sense that.

Who is he?

Written, more than once, in your notebook.

He laughs that afternoon in puzzlement. 'I'm a failed writer. I'm far too old for you. I'm not great with kids. So never ask me that.'

He is the one.

Written, more than once, in your notebook.

'Love has no right to be all knotty and tangled, does it?' he muses that afternoon, more to himself than to you. 'It should be the easiest, cleanest, clearest thing in the world. Don't you think? It can often be so fearful; but you know, with you, I don't feel afraid at all.' He speaks as if he can't quite believe it; the miraculous simplicity, at last.

You breathe shallow; fear he is someone who will always feel strongest when he's by himself, that he will never enfold anyone with the great calm of ownership – so while anyone is with him they'll be obsessed, always thinking, 'when's this going to end?' and never knowing and tormented by it.

This is impossible, you must pull out.

I will change him.

Written, more than once, in your notebook.

'But you are strong,' he is murmuring, more to himself than to you. 'Much stronger than me. And a better writer. A ruthless observer. I know it already.'

'Really?'

'Oh yes. It's in your eyes. You'll write something one day, I just know it. You've got the chip of ice.'

Lesson 114

Tom, Dick and Harry, their brothers, has each had it knocked into him from schooldays that he is to do something, to be somebody

---

Languid in the stillness of his dam. Floating on your back, naked, your arms outstretched.

'Are you ready for my cheongsam?' He teases from the dam bank, holding out the flat black box. You laugh him off in the sparkling light. Take your time coming out. Let the sun be your towel; it leaves you brushed with the finest, silkiest ochre.

You finally smile, yes.

Slip on the dress in the open air.

'Oh my,' he whispers, as he closes up each silken bud of a button across your breast, and sanctifies each knot with a kiss. He takes out a camera from a worn leather satchel.

You step back. Hang on. You weren't expecting this.

'Please?'

You shake your head, not sure you like this; don't know why but you're suddenly thinking of those lost three days and the guests he won't talk about — others, watching; some kind of auditioning shot. For someone, something, else.

'Why are you doing this?'

'So I always have you.'

'Huh?'

'I'm a collector, you know that. Plates, shells, paintings, pencils, ravishingly beautiful photographs …'

'So how many times have you done this bit? With how many other girls, mister?'

He laughs in bewilderment. He doesn't say; ignoring enrages you, it always has.

'Tol?' Serious.

'What do you think?'

You, standing there, stilled by suspicion; he, still fiddling with the lens of a heavy Nikon FM. You've never seen such a camera up close, your family are instamatic people. He, clicking tentatively, once, into your scowl and then again, smiling, moving around; you, now, leering at the lens, crinkling up your nose and poking out your tongue – cheekying up – not giving him what he wants, anything but that.

'Lift up your skirt a little,' he cajoles. 'Just for me. Come on.'

'No.'

His hand drops the camera.

You fold your arms. 'Not until you say you love me, mister.'

A vibrating silence.

Your hands gather the cloth at your hips. Inch it up, teasing. Stop, just. 'I'm waiting.'

He says it.

He *says* it. He says it.

Shy. As if the words are not used to his mouth.

You grin, on that dam bank, in chuff, and lift up your skirt in triumph. Nothing underneath, of course. Freshly bare, raw – your choice. The cheongsam is now bunched around your waist. You spin around, laughing in the light. He closes his eyes for a second then lifts up his camera half playful, half hopeful but your hand snaps to attention and covers his lens, strong.

Blazing. 'Put it down. Say you love me again. Just that. No more photographs. I don't get why you're doing this.'

He looks straight at you. 'There is nothing to "get". From the first moment I saw you I was caught.' Speaking sincerely, it is in his face. You are quiet. 'My whole body resisted … but it didn't work.' A pause. 'And so here we are.' He places his camera back in his satchel. 'I wanted to have you forever, by my desk. That's all. Somehow. However I could. In case you … disappear … somehow, from my life.'

You look at him doubtfully; it will never come to that, how could it possibly? He sighs and picks up your book in the pocket of your abandoned overalls. You let him, you trust. He takes out his nub of a flat architect's pencil and writes in his allotted space at the back, only there.

You must look in it tonight, not before; you must resist.

That is the request as he walks up the steep bank of the dam, without looking back. That you obey, of course.

Because he said he loved you. He said it.

At *last*.

Lesson 115

To 'grow old gracefully' is a good and beautiful thing;
to grow old worthily, better

That night you open his words from under your pillow like
a favourite chocolate you've hidden in a box, for this exact
moment, your midnight treat.

> *I feel there is some obligation I have to fulfil with you, in*
> *the way of a gift.*
> *Something spiritual and rare. We 'fit', so to speak, and*
> *I feel an enormous calm because of it.*
> *Believe that.*

The golden thrum washes through you like liquid sun under
your skin. Does he attract you because of his certainty? You
feel he knows exactly who he is in life and will not change and
there is something so solid, so settled about that; whereas you
are anything but.

Another gift, you have been tardy of late: a battered, rectangular
tobacco tin, words barely upon it.

CAPSTAN
Navy Cut Cigarettes.
W.D. & H.O. Wills, Sydney.

Perfectly the length of his architect's pencils; the entire collection of them.

Lesson 116

How mysteriously soul and body act and react upon one
another

_____

The lessons gather pace. He tauntingly resets your experience
of sex, obliterating every touch, every thought that has gone
before him; wiping you clean, saturating your memory with
his caress and his alone. He slips inside with a groan, as if it's
all, almost, too much. He roams your body, discovering new
nooks, crevices, valleys, new plains of torment.

'I like exploring,' he smiles.

He's meticulously careful never to come inside you; he
ejaculates on your stomach, neck, through your hair, dabs it
tenderly on your lips and kisses it off, spurts it in triumph.
He's always careful, so careful, to never rub away at the skin
around your lips – the moth's kiss, first, always – so as not to
draw attention to any of this. Your father must never know, no
one must.

Now you're on top – 'Throw back your head,' he commands
as his eyes eat your body up.

'Keep laughing,' he commands. 'That's it, *glorious*.' You feel
empowered, strong, lit.

'Love that body God has given you, all its miraculous gifts,' he commands, 'what it can do, what it's changing you into.' As you do, you realise the great secret: an enjoyment of sex isn't about technique, or cleavage, or a perfect body.

It's about confidence.

Lesson 117

The perpetual dread and danger of exposure
_____

Returning, always returning. Because he has burnished your days with light. Your emboldened back as you walk down the corridor of your house, as you roam the aisles of the supermarket. You're sure everyone must know, *something*; it is in your eyes, your shoulders, your new height, spark. Love, you now know, is the supreme propulsion of life – the great repairer, rescuer, uplifter. You feel sexy, sexier than ever before, you are turning into someone else.

He says you have the most beautiful innocence, a radiance. He loves your passion for life, for living, he says it shines from you and is in awe of it. He says you have an absence of cynicism, you're not afraid to lower yourself with enthusiasm and some people think that's a weakness – like a smile or an apology – but he doesn't. He loves that you don't wear perfume. The smell of the earth in your skin, your hair. Under your arms, between your legs. He wants you to love your body, to know it, to not be afraid of it. He says you must never lose your sense of ludic, a word he loves, your playfulness, your spark. You must never be pushed to the side of your life, from the core of who you are, you must never let a man do that.

He could never do anything to hurt you, he pledges, doesn't

want to push you, needs you. You cannot sleep properly, cannot eat properly. You keep running to the toilet, diarrhoea, can't stop smiling, staring into space, lost. You fly on your bike and then fling it aside in its ditch and run up his road; never quite sure if he'll be there, jittery, craving. Turning your head at his gate as you whizz past in the car – always checking – that it's not stopped, this secret Woondala life, that it will never stop.

You will do anything for him now to keep that gate ajar, you are bewitched. He has whispered of collars, of handcuffs, other people, men, women … *let's see how far we can take this.* You do not know what is next. You want it. You trust him. You are ready to be laid bare, stripped.

Ready, at last, for the next step.

As you walk away on a sun-smeared afternoon there's an enormous joyous raucous shriek: a white cockatoo – then twenty, maybe thirty – before you, all around you, playing. Landing on the roof and the falling fences and flimsy tree branches that don't quite support their weight, flopping upside down, clinging to the rocking branches and working their wings, squawking and playing and squabbling and you laugh out loud, at all of it, all, its joyously screechy fabulous magnificence. Seizing life, seizing all of this. You sit in the middle of the dust and extract your battered little book.

I am becoming known. I have found the courage. I am ready. I trust.

Lesson 118

Perhaps she makes a pride, and her husband a joke,
of her charming ignorance in common things

But then other days: a souring. A falling away. No, not today,
you just want to read a newspaper, rest, in stillness and laziness;
put it all aside like the richest of chocolate cakes you have
gorged upon too much.

And then.

The whisper behind your ear.

'I want to do so many things with you. Before it's too late.'

'What do you mean?'

'Explore.'

He turns you around, he kisses you tenderly, once.

'Please,' he says. 'Will you let me,' he says. 'For a lot of women
experimental sex is associated with pain. Coercion. Fear.' His
lips, a flutter of a butterfly against your ear. 'But it doesn't have
to be like that. It can be a gate opening to an entire other world
of … bliss. If you want it. Enough.'

You say nothing. You give him nothing. You squeeze your
legs on your bareness. Gasp, just.

The grand and meticulous experiment.

Lesson 119

Ladies, 'tis worth a grave thought — what would the most
of you leave behind you when you die? Much embroidery,
doubtless, various pleasant, kindly, illegible letters; a moderate
store of good deeds and a cartload of good intentions.
Nothing else — save your name on a tombstone, or lingering
for a few more years in family or friendly memory.

He brings out a small leather suitcase.

'We've only just begun,' he smiles. 'But it all, of course,
has to be on one condition: everything we do is of your own
free will.' You nod. 'Just remember that pleasure is all about
surrendering ourselves, and accepting pleasure is a big leap for
a lot of people. No one's born a lover — we all have to learn.'

'Even you?' You tease.

'Oh yes. Me most of all.'

He opens his suitcase. Takes out a blindfold. The softest
velvet, as black as midnight. He ties it around you; his cock in
readiness, firm into your back. Gently, so gently, he turns you
around. He slips something flat and heavy into your hands.

A book.

The surprise of it.

The Letters of Abelard and Heloise.

Written eight hundred years ago.

'Don't return to this house until you've read it. Until you're ready for the next step. They were medieval lovers. And this is to show you that these things have always been done, and *will* always be done. If you dare. If you want it.' His voice drops to a whisper. 'And I think you do.' He kisses you on the lips, once, the moth's kiss. 'With someone you trust …'

Late, at home, you devour the words, hidden under your blanket as if not even the walls or the night air can bear witness to what you are reading; midges hovering and you slam the book shut on them as you come – your fingers between your legs – and come, with anticipation.

> *Our desires left no stage of lovemaking untried, and if love could devise something new, we welcomed it. We entered on each joy the more eagerly because of our previous inexperience and were all the less easily sated.*

The key word: joy.

Those two deeply religious, searingly intelligent people were having a huge amount of fun.

JOY.

Written in your notebook, in readiness.

You are a foreigner in his country, a child in his nursery; all is new, wondrous.

You are ready.
For anything.
Because you are doing this to learn.
It is, after all, what you asked for in the first place.

VII

'... he forgets his mother and his brothers and all his comrades, couldn't care less if his property is lost through neglect, and, in disdain of all those proprieties and decorums whose beauty he once cherished, he is ready to be a slave, to sleep anywhere he is allowed, as close as possible to his desire.'

Socrates

Lesson 120

Women's work is, in this age, if undefined almost unlimited,
when the woman herself so chooses

He is ordered, he is ready. Before the two of you can proceed
there are two things you must know.

'I want you. *You*. *No one* else. Believe it. And secondly,
stop worrying. About everything.' He taps your head, his voice
lowers. 'Trust me.'

The softness of his cheek against yours.

You have been reading, preparing, priming, learning. For
this moment, the next step. You no longer angle yourself
during sex as if you're viewing the scene from the ceiling, no
longer direct yourself into the most flattering positions. You've
learnt to accept your body, with all its faults, don't care what
you look like.

'I just don't notice, alright,' he's admonished more than
once. 'I'd much prefer you relaxed.'

You nuzzle in gratitude, breathing him in deep, and you
open your body wide, wider to him, wanting to offer yourself
for his pleasure and his alone, wanting to snare him forever
with infinite sex.

And lo and behold, you feel more womanly than ever before.

He is right.
You are ready.
Thrumming with it.

The day is stretching into lengthening light, soon you must go.
He asks you to stand. Naked, still. He says he wants to prepare
you for next time. When it will start. Give you a little taste.

He slithers off the silken grey ribbon from its black box,
kneels, slips it around your waist like a tailor at a dummy and
ties it just above your belly button, in a bow.

A present, to be unwrapped.

'Close your eyes,' he whispers.

The long trails of the satin are teased over your bareness,
goosebumps spring to life under their coldness. Gently, so
gently, he instructs.

'Now put on your clothes and pedal away tall, on your bike,
and imagine all that is ahead. In two days. Don't undo this
ribbon until you're home. Think of everything we've learnt so
far. Anticipation. Secrecy. Imagination. Surrender. Trust.'

He kisses your lids, first one, then the other.

'Love.'

The moth's breath against your ear.

'Restraint …'

The trails of satin whisper between your thighs.

'And release.'

Lesson 121

'To know' gradually becomes a necessity, an exquisite delight

_____

It is the weekend. Two days – two churning days – of waiting ahead. You're like a horse straining at the starting gate, kicking out strong in your box.

You drive past Woondala with your father.

The gates are locked. *Locked.*

Your head whips back.

'What's up? You alright?'

'Nothin'.'

But your groin. Squeezing in want as it bears down on the car seat. Still feeling those slices of satin lingering, teasing, electrifying; long after they've gone.

What you have learnt:
We love the things we are not meant to.

What you have learnt:
Love is a restless absence.

What you have learnt:
You shouldn't be doing this.

What you have learnt:
You are enslaved, you can't stop.

Lesson 122

Published or unpublished, this woman's life
is a godly chronicle

'I need your notebook.' First thing he says.

'Why?'

'I have to write something down.' He smiles. 'One last time.'

'But it's all *my* notes now.' You hold it protectively at your chest. 'I don't want you seeing it anymore. Anyone …'

He laughs. 'Give me my page, *you*. I'm not looking at anything else. Trust me.'

Reluctantly you hand it across; he turns obediently to the back.

'Just one more thing, alright. To mark the next stage, to frame it.' He looks up; a roguish smile.

RELEASE

Ted Hughes wrote in the foreword to Sylvia Plath's journal that even though he spent every day with her for six years, and was rarely apart from her in that time, he never really saw her show her real self to anybody. Including him. Ever.

'I think we can improve on that.'

You bite your lip.

A nervousness has stumbled into your love.

Lesson 123

To many, truth comes only after the self-control, watchfulness, and bitter experience of years

---

'But do you really love me?'

The guarantee that is needed to proceed.

'Yes yes, come on.'

You're holding back. 'Sometimes, I don't know, I think you're too clever to love anyone. That your type only ever love *so* much.' You squint and pinch your fingers as if they're holding a pair of tweezers.

Because he has learnt survival and you have not. Because you fear it.

'Do you love me, Tol, as much as I love you?'

He hesitates.

'I don't know.' Sincere. Honest. Matter-of-fact.

You stop. Look around. In something like panic. You've been colonising his world ever since you set eyes on him and you're still not convinced that he likes it, enough; are never sure.

'I could make this such a beautiful home.' You smile, testing, a game, turning to a wall and sweeping your hand across it.

He doesn't reply.

'I *said* –' you repeat, louder.

He doesn't reply. He's making you feel soiled, suddenly, with his silence.

You snap away. Cut the session short.

The piracy of indifference, and you will not stand for it.

Furiously you cycle home, the light dappling the dirt road in zebra shadows like strobe lighting flicking across your eyes as you wonder how this all ends – it won't, it must.

Feeling as vulnerable as a fontanelle, suddenly, with all this.

Lesson 124

There is no anguish like youth's pain —
so total, so hopeless, blotting out earth and heaven,
falling down upon the whole being like a stone

For four days you do not go back.

Riddled with frustration, hesitation, doubt; shielding yourself against future hurt. You can't give him what he wants because you're not sure he'll ever give you the equivalent in return. He wants so much from you: your deepest thoughts, your truth; but you don't have his and suspect you never will. You are not an instrument by which he will work things out here, you will not let him hone his skills on you for something – some*one* – else. Someone in the past or the future or even, God forbid, the present. Who exactly is in the city, waiting, that he's always running back to? Who's in his other life?

Everywhere, now, little barriers are shooting up.

You try to focus on your school work, finally; you're nearing the end of the holidays and the study's banking up. You've been existing in a golden morass of sex that is slowing you, killing your thinking, you've got nothing done. The pleasures of Woondala have been making you weak, interfering with your focus and calm; it's like a magic spell binding you, swamping you now, snatching your ambition and your strength.

Him, too. You can tell. This is for the best, this being apart, yes. Because something is falling away – sometimes, recently, he hasn't been looking out on the verandah near enough for you; sometimes you've had to wait too long after throwing a pebble at his study window, until finally he emerges as if dragged from his desk.

You, the intrusion.

He's been lamenting recently that he's not getting enough done, he's too distracted, this second book is so difficult; it's like extracting blood from a stone. Lamenting that he wrote his first book with such an arrogance and an innocence, never knowing if it would be published, but now he has the weight of expectation on him and it's clogging him up. Lamenting his fear, the writer's fear, that the urge to think rarely strikes the contented; that he needs the hunger or he will stop.

The wolf-ranginess of the alone. You fear it, that it is deep in him, and it will always win out.

> Someone asked Sophocles, 'How is your sex-life now? Are you still able to have a woman?'
> He replied, 'Hush, man; most gladly indeed am I rid of it all, as though I had escaped from a mad and savage master.'

You wrote the passage down recently while you were waiting for him, flipping through the books by his bed and coming across it. You felt a little whine of frustration blundering between you in that moment, which is growing, now, in this time apart.

Will he break you?

Lesson 125

How the heart leaps up to meet a sunshiny face,
a merry tongue, an even temper

But then. A great surging within you, you can't help it,
you must go back, can't not; shuddering deep inside as you
cycle up his driveway on the afternoon of day four with one
very beautiful art deco tea cup wrapped in newspaper in a
Woolworths bag – from your grandmother, she lost the saucer
decades ago and says you can have it, to find a match.

You flit by something glinting in the sunshine. Stop, turn
your bike around.

A jar, suspended on a single thread of wire wrapped around
its neck.

Inside, a note. On red paper so fragile you could almost eat
it, melt it on your tongue.

> *You soak through and permeate the spirit and skin of my
> days. It is wondrous, torturous, transcendent, crushing,
> tender, all at once.*

The smile plumes inside you like ink through water.
Affirmation – and isn't that, in the end, what we all want. His
writing voice is like a hand reaching inside you and holding

your heart and never letting it go. You place the jar back onto its knot of a bark hook and walk on with your bicycle, the slip of paper in your overalls, spreading its warmth like a heated stone tucked into a pocket in the deepest of winters.

Another jar.

Another note.

Green this time, as fragile as the last.

> *Every conversation I have with you sneaks inspiration upon me. Your honesty, your spark, your enthusiasm for life. I just want to be with you forever, complete and strong, true, moving, growing, binding ... my soul mate, my elemental wife.*

Another, further on.

> *The other day I felt as if I had fallen in love with your soul, my feelings were that strong. I am with you. I am always with you. Never forget that.*

Another. A scrawl on a eucalyptus leaf.

> *Your proud, walk tall love!*

And gouged deep in the bark of the Scribbly Gum it hangs upon:

> *'My spirit so high it was all over the heavens.'*
>
> *Pound*

All of it wrapping you in a gigantic yes.

You drop your bike, you break into a run.

He is waiting on the verandah, sitting on the top step, staring out, as if he has been doing this for four days and nothing else. He calls out your name when he sees you and there is all the loneliness of the world in that cry and you rush up and hesitantly you feel him, like rare china, scarcely believing.

It is as if he will break with your touch.

Lesson 126

When his whole heart and conscience
accompanied and sanctified the gift

_____

You bowl into his study without looking back, heart roaring.
Take the scraps of coloured paper and the gum leaf from your
pocket and open his pot of Clag liquid glue – the glue you used
to eat as a child – and stick each torn strip of paper to his wall,
one beneath the other, in a ladder of neatness by his typewriter.
You varnish them to the old, yellowed newsprint on his wall in
a line of permanency he will never forget.

'What are you doing?' So quiet behind you that you jump.

'Trapping them. With you. Forever. Because I can't have
them at home. My dad might find them. And because you
need to be reminded of what you've written. Every day. Every
single day for the rest of your life. You must never forget.
Alright? _Any_ of this.'

That last sentence raw, urgent, teared-up.

He turns you around. He kisses you. The moth's first kiss
in your trembling.

'I won't.'

He lifts you into his arms and carries you to his bedroom,
pausing just once, to kiss again, on its threshold.

Lesson 127

Human life is so full of pain. The mind instinctively turns
where it can get rest, and cheer, and sunshine.

———————

Nothing more life-affirming than this, now, as he is poised
above you. Something deeply spiritual in it as he moves, in
silence, staring into your eyes. A divinity to it. You know now
it is the most exhilarating mystery available to us, as humans.
You are communicating on the deepest level – in silence. Both
of you cracked into vulnerability and honesty, into light.

You have never felt closer to someone in your life.

'I can just see us in Grandma's feather bed with the two kids
between us,' he murmurs in the golden quiet of afterwards,
as you lie together in his sheets within an afternoon of soft
pattering rain. 'I've never felt that before.'

You roll away and wrap his languid arm around your belly.
Something here is turning, softening, the rabbit sex has died
today into something quieter, more solid. The sweetness of
skin against skin. The stillness and sanctity of no talk.

It has come to this.

Lesson 128

Better beg, or hunger, or die in a ditch —
than live a day in voluntary unchastity

___

But away from him, that night, a warning; no it can't be this, surely not.

An article in a fashion magazine abandoned by your stepmother, about the dangerous allure of first love. That first passion that can whisper through your blood your entire life and become the standard of intensity by which all other partnerships are measured. You sense, that night, a shiver of a truth: that the man in reality will always fall slightly short of the man in your head, the concept of him — that the known will never quite arouse the way the mystery will later, alone. The shock of reality — sour breath, wrinkles, flaccid stomach, dulled teeth — all is forgotten with that precious little bauble of wonder and chuff that you carry to bed with you, every night, into your sleep.

That you love, and are beloved.

There is nothing else in the world that you want.

You have found a love that will be the foundation for your entire sex life to come, you sense this, even now. And God knows if you will ever be able to replicate it — if you are being spoilt for life. Is this Tol's way of expressing his love? Stamping you with these memories so that forever onward you will be dissatisfied, disappointed, until you give up; bound by worship and longing for an experience long ago, ruined by it.

You pick up your notebook.

There will never be anyone else.

Lesson 129

Year by year the fierce experience of life,
through death, circumstance or change,
narrows the circle of those who own friendship

By the dam bank, naked in the softness of the mud, he tells you he wants to marry you out here, that it's like the two of you are welded by the elements, by the land and the water and the air. Yes, you breathe, yes. The sweat and the semen gluing your skin and he suddenly presses in, so fierce, as if he's trying to extract the life-force from you, thudding his torso against yours and murmuring, *it's like we were made for each other, we fit*, as you curve into each other, *you keep me alive*; and his cheek is soft against yours as you stare up at the cloud-dotted blue and feel a peace blooming within you, because this is right, you fit. Yes, married out here – by the sky, and the dust, and the air. Anointed by ochre, and light.

'I'm ready,' you tell him.

'Really?'

You nod. Ready for the next step.

Lesson 130

We take pleasure in tracing the large workings of all things

That night, in preparation for God knows what, you order your notes. Because you have no idea what you'll be writing in the notebook next. So, now, a collation of all you have learnt from this summer about what works. For whatever is next.

It is a gift to experience sex with someone you love: For then the pleasure is multiplied thousands of times over, becomes sex full of emotion, the best.

A gift to experience sex with a man who treats lovemaking with reverence: Because with that comes a generosity of spirit – he won't get you to do anything you don't like.

A gift to be with a man who is not intimidated by you: Who is not afraid of women.

A gift to be with someone who knows what they're doing: Whose touch hums; who is assured, gentle, confident. Who cherishes women so that his love for them – and their bodies – illuminates the experience.

A gift to be with a man who will hold a woman, just that, as she comes: Wrap her in his arms, still her shuddering but

not intrude upon it, share the experience but not snatch the pleasure from her in that deeply private moment.

A gift to be with a man who is kind: When a man is attentive and considerate, when he listens to what a woman wants, then she's gone, like a dog rolling over for its tummy to be tickled.

A gift to be with a man who tells you that you're beautiful: Who instils in you a sense of confidence. Who empowers, not chips away or wears you down.

A gift to be with a man who respects the mind: For some, the best sex they've ever had may well be the sex they've never had. You can be much better at it by yourself, in your imagination.

A gift to be with a man who coaxes you to break down barriers and enter places you'd never usually explore: But gently, so gently, with tenderness.

You shut your notebook and enfold it across your chest, lying on your back.

Poised.

On the brink of God knows what.

Lesson 131

The known face of your girlhood will altogether vanish –
nay, is vanished

'There's something incredibly erotic about a woman –' his voice drops into breath, he can barely say it – 'bound.'

A sharp intake of your breath.

'Hidden,' he continues. 'Wrapped. Think of Heloise and Abelard. Unwrapping themselves, all their clothes, their known lives – for each other, no one else. The cheongsam will be waiting in that ditch where you leave your bike. Will you wear it? For me?'

You nod your obeyance.

'What we're about to embark upon is a form of bondage … but not as you know it. The best type of bondage can be very life-affirming, relationship-affirming; it requires a heightened level of trust between two people, a willingness.' He whispers, cheek to cheek. 'A closeness that doesn't exist in normal life. Absolute surrender, trust; a communion of equals. Are you ready?'

You nod, your eyes dancing.

He picks up a heavy art book. Flicks through it. You

weren't expecting this. He runs his hands over a picture of the *Mona Lisa*.

'Look at her. What is this woman's story? She's a mass of erotic contradictions. There's the sober clothes, the demurely folded hands, but this, *this* –' his fingers trace her lips – 'the extraordinary smile. This painting is all about sex. Don't you think?'

'Yes,' you laugh, seeing it. 'She's just done it. Or is thinking of it.'

'Absolutely. And it's a big reason, I suspect, why this picture is still so alluring five hundred years on.'

You gaze at the sexual contradiction on the glossy page before you. The hints of a private, supremely confident eroticism behind the sternest of public masks; the sombre clothes, the knowing lips.

'Reserve and sexuality.' He looks at you. 'An explosive combination. My favourite. Never forget that.' He buttons up your flannelette shirt, right to the collar, and steps back. Nodding.

'Explosive. 'Til next time, my love.'

You want to crumple to the ground with torment, anticipation, wetness, want; you do not. It is only then you notice the thick rope Tol has taken from the couch, is wrapping around his wrist, pulling taut, jerking it.

Lesson 132

To domineer and to rule are two distinct arts,
proceeding often from totally opposite characters

Two jagged days.

You change your clothes just beyond sight of Woondala. The cheongsam, of course, nothing underneath. The buttons firm across your breast. Restraint, and flesh.

Uncontrollably wet.

He is waiting. He throws up his hands in triumph at the sight.

He takes you by the hand. He leads you inside to the drawing room. He picks up the blindfold that is lying, in readiness, along the mantelpiece.

He wraps it around your eyes and knots it firmly.

'I want you to read Foucault, I will give you a book. He says we exercise control over sexuality by our knowledge of another person – but also, crucially, by a knowledge of *ourselves*. What our body can do, the amazing things it's capable of. That's the secret. The mind is truly extraordinary. And now, an introduction to it. I want you to surprise yourself. Imagine you are unlocking a door to a hidden room deep inside you, and you have no idea what's in there – yet. Are you ready?'

'Yes.' So much.

He is breathing deep. He undresses you, slowly; lingering his tongue and his lips, pausing for a wisp of a kiss, here, there. Until you are quite naked except for the blindfold whose long silk ribbon trails down your back with the deftness and coldness of a lizard. Now a suitcase is being opened – you can hear it – things are being removed carefully, and placed upon the floor. It is taking time. Your legs are almost buckling now with want as you strain for sounds, clues. It is taking too long.

His tools.

A heavy leather collar of some type. Wound around your neck, buckled firm. You gasp. A chain is attached to it, its leather handle is whispered across your pubis. Its coldness is then looped down your back and threaded through your legs and pulled, firmly, once. Again, a gasp. You squeeze your groin on it, into it. Bend, instinctively working the metal deep into your fold. With a steady hand, with firm and gentle fingers, you are led through the listening, waiting house; every so often the chain between your legs is pulled taut – a reminder, a taunt. You are taken to an upstairs room, a room ringing with air and light, you can read it, read the sky in the dark. You are laid down, gently, upon your back on an empty mattress. Your legs are parted. You go to shut them, automatically, they are parted again; firmer. Your hands are taken, they are bound with a thick scratchy rope and secured to the iron bedstead. You are trapped, you cannot move them, you twist on your back. 'Uh uh,' he whispers, 'you wanted this.' Your legs are pulled apart and tied wide. 'That's better, that's what we need.'

You arch your back, groan. We?

'Now,' Tol says, from above, looking down, 'we can do whatever we want.'

The metal chain lying along your spine is jerked up, once, savagely, through your legs. You buck, exposing yourself more. You cry out. Tol pauses, you strain to hear anything beyond him ...

'Or should I say, whatever *you* want.'

A shardy silence. Shuffling in the room, breath, you can't make it out.

'Fuck me, quick.'

Tripping with wetness, coming, too quick.

Now he is unbuckling you, hauling you up on your haunches, exposing you – for what? Who? Opening you wide, dipping in a tongue. Fingers, many. Rim you, probe you. You pulsate, want it. All. *All.* Everything.

'Well done. Perfect.' At the end of it, the delight in his voice. 'This is only the beginning, my beautiful, beautiful love. The very start.'

The tin roof above you talks in the heat, it cracks and stretches and creaks – or is it something else? In the room, watching. A feminine gasp, no, surely not, is your mind playing tricks? You are still blindfolded, you can feel it, you think, perhaps, you don't know.

'Again,' you whisper to him in the dark, widening your legs further. 'Now.'

You have tumbled out of yourself.

Lesson 133

What a future you open for her!

_____

Your love has lost its innocence.

He is greedy. After the librarian, the demureness, the restraint – the whore.

'Let's play, come on.' Gleeful, as if a fabulous world of riches awaits.

He has gone shopping, there are many new clothes, toys. Tassels at the nipples now of a beautiful satin bra, a slit in silken panties he jerks his finger up.

'Be my stripper,' he's breathing softly into the back of your neck, a hand looped around your belly with a finger through the slash in your panties that are soaking wet.

'Why?'

'Because she's such a fabulously glorious mass of erotic contradictions. The girl who promises everything but actually, gives very little.' His voice drops, his fingertip swirls, inside you, you groan and clamp him tight. 'It's all look and fantasise and project – but don't touch. Don't possess. The potency in resistance, remember. She's the girl who's completely in control but she's never quite going all the way and she's revelling in it, that supreme moment of power where she's got the attention of an entire room and is calling all the shots but is always withholding that final moment.'

You gasp.

'Imagine you, here, with a room full of men. Imagine the power of it. All of them. Rapt.' His voice right at your ear. 'But you don't have to withhold at the very end … if you don't want.'

You touch yourself over his finger, you curl him into you, tumble to the ground. He pulls away your panties but before he gives you the release of his own touch he is parting your legs and staring, appraising, teasing.

'You want others, don't you? Watching, touching, wanting; hands, everywhere, all over you. Dipping in.'

His breath brushes your arsehole, he doesn't touch.

'I know you do,' as he spreads your legs wide, wider, 'you're ready, aren't you? Just tell me what you want.'

You arch your back, your nipples erect, you feel all-powerful, tripping with it; you would give him anything in this moment, anything.

He touches you.

You explode.

Lesson 134

Order is heaven's first law

_____

'I must know. Everything. What's in that head of yours? Don't be afraid. I need to know. So I can help. With absolute, utter trust. Always that.'

All his words, words, words, over the next few days of apart. Spinning in your head as you help your father with the engine of his ute, handing across spanners and wrenches and bolts. You're in retreat, here, now – you can't go back, everything is galloping too fast – you don't know what's next, where it's meant to stop, who he's bringing in to this; you're a good girl really, you can't.

You will not go back.

What happens if you've fallen in love with a person who will ultimately destroy you?

It is not the first time you've thought this.

Woondala has woven a spell around you; you are different there. You don't recognise yourself.

Your father needs to fix the chook house. It's falling apart, a big job, you want to do it with him; need his silence, the solidness of hard work, the reassurance. Need the known, everything that is comfortable and secure and known in your life. In the heat that is so thick it is a presence in this place.

You do not go back.

Lesson 135

It often takes years to comprehend the peculiarities of one's own constitution

___

A letter. Your name and address on the envelope, typed. Businesslike, anonymous. Your stepmother turns it over curiously, goes to hold it up to the light.

You snatch it from her. It is typed with his old typewriter, you just know.

'It's from my drama teacher at school. She said she'd write.' Nonchalantly, already ripping it open. 'It's about the school play, next term, my lines. She promised.'

Rushing it to your room, as bored-looking as you can.

There's a joy and trust and innocence brimming within you, and a depth which caught me unawares. I'd never want to hurt any of that in you or see you lose it. I feel old and cynical. Don't inherit that from me, racked with all my doubts and worries. I feel I could poison you. Bring you down. Leave you bereft ... but to capture that acuteness of being alive! That razor-edge quality, yes, that's what being with you is like. I feel like you help me to live. You are so much stronger, freer, braver, than me; I must learn

from that. I was feeling so crusted over, so weary of life –
and then you came along. I want to make love with you
madly, maddeningly. However you want.
Longing for you.
Now you must hide this, burn it. And then come.
I need you.

You run out the door with a slap of the flyscreen and leap off the verandah – clearing, cleanly, six steps.

Lesson 136

Be scrupulously honest and truthful,
in the smallest as in the greatest things

_____

Sobbing as you're pushing him away then pulling him to you, animal fucking, eating his flesh, biting, branding him, feeling his seed dribble from your stomach as you lay back on a huge slab of rock and it scrapes your back and you want it to, need it, to be marked forever, scraped by this grit; need it to hurt, to always remember this; want this day's rawness and hunger tattooed upon the flesh of your back.

'Deeper,' you command, craving. 'Fill me up.'

'You're the best thing that's ever happened to me,' he says in the thick of it.

Holding you tight, thudding you into the rock, scrunching into your body as if he is clinging onto a lifebuoy in a wide ocean of fear, not wanting to let go, not wanting this to stop. He smells good, he always smells good and you nestle your face into his armpit, its animal smell, and drink him up – intoxicated, with all of it.

Soaring with happiness. That he could be so open, honest.

'You're the best thing that has ever happened to me.'

You love the vulnerability, the anchoring power of it.

A dome of secrecy over you both. As you lie there, limbs strewn, inside the raucous, ringing, bang-smash bell of heat and noise, cockatoos screeching above and the wheeling blue, the bubbling creek.

You look straight into his eyes which laugh back.

So, now you have it. That bloom of certainty that women who are anchored by a relationship have, that you have envied and craved your entire teenage life. A love that scorches self-hatred and insecurity and doubt. You are the love eaters in this place. Love gorgers.

Life eaters.

Yes. You feel so alive with all this.

You tell him, at last.

What he wants.

Lesson 137

It matters little when, or how, or by how many, truth is
spoken, if only it be truth

You are thinking of someone else. Other men. He is the trigger;
he is only the start. It is all in your head, the movie running
concurrently with the physical action, it needs momentum, it
does not need his talk crashing into it.

'Men,' you whisper, 'a lot, looking at me, all around me,
running their hands over me, dipping their fingers in. A dog,
brought in on a leash. They are all watching, my pleasure,
someone ... someone parts my cheeks. They all fuck me, one
after the other, again and again. I am favoured, caged, bound,
handcuffed, displayed – the object they all want.'

You are deeply red, deeply shamed, at the end of it. Your
face is flaming. You are quiet, cannot look at him, cannot say
anything more. Can't believe you have allowed this.

He turns you around. With great certainty, with gravity.
In silence.

'Thank you for trusting me. I'm your helper, your facilitator.
I will never hurt you, I will never exploit you. Let's see how far
we can take this. But only if you want to ...'

His tongue flicks into you, as deft and cool as a snake.
You clench on it, groan.
His answer.

Lesson 138

A *friend*. Not perhaps until later life do we recognise the inestimable blessing, the responsibility awful as it is sweet, of possessing or of being a friend.

Later, in the kitchen, cradling a mug of tea.

'But how can you love me yet even think of doing … everything … that I said?' The blush is deep; what you have revealed, oh my God. 'I don't get it.'

'I love what you have given me. What we are doing here. You will never forget it and neither will I. We have released you, and so few women get that chance. We are doing this together. You're a work-in-progress, but then so am I.'

He comes right up close, his face tells you he is confident that no one, ever, can take his place, no matter who comes next; he is inked through your heart, through your blood, until the day you die he is there and he knows it. His smile tells you your pleasure is his, that he knows he will have succeeded if he sees you gaining ultimate pleasure, beyond him, beyond anything he can do; it will be his greatest gift.

'But *how*?' You furrow your eyebrows, frown, still don't get it. He tells you he is doing all this because he is a student of women and he needs to learn, as do you, it is the writer's curiosity – he is a student of life, of living to the limit in pursuit of love, connection, soul-sharing, radiance.

He loves you, never forget that. No matter what comes next.

'I want to unlock you completely and fully and absolutely. Give you the tools of womanhood, the most splendid of experiences. My ultimate lesson. I want you to know the choices you will have – the breadth of the experience – and believe me, many women, most women, don't. Consider it an act of generosity, if you like.'

'But what's in it for you?'

'It's exciting. I want to watch. I want to see your pleasure and know that I, ultimately, am responsible for it. I want to give you an experience that will be with you for the rest of your life.'

He asks you to shut your eyes.

He leaves the room and returns; buckles the collar around your neck. You are free to look but don't, in perfect obeyance.

No more words, as his rigid cock presses firm into your flesh.

He takes the collar off.

The breath of a kiss, on the nape of your neck.

'Friday. We'll be ready.'

Before you can ask him what he means, again, he is gone, he has shut the door on you, the study door that is always locked now; his secret refuge you are not allowed to trespass across anymore. You walk out of Woondala. The afternoon has turned, is now grey, sullen, waiting. You retrieve your bike. You don't have to return. You don't have to ever see this house again.

'It's your choice.' The yell from the verandah to your departing back. 'It's always your choice.'

You do not turn around.

Lesson 139

Be honest with me. I don't expect from you more than human nature is capable of.

Running to him two days later, in your overalls, the shirt flung from underneath them as soon as you have slipped through his gate and tossed your bike aside. Running to him, for him – you can't help it, he has you snared, trapped. He loves you earthy, sweaty, loves you brimming with vividness, his child of nature, that girl he first knew, and so you are running and running in your Blunnies, through deep fern gullies and over rocks and through his creek; thudding away spiders and cobwebs and snakes; grimy with sweat and exhilaration and the slap of his bush; grimy with its life. There's the crispness of an approaching storm in the air, an exhilarating readiness and you feel alive, on edge, shivery on the precipice of a something – God knows what – and you are poised to leap off and you are so ready, trembly wet, laughter shooting out. Ready to act volcanically however he wants, your heart pumping with greed and hunger and dread and desire; you are pure emotion now, shameless, unmediated by discretion or convention or decorum. You have entered a new world. You are someone else.

No name, no age. No future, no past.

Just this, the varnished present. Pure, lovely, ravenous want.

He walks out to greet you.

As if he knew it would always come to this.

The curve of his cock, erect, through his trousers.

He is holding a black silk blindfold and a pair of black opaque stockings and a suspender belt in one hand, and in the other, some beautiful Manolo Blahnik stilettos, of spindly black velvet, exactly your size of course. He places everything down, methodically, he has thought carefully about all this. He unclips your braces, pulls them down. You are wearing nothing underneath and you are shaved, in readiness. He shuts his eyes, briefly, as if he can't bear to see it. He asks you to put on the stockings and the shoes. You have never worn anything like this in your life.

Trembling, you obey him, breathing deep.

He turns you around. He covers your eyes.

Blindfolded by the softest of black silk. Two tiny metal weights on the ends. They slither, icy, against the skin of your lower back, a thrill of cold. Your flesh springs into goosebumps. He buckles the heavy collar around your neck.

All sensation now. Nothing else.

He dribbles the lead of the collar down your stomach then threads it between your legs. He pulls it up sharp. Between your lips. Forcing them apart. Exposed. You wince, with exquisite hurt.

'Steady, my beauty, I'm with you,' he whispers, a calming

hand on your back, murmuring as if you are a wild brumby he has to lead into a horse float for the very first time, guiding you gently, all the way, every step.

'Remember, confidence.'

He leads you into the cool dark house you know so well, every crevice, wall, crack. He leads you into the main room, his hand still holding the chain taut at your back. You grip his arm tight, blinded, breathing deep. The chain cuts through you. Flipping open a lip. You are ready. Your nipples ache with anticipation. All your senses on alert.

He stops you.

Works the chain up higher, higher, so you have to spread your legs, open yourself wider, groan. You hold your voice, leaning your back against his stomach with his fingers in your bare cunt, splayed; as if on display.

All is still, all is quiet.

Just the tin roof above you, cracking and ticking in its heat.

The roof you know so well.

The only thing you know, now, in all of this.

Lesson 140

Our interests gradually take a wider range

Gently, so gently but with firm authority, like a doctor before an operation, he lies you, belly down, on the couch. Your buttocks are placed over the roll of its arm. He trills his fingers up and down your back, then your thighs, dipping inside, further and further, soft, so soft and you lift up your arse, out, up – have to. His hands help you, his knowing hands, you open yourself out, groan, it's unbearable, you want him, here, now, so much. You are left alone. Your body keeps pulsing, opening out. Then you hear another noise, the sound of a belt being taken off, trousers unzipped.

In the room.

With you.

Who? You don't know, who else, how many.

Yes, no, you can't make it out.

'Only do what you want to do.' Tol is back, beside you, whispers his soothing words, 'I'm here, I'm with you, everything's your choice, it's what you want.' Then he leans close and his fingers continue murmuring over the back of your thighs, loving, so tender – it moves you to tears, it's unbearable, you spread your legs wider, you want it, want everything, all your clothes gone, on show for anyone here in this place, men, women, whoever is here, everything, trying to scrabble off the Manolo Blahniks, the belt.

'Yes,' you whisper, 'yes.'

'Good girl,' he whispers, slipping down your stockings, unclipping your belt, parting your cheeks, for them, for the room, for whoever it is. You hear a gasp. His, someone else's, you don't know, don't recognise anything anymore. It's your cue. You lift yourself higher, higher, giving yourself to the air, rocking with it, displaying your arse, for God knows who, what.

'Come on, come on,' you whisper under your breath, urging it. Ready for him, his mates, his possession. His creation, ready for whatever he wants.

'This is only the start,' it is whispered.

Gently you are turned over. Instinctively you spread wide. Your hands are taken. A belt you don't recognise – you can feel its difference, its heaviness – someone is binding you with this stranger's belt. A knee is holding you down. You submit, you trust, the knee is removed, you curve your back, splaying your wetness, your readiness. Strain to hear – you can't make it out, another presence … or several … movement. Something else in this room, breath.

'Well … well,' in appreciation, as hands are directing you to the ground, some kind of platform. Hands, you don't know whose, gently someone blows upon you and you bow your back, you arch your buttocks out, ready, so ready for this – trembling, wet, you feel as if your insides are tumbling in slow motion, with all of it. It is fear, excitement, anticipation; power, surrender, want.

A finger, you don't know whose, touches your cunt. Softly, brushing the underside of it, parting your lips. Inspecting.

'Sssssh,' Tol whispers, reassuring, in your ear. 'Sssh.' He angles you head down, so you are opened wide, wider, dangling the collar's chain – its cold, brutal metal – across your wanton cunt.

Lesson 141

Come, just as you are – ragged, dirty, dishonest.
Only come, and we will do our best to make you
what you ought to be.

———————

Fingers, everywhere. You don't know whose. You arch your back, giving yourself to them, wanting it all, all, everything. In your arse, in your cunt, your mouth, between your breasts, all at once, blinded but seeing all, in your head; but they don't let you come, they stop just short.

Saving you for something else.

'Surrender,' Tol whispers.

You groan.

You are humping a tongue. Urging it deeper, deeper. Something slips into your arse. You fuck it all, all. You want everyone to see, you arch your back, you love that you are giving pleasure, dispensing it; you feel supremely in control – strong, victorious, holding this room captive. Wanted.

Noticed.

That you can have this effect. You.

The power of it.

The gift of attention.

*

Sounds, coming from you, that you did not think you were capable of, in a register lower than you have ever uttered in your life. You are split wide open, stripped, they have seen the core of you and you have never seen it before, in yourself and you marvel at that; the next step. That such a thing exists. That your body is capable of this.

This tsunami of ... *pleasure*.

Lesson 142

We feel we should like to go on living,
were it only out of curiosity

As you come and come you push away, all of it, not wanting anyone, anything, curling in exquisite aloneness, need to savour, scissoring your body again and again and turning brutally, in this needing to be alone.

When the spasming has finally died down, Tol enfolds your trembling in his arms and holds you and holds you until you stop, until all is quiet. *Sssh*, he is whispering, smoothing back your hair, again and again, *sssssh*.

'What exactly is freedom,' he muses later, close, and you can hear the smile in his voice, 'but doing exactly what we want to in life?'

Then he kisses you. Just. The moth's kiss.

'Thank you,' he says.

You are still blindfolded.

He slips it off.

His eyes, soft, into yours. Just his eyes, nothing, no one else, in the room. He lifts you like his bride with the dearest and most sacred tenderness and he carries you across the threshold of his bedroom again and he lays you on his mattress with consummate gentleness.

You have no idea of anyone else.

No awareness of anything, only him.

His gift.

Lesson 143

Where shall we find the light? In the world and its ordinary code of social morality, suited to social convenience? I fear not.

One last fuck on that seared, soaked day: lying with his stomach pressed into your back, one of his hands across your mouth and the other strong on your pubis, fucking in silence, stifled. Muffling your cries with his hand, *you must be quiet*, he is giggling, *sssh*, as if he is not meant to be doing this, others are listening, they're not allowed to know he is sneaking it.

'I want you to be my woman forever,' he is whispering deep inside you, moving so slowly, almost imperceptibly as his words pump through you, filling you up. Glow girl. Have you ever felt more alive, more sated, than this? He has removed you, shut the door on everything else, you are his only now, *his* – his woman, his world – and when he comes it is with a great cry of agony and distress and release, his whole life in it, all his past, all his future.

'Thank you,' he breathes again, panting, and then tells you he will never forget what you have given him – your trust, the gift of it through all these summer weeks. He will remember this golden, burnished time for the rest of his life – your love, what you have done, all of it. And then he starts to weep.

The shuddering pressing into your back.

The tears, the wet, the weight.

You stay still. You do not turn to him. It is something deeply private, and you do not want to intrude upon it.

Lesson 144

The wretched girl lives in terror of being turned from an
angry father's door

The house feels completely empty, except for you two. You
have heard no one leaving, moving about, no cars, nothing.
Just you and Tol and a world you have created for yourselves.
You lie there and smile in the infinite depths of the silence of
the softening day and the stopping and the rest. God in the
quiet. Grace. You know now what it is to be a woman who
radiates peace. Serenity.

In a life driven by love.

You sleep, you stir, you are the salt sweeper now, mining
Tol's body with your lips, your tongue, your breath. You
taste regions, delve. The velvet softness of his flaccid penis,
the toadstool head freckled softly, endearingly. You remember
walking through his drawing room door once, unannounced,
and Tol coming at you, rising from the couch, and in that
instant you had a vision of him old – the thickness, the
tiredness, the slowness – and felt an enormous tenderness for
what he would become. You will be beside him, of course,
you will not recoil from it; charging like crazed warriors at
convention, still. You can see it.

You float your lips over his body like a metal detector at a beach, trying to know him, extract him, his essence. This man in your life who touches the world so lightly with his living, who has no need of anyone else. With his constant capacity to surprise.

Now, with stillness.

The coldness of night is leaking into the air. The real world awaits. You get up. You shower. You leave. With a breath of a kiss on the nape of his sleeping neck.

Your little Victorian volume is waiting for you on the verandah doorstep, your little manual of scrupulous honesty that has accompanied you the entire time you have been in this house. Smeared by insects and ink smudges and mud from a dam. You pick it up, puzzled. You'd left it in the pocket of your overalls, in the ditch.

Inside is a fresh inscription.

Up front, roguishly, in an area that has never before been written in – the writing messy, hasty, not his usual neatness – a person who has been shaken from themselves.

This place can teach you so much.

Lesson 145

From that day this girl never was dependent
upon any human being
_____

Your father looks up from his tea and chocolate biscuit as you enter the house. As if he knows, as if he can smell something on you. Change, perhaps, as simple as that. Bruises are pluming on your thighs and your upper arms but he cannot see them; you do not know what he senses but it is some subtle thing, perhaps a ripening, a readiness, just that.

'How old are you again?' he asks absently.

He always teases you with this, on the birthdays he invariably forgets or ignores, to toughen you up, to get your indignant reminder. He asks you now like he can't believe you're growing so fast; he needs affirmation of how young you really are.

You just roll your eyes and smile the disbelieving, mock-disgusted smile that you always give him at this question then retreat to your room – have to, suddenly an uncontrollable trembling in your legs. Have to rip away your clothes to examine the vivid map on your skin, the imprint of what went on: the bruise on your left breast, deep and angry, the strange colours dancing up. No idea how it got there. The savagery of the lovemaking, all over, an elbow, or a chin, a knee. Embedded.

Your nipples shrivel like dried grapes at the thought. The tingling between your legs, at all of it.

Wanting it, all over again.

But you must wait. Tol would want that. Restraint ... and release.

Lesson 146

'To love' is by no means the sole verb in the grammar of life

_____

Over the coming days you sleep and sleep, gulping up rest, burrowing deep into your lovely bed. Outside your father is burning off and the smoke wends its way through your clothes like the smell of a lover and you turn and smile, scrunching your body in its pyjamas as you repair, and rest. There is a prickling in your cotton pants as the hair starts to grow back; the itch of it, the grate. For three days you can barely get out of bed at all and your father comes to the door of your room and stares, perplexed. Unable to ask, unable to articulate. The great clotted silence of the Australian male, you know it so well – from him, from Tol. So apart yet so similar, the two men in your life, who cannot properly talk out their thoughts except in writing or in work, as they're distracted, as they teach.

Sometimes your father comes back and strokes your cheek as he used to once, long ago, before stepmothers and boarding schools, before any of that, when it was just him and you, untugged, pure and solid and known and quiet. In the silence of the gesture you hug your glow to your chest and let the stillness seep in, vast and rich.

When he's gone you roll over. Wonder what on earth's next. With Tol. So much you want to do and have done; so much you want to do to him, to find out.

It is his turn next. What's in his head, what he really, deeply wants.

Let's see how far we can take this ...

With knowledge comes generosity. You have learnt that.

Lesson 147

Work is a natural and most holy necessity

Day four. You go back. Whole.

The gate is locked.

It has never been locked, except for those weekends when he's away or has guests and it is not a weekend now, it is a Monday, your heart is thudding, no, this can't be.

The shock of it. The disbelief. You shake the gates and shake them but cannot get in. Stunned. You sit slumped by the road, waiting, churning, for goodness knows what. Sit there, a great spanner twisting your heart. You sit there deep into that afternoon, into dusk.

He doesn't arrive. He doesn't leave. There is no letter, no jar, no scrap of a note. *Nothing*. You are swamped by loneliness. The chill of the truth, now, of bereavement. So, this is how he will whisper through your blood for the rest of your life – of course – by abandonment.

By silence.

The most torturous experience of the lot.

On that long afternoon you see your whole life ahead of you … You will live, now, the worst kind of life: within a question.

Over those waiting baffled hours you interrogate the last couple of months, everything that happened, but they stubbornly refuse to yield any answer. You gorge and gnaw on everything that went on inside these gates until you feel ill with it; every sign, signal, every conversation scrap. Everything thrown into confusion by these firmly shut gates. You do not know anything about him, why he did what he did, what he turned you into or why. You are just less when you should be more, so much more.

Why has love done this?

Lesson 148

Kindliness, unselfishness, charity, come to us by nature:
but I wish I could see more of my fellow souls practising
what is far more difficult — common justice, especially towards
one another

You wheel your bike home as dark comes crowding in.

Keening.

So. A new existence now. An ice pick crashed into the underbelly of your life.

That night a rush to words. Feverishly galloping the writing into your little book. It's all you've got now.

Your honesty.

That you gave him.

The sacred, solemn gift of it.

That he has abused most monstrously.

Lesson 149

It is safest, on the whole, to treat people as better than they are, than to check all hope and paralyse all aspiration

---

Every day you go back.

Every day the gate is locked.

Inexplicably padlocked.

You know him. He would never be so uncaring. Destructive. Cruel. It doesn't feel right. You *know* him.

You don't know him.

Newly alone, eyes glazed, stumbling through your days. You feel quarried. Physically, mentally, emotionally. Can you bear the truth? You don't think so.

His cold pleasure, it doesn't make sense.

I feel like you help me to live.

His words are re-written in your book, your heart tells you they were the truth. But every day now, cycling home in shock, every day now, disbelieving, as you turn from the padlocked gate. Like the lion's victim who is anaesthetised before the kill, a strange, floating calm carries you on, gets you through your days. The love, the God-given love for him still so big and strong and pushing and pulsing under all the bewilderment; the love that is Grand Canyon vast, that you do not know what to do with. Now.

I want to stay forever in your life.

He wrote that once, on his back page, and you know now that 'to stay' means as torment, affliction, weight. How could you be so deluded. *Young?*

A weight like a chain attached to a safe is pulling you down, down into the inky depths; and you cannot untangle yourself.

But you collect yourself, always, as Beddy looms into sight; plumped with tears but walking tall and nonchalant through the front door of your house. If you were pricked by a pin the howling would come raging tumbling tearing out in a great torrent but you cannot do that, you have to hold it all in – as you study at the dining table, as you peel the potatoes, as you clear out the garage, as you hand across the hammer and the screwdriver and the wrench.

Every day a Sunday expanse of loneliness and emptiness. Every day.

Lesson 150

As for resting your heart upon such a person, you might as well rest it upon a burning rock or a broken reed

---

Wailing in the rare alone in this tiny, suffocating house. Wanting, wildly, crawling on your knees; madly cramming your face when everyone's out and you're alone, stuffing yourself full of chocolate, biscuits, ice cream; forgetting for an instant the power of slim. Your skin loses its glow and its freshness, he has destroyed your equilibrium. Too big in you, all of it. Your love like black market currency now – vast riches but nowhere legitimate to deposit it. You fear his hesitancy, hate it. His cowardice. His cruelty. His silence. His motive. Grubby with it.

As you hunch over your textbooks, seeing but not seeing, keening under your breath, your father stops at the door and shakes his head, looking at your hands gripping your skull in frustration, your knuckles white, and he murmurs that he wishes for you an ordinary life, that's all. A solid, ordinary, happy life.

Then he walks off, leaving you to it, all your books. The weight of study, that he has never known in his life.

The dream. Crazed by it. The gate is open, you have stayed

and slept beside him, there is the stilling calm of skin to skin, of luxurious hours, of certainty; the feel of his hip, his tender earlobe, the back of his neck. Your bodies softly, rightly, moulding into each other then falling into slumber – what he always dreamt of, just one night, where true love lies, beyond words, beyond sex. He is kissing you in sleep and murmuring how good it is to have you with him then he wakes, boy-startled, a face of light, and smiles to see you there. That moment of vulnerability, of truth; you tuck it into the pocket of your heart, to always have, to always be able to slip out.

Crazed by it.

My heart is now shrouded like a cloth drawn over the dead.

You write in your notebook, can't haul yourself out.

The only soundtrack in your house, besides the ticking clock, is the talkback radio and once, in the morning, in response to the strident tones of a shock jock is a woman's steadying voice, all the wisdom of all the ages of all the women of the world in it.

'God gave us the gift of suffering,' she says calmly, matter-of-fact, as if her life is lived by this understanding, this truth. Yes. You have to learn. From her, from her voice. From other women.

To dive into the world with grace.

You have to start.

Because you know now that you feel too much. And you will be cursed by this fragility your entire life. Raw, skinned, with a huge open heart and what a combination to set forth into the real world with.

And him. The opposite, of course. What has happened has taught you that.

The authority of removal, absence, lack.

How *dare* he.

Lesson 151

Kittens and boys — the former being the least troublesome of the two

---

A cold that lingers for days. Your body crying. Eyes scratchy with tears and hurt. You wrap yourself in defensiveness. Inside, a quivering core of self-hatred, shock, doubt. He has stolen your confidence. Strength. Spark. The lack of him has become enormous, larger than anything that ever existed between you, fizzing and spitting like an insect caught perpetually in a trap.

Your stepmother comes into your room without knocking, doesn't tolerate sickness well, is rarely sick herself. Throws a letter onto your bed.

'The drama teacher again.' Walks out.

You snatch it up.

Do you dare open it? Your breath hovers at it. The type you know so well. You put it down, can't bear any more hurt, it will fell you, this.

Our time is up. I have to leave now.
You must live your life. I cannot stop you living it.

I have faith in you to do great things.
I will always love you. I will never forget.

Tol xxx

That's it. *It.* Not even his name handwritten, not even the solace of that. Your twisting heart, you clutch your chest, the paper drops on the bed.

You don't get it. Just this. After *everything* that went on, after you bared yourself.

Then the anger comes.

Is he afraid of women? Is this his revenge? You thought you had a friendship as much as anything else. Is he one of those men who saps a woman's self-esteem – by reducing, depleting, chipping away at. It never even veered into sourness or stalemate, just abrupt end. Blown out like a candle. The worst kind of love, because you have no explanation, no closure. Certainly not from this letter.

So, it will never let you go now. The only thing known in your life at this point. And now you are so ashamed at what you did, what he made you do. Did he record it, photograph it, will he write of it?

You pick up the letter and slip it into the back of the notebook that you will never write in again. You are on your own ship now, the good ship heartbreak, lonely at the wheel and not knowing where you are steering to. The storm is endless, the skies iron; when will the clouds break? *When?*

In passion that has failed is a seed of insanity.

The last entry, from yesterday. Ten days since the padlocked gate. Outside your night is softly spitting tears. The sky is crying and you cry with it, you weep, silently, so no one hears, of course.

It feels so long since you were young.

VIII

'illum absens absentem auditque uidetque'
(him not there not there, she hears him,
she sees him)

Virgil, *The Aeneid*

VIII

Lesson 152

She has opened a gate of misery so wide
that one almost shrinks from entering it

You emerge into the light as if from a coma, a sleep of a thousand years, a death. Your girl-face is gone.

The anger, still. That you were a lover before you were entirely a person. A lover before you were a woman and something is wrong with the natural order of that. Perhaps he has gone back to his Cecilia, perhaps she was in the room that final afternoon; it was all for her, a porn movie sprung to glary life.

Now the shame washes through you as stately as hemlock, shutting you down. Retracting from everyone and everything. You wrap yourself in black, forget to wash your hair, ugly yourself up.

His plaything. His doll.

How *dare* he.

Oh yes. Anger, now, sludgy-black through all your days. At his weakness, his cowardice, his selfishness – alone in his tower, unable to face life. Such a little man.

How *dare* he.

Lesson 153

By choosing a definite profession, a woman must necessarily quit the kindly shelter and safe negativeness of a private life

You go back to school, plough yourself into work. You have the gift of an excellent memory; it sees you through. You do not consider yourself especially clever, you can just recall so much, fool everyone.

As the anger congeals it hardens into aspic. But you have a life to live and so you must. Apart. Alone. Doubt and rage still there but it is as if a layer of skin has been peeled from your eyes. The desolation is wolfish, jagged, hurting. This is a stepping stone to the new – your next love will be more owned, more adult.

You are growing up.

You see Tol now. His running life. No woman's to have or hold. See the essential loneliness of the soul; he demanded it and he has infected you with it. But you don't like the solitude anymore – he has made you lonely in it, for the first time in your life.

And he has robbed you of your youth.

Lesson 154

The chief canker at the root of women's lives
is the want of something to do

You pass your Higher School Certificate. Triumphantly.

The pride in your father's eyes that he cannot articulate – he recognises that education is the way out. The only way out for his daughter; the only way to escape the life of his wife and all the women around him.

'I support you in whatever you do,' he tells you quietly on the day the letter arrives. But you know what he wants. There will not be poetry in grimy attics or acting courses or novels by the sea; none of that is a proper, solid, paying life. You are the first in the family to ever finish school let alone university and you have no choice. It will be a prestigious profession, law or medicine, at one of the nation's top universities. You cannot let him down. It is unspoken, of course.

What has characterised the relationship between your father and yourself as your teenage years gathered pace: silence, absence, a pulling apart. Perhaps he has sensed you slipping away yourself, that you don't need him anymore, and it's his way of connecting – barbing you, hooking you, in the only way he can.

Through withdrawal and silence, the hurt of that.

But you smile now with the release of forgiveness. It is time to pay back all that love, so awkward and unspoken; but constant, like an underground river deep through you; nourishing, replenishing.

Everything Tol isn't.

Lesson 155

Happiness itself has become to her an accidental thing

_____

Sydney, now you're an adult, feels like a rangy dog in the back of a ute, pacing, cagy, unwilling to rest. The loneliest place you have ever lived in your life and sitting in your local café you are like a blind person, all senses reeling. At the relentless traffic – sirens and accelerations and buses braking with a great squeal – at radio jabber, car fumes, crashing tea cups, clattering cutlery. You understand now where Tol was coming from: yes, this city is too noisy to write in, too aggressive to ever find calm. The exhaustion of just getting by in it.

You walk onto the university campus on your first day feeling completely out of your depth. Old, already. But with no idea who you are. You have to find out. You only know you want to be in London by the time you're twenty-five, New York by thirty.

And always, your soaring heart when you board the train for home. For your quiet. Your air. Your hurting sky. His too. On the train speeding you home you squeeze your eyes on tears as you take his earlobe in your lips, his vulnerable, creased softness; you know him like a landscape you have played in endlessly, want to enfold his body into yours as the train clacks you on, want to wrap your limbs around the foetal curve of his back, and hold, just that. Want. Want. Want. As the train propels you deeper and deeper into a secret world of memory – your land, your sky, your learning.

The gate is always locked.

Every time you cycle back. Just in case, just to check.

The weeds grow over it, the scrub grows tall, the land reclaims as it will always reclaim everything, eventually, in this place that is not meant for humans, that will always draw you back.

And then the mornings. Every morning, in your old childhood bed, just before wakefulness. The aching stab of wanting him to touch your cunt, a whisper of a touch and the thrum spreading through your body, from your explosive core, and you are burning with it and you jerk into waking, into emptiness.

For so long you wander, desolate and alone, in the bleak borderlands of the soul. Head down, flinching people off. No touch. Never that. Nothing physical with anyone, couldn't bear it, the disappointment. All you have to anchor you is work.

Lesson 156

She should rouse herself with the thought:
'Now, what have I got to do today?'
(Mark, not to enjoy or to suffer, only to do)

Those rogue Saturday nights when you haven't been able to organise going out. Those endless New Year's Eves by yourself, raw with the alone, in your bedsit. Those keen questions at Christmas from grandparents and aunts: *when are you getting a boyfriend, love? When are you going to settle down? Are you happy? Is anything wrong?*

He has sullied your idea of passion. You have lost all sense of love as rescue. You are becoming desiccated and crabby without love, can feel the sourness. Cross and short with people, losing grace. Once, the more sex you had the more you wanted; now the less you have the less you want until desire has stopped, entirely.

For years, the flatlands.

For years, the soft patter of rain, from your heart.

Lesson 157

She should be judged solely by what she is now,
and not by what she has been

———————

A dinner party. In raffish lovely seedy Darlinghurst – Darling it Hurts in local parlance. The intense curiosity of the boy opposite. Firing questions, rat tat tat, drinking you up. You lean back and smile a crooked smile at his enthusiasm, feel so old within it. You used to be him once, vivid with curiosity, eating up life.

'So, do you have a boyfriend?' He's asking playfully, greedily. 'Have you ever had one?'

You bite your lip. He thinks you've never had one. Good grief. Because there's something so closed about you now, demure, shut off, in your fifties cardigan and dress.

You are twenty-two. Something snaps in you.

Once, you were a collator of experiences.

Once, you were conducting a grand and most exhilarating experiment.

You smile at him, a new smile.

Ready to begin again. Just like that. To unlock the more dangerous side of yourself, to take her out, to drink his enthusiasm up.

You cross your legs, wet.

Lesson 158

The happy duty of helping others

'I bet you don't even fart,' he says, working his finger into your arse. You wince. 'Real closeness between people is when they can fart in bed, don't you think?' He's a talker, he giggles, wants you loosened, wanton, he's roughing you up.

You let him go on.

You use him.

Ask him to shave you. To bind you to the bed post. Blindfold you. Later he asks if he can get out his video camera. You just look at him.

He'd never get close.

You knew this from the first kiss.

You get up. You leave. Without saying anything, without looking back.

As you have learnt.

But he has served his purpose. You are woken up.

Lesson 159

Counting-house, shop or college afford him a clear future
on which to concentrate all his energies and aims. He has got
the grand pabulum of the human soul – occupation

_____

It feels as if you are being returned to the world in a wheelchair,
crippled and bowed but ready – you have survived. Suddenly
it is different, the way you look at men. Every one a prospect.
The old carnality back. Curiosity is how you began and you
still have it in you and you smile at that, slipping it out like a
long forgotten book that woke you up, once; thrilled you into
life like a golden varnishing washed over a painting.

So. Other men, viciously now, other sexual experiences.

You have developed a laugh that could be described as filthy,
at odds with your image of containment. It is an invitation.
You use it often.

It works.

Lesson 160

These chapters do not presume to lecture the lords of creation

---

What you learn, what you jot down in your Victorian notebook that you vowed you would never write in again, in another life:

Example One: The shopping centre executive twenty-two years older than you. Because perhaps he, too, can teach.

He fucks you from behind with your legs clamped together by his as if he wants you a virgin again, wants you snug and tight. Cries take me, take me as he comes. You don't want to. He tells you confidently you have not yet discovered your sexuality. You don't tell him that with him you've shut your sexuality down like a snail in its shell, everything in retreat. He does not like women, you sense that from the start. It will never work. You walk away, you do not look back.

Example Two: The perfectly decent, gentlemanly, engineering flatmate you are not remotely interested in, who blackmails with generosity.

O worst kind! Crowding in, hovering, leaving roses by the bedroom door, chocolates and favourite books. You can't ever hurt him but you will never sleep with him. You can't bring yourself to say this. Don't they realise that this knowing comes within the first seconds of meeting? He is not a possibility. You can't be veered into that path. Love is an energy between two people – a recognition, a likeness – you catch something of yourself and it is there or it is not. As simple as that. It cannot be manufactured.

Example Three: The colleague. Almost.

His touch an echo of Tol's, the tenderness and the expertise in it and you think, perhaps, oh my goodness, is this love, yes, and you open out, become younger for him, shed years, shine up. Fuck like a teenager again, abandon yourself.

But my God that vulnerability of saying you love someone – and feeling stripped. The solitude of love. Not hearing from him for a week and you're going to pieces: unknowing fells you. Just tell me, you beg on his answerphone, so you can have your strength back. When he finally calls he tells you he's slept with men, occasionally, and something contracts. So. It will never be. Because he may go back at some point, maybe you're just an experiment, a one-off, and you can never compete with that thought. You walk away without looking back.

Example Four: The college boy into anal sex.
His reasoning – it's quick and easy, and there's no risk of pregnancy. He tells you of a Uni Drinking Society toast –

'To anal sex!' – and that it's the girls always cheering the loudest.

'Because if they're tired they can just turn over and let the guy get on with it.'

They have a point.

So much energy expended now trying to make unsuitable men suitable, so many wasted fucks. The bleakness of it. The astonishing emptiness of one-night stands where naked, with another person, you've never felt more lonely in your life and the trembling never comes again and you're faking so much and they never know it. It's easy, just as Tol said; you're becoming precisely what he didn't want.

Inauthentic.

Searching, searching. For something to wipe away Tol, to release you into the light.

Example Five: The actor.

Textbook handsome. The remoteness, the bloodless sex. As if he's never had to try too hard, never got his hands mucky in the mess of life. He never engages too deeply, leaving you cleaving to him. He says absently one night he doesn't have a passion in life, for anything, and he's right.

But then you. A world apart.

At night, late, after every one of them, taking out your little Victorian volume and flipping through the pages crammed with handwritten notes from both Tol and you, among rain spots and sap and bicycle grease and snail's trails and the knotted remains of clamped ants. So much text, from all those years ago – duelling, fuelling, itemising – that you have to scribble any new notes up the sides and in between and then leak them through all the Victorian declamations of the anonymous woman who would have applauded, once, long ago – for what you had, what you learnt, what you felt.

Then Tol's hand, strong at the end of it:

> *'Sex pleasure in a woman ... is a kind of magic spell.*
> *It demands complete abandon; if words or movements*
> *oppose the magic of caresses, the spell is broken.'*

Simone de Beauvoir

Did your Victorian author ever experience something of that?

You are sure. It is in her voice. You envy it.

Lesson 161

All the rest are a mere atmosphere of nobodies

It was love at first sight. A spiritual recognition you knew instantly and it cannot be cultivated, it is there or it is not.

'Don't talk. I don't want it. Just be quiet.'

Your command to them again and again. So you can be alone, in your head. So they don't crash into it. The movie that is bringing you to orgasm, that they know nothing of.

Reliving his tongue as thrilling as a trickle of water; reliving his touch springing you open like a trap released. You can't expunge him no matter how hard you try, he is like a stain on a favourite dress that cannot be removed and has spoilt it now, you can never wear it again. Can never recover that girl from long ago, in her cheongsam.

Except in your head.

Lesson 162

A very large number of women
are by nature constituted so exceedingly restless of mind

Graveyard sex.

Lune's expression for sex with an ex. She's the only person you have ever told about Woondala. Had to tell someone, as if to anchor it in reality; it wasn't a dream, it did exist.

'If you went back to him, sweetie, it'd be graveyard sex. There'd be something so sad, so deadening, about it.'

You laugh, shaking your head. It could never be that with Tol.

'Don't even *think* of finding him,' Lune warns.

You hear rumours, in literary pages and from bookshop owners when you enquire about his next book. He's disappeared, he's still writing. He's given up. Is changing tack. He's working on the great Australian novel, a love story; has crippling writer's block. There's occasional speculation that he'll publish something soon, next year or the year after, but eventually it dies out as new successes bloom for the media to gobble up. He's vanished from the face of the earth. You have no idea where he's living. Your worlds never collide.

You had nothing in common except love.

'Stop thinking about him,' Lune snaps.

Can't. Imagining the coming together again after so many years – the matey, laughy, fragile tenderness of old lovers, the intense familiarity. The strangeness. Wrongness. He harasses your dreams but you cannot tell Lune that – how you hold and hold him, stirring him just as you used to, urge him deeper and deeper and wake up gasping, wet.

He is holding your life hostage. You do not know how to escape.

He is the roadblock on any experience of love you've had since.

Lesson 163

Men may laugh at us, and we deserve it:
we are often egregious fools, but we are honest fools

———————

Lune despairs she's being 'flattened' by her divorced lover, Luca, who she has brought back from France, yet does nothing to extricate herself.

'He is the rock upon which I break, and break, and break,' she sobs, one red-wine-fuelled night. She's given up her Economics degree for him, the first man she's loved in her life; is becoming dependent, fragile, weak. It's as if she now has an obligation to succumb and there's nothing her friends can say to stop it. She who was so striking once. Losing all ambition, confidence, strength.

You become a shoulder to cry on. A wise one. Yet she will not listen to reason; is throwing away her future for this one thing only – a man, an unsuitable one at that.

You can see it in another person but could never in yourself. Tell Lune we mustn't let ourselves be dampened by the confidence of men, their unquestioning sense of rightness; we mustn't ever be the yes girls Tol hated so much. *We won't capitulate, alright?* We must never have that gulf of loneliness as we make love, in a marriage; that poison of never feeling more alone in our lives than within the thick of a relationship. Which Lune will, if she stays with Luca, you just know. So easy to say.

What you cannot tell her is that you crave connection on the profoundest level. Wildness, madness, edge. Again. A holiness fluttering in both Tol and you – no one else – and it is a weakness you can't bring yourself to articulate. You need obliteration, cleansing, a wiping of every memory of his touch. It was a spiritual intensity and it could never be replaced cheaply; this is the lesson you are learning.

He is the only one you want. If not him, no one else: you will wander the earth crazed, celibate, lone. Riddled by his ghost, a luminous light.

The price of love. So be it. You had it once, and so many don't.

Lesson 164

From his silence she had been driven to go desperately and sell herself to the old fool opposite

As your twenties gallop on you feel like you're swimming against the waves of a cold, choppy lake; the waves are slapping and butting you sideways and you're getting nowhere. Your world encompasses enormous stretches of alone and the bleakness of one-night stands and relationships never quite right that peter out after three months. How easy-perfect the lives of some of your friends seem. Everything, for them, is falling neatly into place.

Saturday night, late. Racking sobs into the dark. How has your life come to this? You're a bush girl who hauled herself out, became a lawyer in Australia's largest metropolis. You're strong, independent, self-sufficient – and swampingly lonely.

Couples, all around you. Reading their weekend papers, holding hands as they walk across a city street, piggy-backing in play in the park. But you.

'Live audaciously,' you tell yourself. London then New York, the dream, don't lose it.

You have to get out of this.

Walk away from these years infected with their sourness.

Lesson 165

Have faith in the wisdom of that we call change

_____

After all the broken days, your face is returning.

Well hello again, you.

You still wear your armour – the vintage dresses, severe hair, glasses – the carapace of the respected lawyer. But you're rangy now, for out. You've always had sunshine at your core and you'll find it again. Sydney is too small for the two of you; one day there'll be a party and your paths will converge and you never want to come across him, now – betraying the trembling and the blushing of the life held in limbo, the weakness of it.

It's time to crash rupture into your life.

Too often now, the feeling of being trapped. At weddings, engagement parties, birthdays. Placed next to someone you barely want to talk to, having to endure endless speeches, unable to pop in for just twenty minutes and then scat. Weighted by obligation, every weekend and most weeknights. Weighted by your stepmother, who betrays her jealousy and bewilderment of the life you have forged for yourself with her silence – she never once asks you about your work, never feigns an interest. Weighted by your father, who just wants you settling down and giving him grandkids, it's all he can tease you with now. You have a terror of this life closing over you and at dinners you don't want to go to you step outside for great gulps of clean night air, and space, and quiet. Needing to get away from all this. A world too known.

Lesson 166

The sufferer has learnt that God never meant any human being to be crushed under any calamity like a blind worm under a stone

———————

When you hand in your resignation at the law firm your middle-aged boss tells you that the readiness to have children is oozing from you, that you must have them, to complete yourself. You laugh it off. You're going to London to be a lawyer. Just that.

But your periods are becoming heavier, your body is urging you to hurry; there's the prick of the Saturday afternoon couples as you wander the city alone, in your final weeks, all-seeing, all-alive, in your singleness.

What you have learnt:
The importance of not giving all in a relationship, of retaining something of yourself, for yourself.

What you have learnt:
Love should be empowering not eviscerating.

What you have learnt:
You will always make sure the other person loves you more. From now on. It is the only way to survive.

What you have learnt:
The authority of distance, removal.

You feel like you're extending a hand – calmly, strongly – to destiny. You need to, to feel alive again.

Lesson 167

Bid a woman lift up her head and live
_____

And always you flick a glance as you drive past the gate and always it is locked. As if no one ever goes near it, it was a mirage, a dream, he was a ghost. It never happened, it was all in your head, you were so young, addled by hormones, delirious. Occasionally you stop your car and get out, bow against the chain and bounce your weight into it. It doesn't give. It never gives. Never spills its secrets. You stare through the fence, your fingers looped in the hurting steel that your bare feet couldn't climb once.

The cairn of him before you.

The shudder beginning in your bowels and travelling deep to your breast, almost hurting, thinking of him and of everything that went on beyond this gate and you squeeze your thighs tight. He is not here, it is obvious.

No one goes in.

Or out.

You turn away, you will never come back. It is time to hold your face high to an unknown sun. To allow forgetting into your life.

That night, as you fall into sleep, you put out a hand to God.

Lesson 168

Rescue, then, is possible

With Tol your name was Ripe.

In the years that followed: Husk.

Your name now: Ready.

Because as your twenties gather pace you know that women have to go after what they want. It's no use waiting for the phone to ring or the email box to ping – you have to make it happen yourself. Have you ever acted as you've honestly wanted? You need a recalibrating. You will make a living in a new world; forge your own life, your own way. Not with anyone else's expertise or money but with what you have earned yourself. You have your father's work ethic for that. You will act with audacity. Take full possession of your life. The experience with Tol and its aftermath has taught you one thing: bravery.

You are ready.

To stand at the bow of the ship and feel the salty slap of life firm and cleansing in your face. You take out your Victorian volume. Under the scrawl at the front – about a place that can teach you so much – you jot a scrap from the journal of Katherine Mansfield.

Here is a little summary of what I need – power, wealth, freedom. It is the hopelessly insipid doctrine that love is the only thing in the world, taught, hammered into women, from generation to generation, which hampers us so cruelly. We must get rid of the bogey – and then, comes the opportunity of happiness and freedom.

You shut the book and smile.
Ready.

IX

'Still
I have not opened my eyes to this world'

Don Paterson

XI

Lesson 169

O women! Women! Why have you not more faith in yourselves — in that strong, inner purity which can make a woman brave

---

It is 9 p.m. Time for bed.

'What's wrong with me?' you enquire into the ether.

'Marriage,' comes the voice from the couch.

You retreat, chuckling, reminding Hugh to check that Jack hasn't thrown off his blankets; you can feel in your bones an encroaching cough. You never fall asleep with your husband now, he always dozes on the couch and gets to you at 4 a.m. or thereabouts. His hot water bottle. That's all you're good for now, it's become a running joke.

You move into your bedroom, your sanctuary, close the door and breathe out. Uncurl in your bed. It scares you how much you love the alone, but you will never leave Hugh, and he will never leave you. It is unspoken. This is your existence together that you have welded on the great forge of your adult lives, over many years, imperfect but solid enough: it will hold.

So. Now you are middle-aged.

Dipping your toes into the vast zone of invisibility. The signs of slippage everywhere. Your body thickening after its quicksilver years of slenderness, finally you have lost control of it. Your metabolism is slowing, you cannot keep the weight off. Hair is growing in places it shouldn't be, with vigour – the only vigour in your life it seems. You are tired, so tired, constantly. Your eyebrows have learnt disobedience, are constantly going off-piste – when you pluck the wily ones there's likely to be a sudden bald patch; some are wilfully grey, others thickly curled. The most important item you now pack on holidays: tweezers. Not just for eyebrows but for your chin, cheeks, upper lip, belly. Greying pubes are around the corner, various girlfriends have warned you of this. The talk is of dyeing, perhaps, no one's daring to go first. Liver spots are vivid already on your hands – retribution, finally, for a childhood assaulted by its different sun. When you pucker up your lips for a kiss, from child or adult, you can feel the lines cementing into your upper lip. And you think back now to those years when a woman never knew what it was to be dry, internally, those slippy zippy easy years – and laugh.

'Is that blue ink on your leg?' Hugh had enquired absently as you passed.

'No. It's a varicose vein.'

He shrugged. So what.

You love him for that.

You think about sleeping with every man you meet. You do not want to sleep with any of them. You are too tired, too cold and you wouldn't want to take off your clothes for anyone. Your body has rusted up. Your husband doesn't mind. So be it.

But sometimes, at night, the memories. Screaming of the sun. A different life. Being caressed by the air. Lying belly down on the beach with the heat tingling alive your weary back. Here, in deepest England, in mid January, the cold has nestled into your bones like mould and you feel that this world has grown over you, and you will never climb out.

You rarely speak to your father now. He's a hopeless correspondent, doesn't do letters or computers, never rings on your birthday or special occasions. You used to call him religiously for his birthday but often it was your stepmother who answered and she would say without warmth that she would pass on the message, and he never called back.

Like a piece of ragged tin cutting into your heart, years and years of it, the pain of the silence still fresh.

You need to get back.

Lesson 170

Thoughts do not concern married women

Ari is the shining school dad who you just know would spring you alive. He followed a woman to deepest Gloucestershire but they are separating. He does the school run every Thursday. Often you are both the only two parents early, before the school gates open, and you've fallen into bantering. Ari is Israeli; sparky, loud, warm, full of shooting laughter and teasing and flirt. You'd forgotten what it's like to be with people like that. You feel yourself becoming looser, lighter in response. Remembering a woman you once were. Every Thursday now, when you see him, he reminds you that you've been in England too long, weighted down by the sheer energy it takes to get by in it. Such a crowded, aggressive, uncertain land – uncertain about where it's going and what it's become.

On the last Thursday in January you look at Ari as he tumbles his young daughter around his neck, look at his easy smile and shining teeth and know, beyond anything else, you need the WD40 of sun. Or you will go mad. It is as simple as that. You do not have a sense of belonging in this land, no matter how long you are in it, and as you get older you want the balm of that. You need to get out, get home. The cold in you like grease, sludging you up; the homesickness corrosive now and something has to be done about it.

But what would you be going back for?

As if on cue Pip propels himself into your arms with a flying leap, almost knocking you over and his little legs lock around your back and you laugh and twirl him around, just as Ari has done, everything else forgotten in the great burning furnace of your son's love as you bury your face in the warmth of his lovely neck. Everything repaired, forgotten, wiped by the sheer urgent magnificent heft of this.

Lesson 171

Dark deeds and ill feelings can only be conquered
by being brought to the light

_____

Hugh forcibly lifts up your feet. He polishes your Blundstone
boots. Despite a deadly serious protest. You pull your leg away,
viciously. He grabs it back – he will win this. He is doing all
the kids' shoes and his own, it is the night for it, and by God
he'll clean yours too whether you like it or not. What began as
a game is now more, much more, than that.

The anger so pure and festering in you that you just want to
run outside and gulp the fresh air, run and run and not look
back; in this moment, the voice from the woman you don't
recognise roaring inside.

Stooooooooooop.

The boys are watching. They keep you here. Silent. Seething.
On a Sunday night. Before a new week begins, as it will always
begin now, over the years and years to come there will be this
little ritual because Hugh has discovered an Achilles heel, a
new teasing point, and you know him, he'll be seizing it from
now on.

Seething.

At the man who insists on turning the car air conditioning

on in summer even though you crave the slap of fresh air. Who drives too close to the bumper bars of the cars in front and brakes so abruptly you gasp, and never changes this habit. Who litters the house with black crows, the endless clothes he never puts away. Piles of change. Receipts from God knows what. Who leaves the toilet seat up and the toothpaste lid off and who has never learnt, over ten years of marriage, to make tea the way you want it – oh, he'll make you a cuppa, but it'll never be right – he's never bothered to know you enough.

Seething.

At the little snippets of ownership he always has to exercise, all through your days and months and years as the little wife. You stare down in silence at your Blundstone boots that were scarred, once, with the history of your bush life. Now shiny black. As if new.

Seething.

At a marriage that is sapping your confidence, your will, your flinty self-sufficiency. You do not even fill the family car with petrol anymore let alone change its tyres; and once you did all of that. You eat baked beans and fish fingers because Hugh did once, as a child – forcing his habits upon you. You use a microwave even though you don't quite trust it because Hugh bought one, insisted, just came home with it one night. Within this marriage you are changing, retreating. Becoming as soft as a pocket. And you don't know how it came to this. Mel's caress jolted you into life. The tenderness, the caring, the *noticing*.

Seething.

As you stare at the gleaming Blundstone boots you have had since teenage years, that you barely recognise now.

You have to get back.

Rough them up.

Reclaim the woman you once were.

Lesson 172

Leave no odd hours, scarcely an odd ten minutes,
to be idle and dreary in

_____

You dreamt of Tol last night. For the first time in years. It was strange how fresh it was, rushing back his mannerisms – the feel of his hip under your hand, the softness of his belly to yours as you lay in perfect peace, socketed – the dream bringing it all back with a clarity your memory never could. His voice dropped down to you. He was saying your name as fresh as if it was being spoken aloud at that very moment, as fresh as twenty-five years ago and you jerked awake at his talk, out of the blue, speaking your name as he always said it – with wonder, delight, chuff – the inflection downward, soft; more to himself than to you.

And then the name Woondala sings through your blood like an illicit drug you have long turned your back on. _Woondala, Woondala,_ it lures, whispering you south and you stretch languidly in your bed, like a cat thrumming in the sunlight, and feel a familiar tingling, after so long, after years and years of not.

Woondala.

The great unanswered question of your life.

The disease lying dormant in your blood. Still.

Unless something is done about it.

Lesson 173

It is not responsibility, but the want or loss of it,
which degrades character

'What are you doing?' you ask.

Hugh is leaning against the bathroom door, staring as you shower, throwing peanuts into his mouth.

'Examining the goods.' His eyes are laughing.

'You never *bought* me.'

'Oh yes I did.'

You shut your eyes. The authority of his ownership – the sense of entitlement – enrages you. You snap off the shower. Step out, grab a towel.

'I want to go home.' Just like that.

Hugh's fist suspends a peanut high, he is speechless.

'For three months. I've been thinking about it. I'll take the kids. Just for a term. Put them into a bush school. It'll be an adventure. Be near my dad. He's getting old ...' You stare imploringly at him, rush on. 'I need the sun ... I'm going mad with the cold and the dark. Every year it gets worse, not easier; I don't know why.' Clotting up as you speak, needing this so voraciously, can't articulate the enormity of the want, just needing to live in a place with melodramatic skies again and a hurting light. Needing a gust blown through you, flushing you clean, needing out.

Hugh is nodding, absorbing.

'Alright.'

Finally. Surprisingly. As if he knows how far you have changed from that woman he fell in love with, so long ago, that he suddenly remembers that bush girl bursting with smile and sun.

'You're mad, you know that, and you'll only get madder if you stay,' he smiles. 'Off you go. Scat!'

You know in that moment that he, too, needs a break. And is confident enough in the relationship to let you off the leash; confident you will come back. The rivets are strong in this marriage, you have welded them together, hand over hand. Despite all the little irritations – the little snippings and snappings, all the erasures of wedded life – he never doubts. He knows you. It is as simple as that.

He doesn't. At all.

Lesson 174

Not a cloud comes across her path – not a day of illness,
her own or her little ones', shadows her bright looks

You Google Tol every so often as you prepare for the trip. He must be on the internet, somewhere, there has to be some clue to his whereabouts – his writing, his family, his life for the past few decades.

Nothing. How can someone just … disappear? In this world, now. He has vanished from the face of the earth.

It is bizarre. You refuse to believe it.

You will find him.

There's a young girl in you who refuses to die – she is uncurling, she will hunt him out. You have friends a few years older, in their mid and late forties, who are lost, keeling, depressed, dramatically changing their lives and their careers at this point as if eager for one last shot – one last go – before it's too late.

This is yours.

Act with audacity, he told you that once, yes. You crawl into the dust under your bed and pull out an old cardboard suitcase that is crammed with the detritus of a former life. In it – wrapped in your mother's cashmere cardigan, cradled in the crown of an Akubra hat still with its smudges of valley earth – is a tiny, leather-bound book. You breathe its pages in deep, the musty, papery smell plunging you back. You flip to the very end, Tol's page. It's been so long since you have opened it up.

Act with audacity because you are a woman – and because of that you must always do it more so than men.

To be noticed. Free. Strong. To live life the way you want.

That is your burden – and the great adventure ahead.

It is written. In the book, which you pack, of course.

Lesson 175

An ever-haunting temptation

The light assaults the four of you as soon as you step from Sydney's airport terminal. Three little Pommies beside you squint in horror as you stand there tall, drinking it up. Can feel it already spining you strong. You breathe in deep the paperbarks in their ragged skin by the car park, willing you home, to your bush. Hire a car and head north along all the roads of your childhood, to your land, your soul place, and know with certainty now you want to slip into this earth in death, the soil you know so well; you never want to be buried in the dark, crowded damp of England where your bones would never dry out.

The prospect ahead: a renovation of your serenity.

You want to be good at being alive again. You have lost the knack in England; need the solace of home. Need to be marinated again in spareness, and space, and light. To find stillness, and rest.

The house for the next three months is a one-bedroom weatherboard cottage found on the internet. In the town that your grandfather was born in, a stone's throw from your dad. A humble place. White-painted floorboards, clean sun through the windows, bits and pieces of furniture from various old folk. A perfect place. Three tiny camp beds for the boys, and you in the main room on a high single bed in a corner. You revel in living a lighter life. No DSs, no Wiis. The boys have to make do with slingshots and skateboards and an old cricket bat and a nearby creek, a waiting tyre hanging from a branch.

They're stolen, often, by their grandfather. It is OK, you just needed to be physically close by; you were too far away in England, lost. The boys are whisked away, often, for fishing trips and sleepovers, movies and larks in the park. He lives for family and there is a beautiful, old-fashioned simplicity to that. It is quiet and unspoken and good and it motivates everything that he does. You know now that your boys are your greatest gift to him. You have receded in his eyes, it is their turn now – your job is done.

Nothing has faded.

You write, up the front of the book, the only blank space left in it.

Lesson 176

The natural calming down of both passions and emotions

_____

Nature presses close. You can feel the great thumb of it on your back, forearms, hands, in your face. Soon you wear it like a mark. You look up often, saying hello to your sky in gratitude; scarcely believing you are living under it again. The sun's stain is at your neck and on your right arm hanging loosely out the car window or tapping the roof along with the radio, just as your dad always drives.

You watch your three Tigger boys grubby up in this land, grow lean. Lose softness, gain muscle definition, tan as golden as honey – become the little men you always dreamt of them being. Running and swimming and mucking about under this wide blue sky, learning to walk through tall grass with caution because of snakes, to shake their shoes out every morning because of funnel-webs, to swing on their tyre over the creek and make slingshots and billy-carts.

And oddly, achingly, you miss Hugh; the feeling of separation is acute. Your love for him is freshened. You want him to see all this, be in it with you, revelling. Watching his boys, stripping down to his shorts, laughing with them.

A smile fills you up at that.

The man who makes you laugh. He always has. It is the secret, you think, to a good relationship.

Lesson 177

We do not present so many angles
for the rough attrition of the world

Your father has stolen the boys again. Taken them to a rodeo and his favourite, secret place that your stepmother and you don't approve of: McDonald's. The one thing the two of you have in common.

'Sssh, don't tell your mum,' your father conveys in a conspiratorial mock-whisper when you drop the kids off and they shiver in delight. They adore him. Call him Eddie, his old name from your childhood. The past has won out.

You do not linger. It is still your stepmother's house; she still makes you extremely aware of that. You are both wary, polite, but you know she will never invite the boys and you in for a big family meal – she cannot bring herself to widen her heart to that extent.

No matter.

She is of another era, a lifetime ago, you have let it go within the busyness of your own life. You wave the boys goodbye and jump in your hired car feeling loosened, lightened. Your father grins at you and there is a sudden recognition – as you flash a smile back – of your face, absolutely, in his. It's something your stepmother can never take away and there's a giggle in your heart as you accelerate.

Along the deeply known, sun-dappled roads, under your deeply known sky, the girl you used to be is uncurling.

It is good being back, right. It's about the serenity that comes from belonging, the *ease* of it. After fifteen years away you can walk into an Aussie shop and yak away to the stranger behind the counter – because you speak a common language with codes and nuances and subtleties that are utterly familiar. For years you have been an outsider in a foreign land and revelled in that status. But my God, the relief of belonging. Perhaps it has something to do with ageing, with quietening, but it's hitting you now like a long cool drink after a sweltering summer's day. Life is easy, known, navigable again. The bread rolls are the same consistency from your childhood and you gorge on them. The cereal hasn't changed, the apples taste the same, the mangoes, the grapes; there is a comfort in all of it. You'd forgotten what it's like to live like that.

The windows are down, the music is up. Triple J, the station you used to listen to religiously. Elbow hanging out, sun and wind-whipped. Feeling such an uncomplicated, strong, pure happiness. It is dangerous, this.

You stop to fill up. Wander into the coolness of the milk bar next door through coloured plastic fly strips. Buy an ice-cold strawberry milkshake in a silver canister and drink it through a waxed paper straw. Laugh, at all of it, full of delight that your old life still exists! At a laminated table rimmed in a silver metal strip you slip out the little Victorian manual. Of course you have brought it with you, on this day, this trip into the bush, to God knows what.

You feel completely alone, for the first time in so long – years – and you adore it. You could never tell anyone that.

Lesson 178

If she knows herself to be clean in heart and desire,
it will give her a freedom of action and a fearlessness of
consequences

You sit in the milk bar with the book before you; the handwriting flooding him back. What was it about his touch that is so insistent, still? Now that you are an adult yourself with years of living behind you?

A cherishing, combined with authority. And not just a cherishing of the female body – a cherishing of sex. All the wonder that is in it. He'd done this many times before, that was obvious, but he made it feel exploratory, fresh. His dubious gift was to make you feel you were the one. The only one. With how many women had he spun that trick? He was like a politician with the knack of making every person they talk to feel special, wanted, unique. It was all to do with focus. The gift of attention, of course.

The knowing that came only once in your life.

It is why, of course, you are back.

Lesson 179

That grand preservative of a healthy body – a well-controlled, healthy mind

No.

You cannot drive past the gate, so close to this milk bar. Too afraid of being caught – your face, what is in it, after all these years. Still snared. What will he make of that? He is a love object, of course, he has shifted into that. Was *always* in that realm. You cannot even describe him properly; he is not fully rounded, fully human. You never knew him, you only recognised him – as an archetype. Every girl needs one, the obsession, at some point, to learn about life, to grow. To marry the one that is not.

No.

The man who had grown used to sucking on the marrow of other people's lives. The man who did not like his stillness rattled, his stillness so necessary to create, he made that clear from the start.

But then you.

Does he ever even think about you? Does he ever recall that summer and the whole roaring tsunami of experience that transformed your life?

Or did it just roll off him like water from a duck's back? His fucking-toy, his summer project, his experiment to some day write about. The distraction. The annoyance. He never gave in, never loved enough; he was too disciplined for that, feared the consequences too much.

You stand abruptly from the table. Snap through the plastic strips.

Need it gouged out.

Lesson 180

Wives either sinking into a hopeless indifference,
or wearing themselves out with weak complainings,
which never result in any amendment

Finally, the courage. To face him.

To offload him from your life.

Churning through you, churning, as you speed down the roads that your bicycle flew over once. On a day of ringing light, ringing out like a church bell. The little manual beside you, as if to anchor the reality of what went on once. *It did happen. This is proof.* And a plan, perhaps, to bury the book like a time capsule deep and forgotten under the earth. At Woondala. To return it, to stem it. You slow along the final dirt road that meanders like a pale river amid the green. The deep gash of a wound through the impenetrable wilderness. You do not know what is ahead, you slow in wonder at the dips and curves once soldered upon your heart.

The gate is open.

After twenty-five years.

You gasp. You weren't expecting that.

You park. As disbelieving as that time when you came upon the gate locked. How long has it been like this? You slip through, just like that. The breezy blue-sky day is so crisp it almost pings; there is a knife-edge sharpness to the light, a tenseness.

Light-headed. The blood pounding in your ears. Breathing fast.

Can you just step back into this life? What is ahead? Can you bear it? You *must*. A beautifully renovated mansion, perhaps, a solid country wife, roses around the verandah, three kids, Dad at work in the city, he'll be back tonight, *come in, have a cuppa, wait*. The blood pounding in your head. What madness to do this? What right do you have?

The right to your own life.

Lesson 181

They were honestly in love
_____

Scored deep in the bark of the Scribbly Gum, still:

> *'My spirit so high it was all over the heavens.'*
>
> *Pound*

Your fingers trace the knobbly words gnarled over by a sap as rich as amber – as if the tree bled with it in the years after you left – and you hold your cheek to its coolness, allow yourself this, your heart racing and then you walk on, around the curve in the driveway and past the ditch where you'd always drop your bike, that you can barely discern now the bush has claimed it so triumphantly, and then there it is. Woondala.

As you left it.

That last time.

All those years ago.

The canvas water bag still looped over the knocker by the front door, the nameplate still bruised with neglect. No cars. No bike. No life. Nothing.

As silent as a church.

A ruined church, abandoned to its ghosts.

With the air of a building affronted by its emptiness; that it should ever have come to this.

Lesson 182

The very element in which true friendship lives is perfect liberty

———————

There is no one here. Time has stood still. You step inside and graze through the rooms. Linger over the candelabra in the wide grate, the crazed china tea cups, the piano with its possum droppings, the gutted stool spilling its hessian.

So little has changed. You don't get it. It is as if time has never passed. But of course it has, so much: your life since – full rich busy bursting – in all the ways! Several rooms upstairs now have crude padlocks on their doors. You peek through a keyhole to a solid wall of furniture. So, what looks like a household of junk. An entire life packed up.

You return to the ground level, to the bedroom with its mattress still on the floor and pull up the jumble of quilt over the pillow, and straighten it, like it's a dead man's bed and then you lie belly down on the couch in the drawing room and breathe it in; still the same smell of age, and love, and wisdom, and weariness. Your arms slip around the padding in a gesture of embrace and you stare at the air all a-hover with its dust, waltzing in the disturbance you always make, spinning and whirling so stately in the slanting lemony light. All is quiet, except the tin roof cracking and pinging in its heat. You let the stillness wash over you – from twenty-five years ago, from when everything was suspended, tremulous, in the now. No future, no past. Just … this. Exactly this.

Did those days ever really exist? Was it all in your head? Your addled, hormonal, aching-with-loneliness teenage head. When love was this truancy from your normal life.

You have your book. Your manicured fingertips idly flick the pages, halting at the ones so busy at the end. Proof. You turn onto your back, vividly wet for him again, for all of it.

To be combusted once more into life, to be turned into someone else.

You squeeze your eyes in pain at the memory of him grabbing your chin and turning it to him, savagely, *my wild sweet girl*, he'd whisper urgently and it is the voice you hear now.

But who was the ravenous one, the devourer? Who the submissive? *Teach me*, you demanded, urging him on, further, always further, high on glee and the new, the constant new; the neophiliac, he called you once.

'I can't keep up, I need a two-day break just to rest. All that teenage energy, good grief, the sheer overwhelming force of it!'

You still think there is something courageous in the constancy of your love, wrong and ridiculous that it is.

He is the love thief.

Your entire life he has been that.

As were you, once. Sucking at the marrow of his experience.

Lesson 183

In the world's harsh wear and tear many a very sincere
attachment is slowly obliterated

You sit up.

The study.

You haven't checked it yet. The door always locked.

You passed it before, closed, and assumed it was out of bounds as it always was to you — but you should check. His inner sanctum, workshop, sweatshop; the nub of his life. You rush out, heart pounding, to the door with its battered iron knob.

It swings open at the lightest of touches.

Waiting for you.

Can you? Should you?

Stepping inside, gingerly. Breath held.

As if lifting the shroud from a dead person, lying in state.

Lesson 184

Her conduct and character as a human being is accountable to God as much as the greatest woman that ever was born
_____

A room bare, of everything.

Except your gifts.

Every single thing you gave him, once.

All the books taken from the shelves, all the magazines, the pinned quotes on the notice board, the piles of papers and the manuscripts. Everything of him. Every word, except the words glued in a ladder of permanency once, in furious, tear-brimmed need.

'So you never forget, mate.'

> You soak through and permeate the spirit and skin of my days ...
>
> Every conversation I have with you sneaks inspiration upon me ... I just want to be with you forever ...
>
> The other day I felt as if I had fallen in love with your soul, my feelings were that strong ...

On his desk: the old Capstan tobacco tin that fits, perfectly, his architect's pencils. You flip it open. Empty.

On the blank book shelves: the old blue bottle with its bubbles of clearness. Two desiccated willow crowns. A line of photographs, perfectly neat. A girl in a cheongsam dress. Leering at the camera, poking out her tongue, scrunching up her nose in cheekiness. Her long blonde hair ratty across her face, freckles smeared across her nose, sharp teeth. A cheeky gap in the front, now fixed. A girl who owned her sexuality – that young, ready body – filled up with sun and wind and light.

Over the writing chair: the dress itself in the faded Liberty spring print. You stare at its slimness that once fit you perfectly. How on earth did you ever fit into it? It still smells, faintly; cripes, never washed.

On an old wire coat hanger hanging from the door: a flannelette shirt with the sleeves torn off. How he got that, God knows. Can't remember leaving it.

On the floor, some French homework you must have left behind, your funny looped handwriting back then that still had the nuns' imprints upon it, but was trying to cut loose.

Against a far wall, propped: your old bicycle, Peddly. You kneel down in wonder at the trusty wheels, the dusty spokes, the chain that always fell off. Your dad had tossed it, that much you know. Abandoned it by a roadside or the local tip. And now, here. Gosh.

In his typewriter: the sheet of paper you scrawled *yes* on once in gleeful blobs and scratches. When you finally had him caught. That moment of knowing, in your exuberant script.

Beside it: the very first souvenir, the scrap of checked cloth from a cut-away shirt, still with its tractor treads of grease. From your grandfather's drill, long lost.

Now, here. All of it.

You spin around, in bewilderment, the old tobacco tin in your hand. A tear splashing on the scurried surface, varnishing it up.

A shrine ...

To a girl, once. Long gone.

You sit gingerly on the hard, worn saddle of your bike. Trying to work it all out. Your fingers fit perfectly into the handlebars worn into a smoothness on their undersides. A whole other narrative – a whole other book – in all this.

The other side. Of a secret life.

A man you know nothing of.

Lesson 185

The greatest blessing of all external blessings is to be able to lean your heart against another heart, faithful, tender, true and tried, and record with a thankfulness that years deepen instead of diminishing, 'I have got a friend!'

———————

A museum of you.

Nothing else in the bareness. An emptiness that is beautifully clean, swept.

Tended.

You gasp. Everything here is kept, as opposed to removed and you weep at that for it is the exact reverse of your father's house; it is the way you always wanted, dreamt of your childhood world being preserved – everything of your mother's stark in it, vivid and cherished, highlighted by the absence of everything else. But of course it never was, all of that was tossed out in the indifferent vigour of the new marriage.

As it should be, perhaps. As life goes on.

But this.

One searing summer, thrown into stark relief. As if it was all that mattered in the end. A secret place in the wilderness, washed by its beautiful light. Commemorating a moment in time when you were both haunted together. *Both* of you. That is clear, from this, and your hands are now at your mouth, in shock.

Lesson 186

Her own sphere cannot contain her
_____

You ring your father on the iPhone – you're with an old friend you've run into, you have a lot of catching up to do. He's fine with that, the kids are tops, they loved the rodeo – wouldn't get off the bucking bronco, had three goes each, are covered in ice cream and dirt.

'As little boys should be, mate,' you laugh.

You stay in Woondala deep into that swirling evening, roaming the rooms, lying on the couch and the mattress and then belly down on the floorboards of the verandah, listening to the bush settle into its quiet, trying to work it all out. You'd stay longer if you could but the blankets on the bed are musty, the sheets are stained by too much living, too long ago. And this is a ghost house, a dead house. You'd always felt it would be a different entity entirely, at night.

In two days you go back, and then again.

Drawn to his study, the vivid core of him, then.

You begin to write.

It feels right. At his desk. On his chair. Your little volume beside you, combing through all the words with the perspective of a middle-aged woman who's lived a crammed life since. Writing to understand, to work it all out.

Lesson 187

There is a solitude which gradually grows into the best
blessing of our lives

You used to swim laps, several times a week, and then you went
to church, evensong, on a Sunday night; and then you sat and
typed, in a room that catalogued a relationship once.

The feeling at the end of each activity the same: a cleansing,
a serenity. That you have done something solid. Good. Right.
Seizing the alone, and lit with it.

No longer feeling you are the rubbed-away housewife
with absolutely nothing to contribute, the little woman being
pushed to the side of her own life. Here, anonymously, you are
the pulsing beating glittering centre of it. Secretly, deliciously.

It feels good. To have found a voice.

To be honest, at last.

Lesson 188

After marriage, for either party to desire a dearer or closer
friend than the other, is a state of things so inconceivably
deplorable that it will not bear discussion

It is Friday. You are staying late. You have told your father
you're at your friend's house again; not sure why you want to
be here this night, alone, can't explain it, even to yourself. But
it is a Friday, a weekend is ahead, when people pay visits to
their country places …

Perhaps.

You couldn't bear it.

But what if …?

Just in case, you've parked your car at the back of the house,
near the bike shed, so as not to spook anyone arriving late.

A little after ten o'clock you hear what you have been waiting
for, dreading, anticipating. A car. As you knew you would. A
beam of light through the trees, twisting and turning as the
road to this house twists and turns, every bend you know so
well, and you rise in a rush from his desk like a schoolgirl caught
in the headmaster's office. You run outside, drink up the air,

the sexy pungent air of this night, waiting on the verandah, in the shadows. Your heart pounding.

The moment you have been waiting for.

Your entire adult life.

Lesson 189

Nature as well as custom has instituted this habit of life
_____

It is Julian.

You pull back in the darkness, behind a pillar, he does not see you.

Physically, he is much changed. Thickened, with completely grey and receding hair. Shorter, yes, you're sure. He stops to light a cigarette. Tiredness has dragged down his eyes, dulled his glow. So, a small-of-stature, balding, middle-aged man now, with all the anonymity that comes with that. As if his life has become one huge sigh, of regret. It is in his stance. His face. The way he drags on his cigarette. You always think men age more startlingly than women and he is the proof.

You galvanise yourself, take a deep breath, this has to be done. You step forward, emboldened. He starts in shock, a hand grabbing a verandah post to steady himself.

'Hello you,' you say low, strong, warm.

He knows instantly who you are.

'Where is he?' you ask before he can say anything. He steps back down the steps, looks around, bewildered, panicked, can't quite believe you're here.

'D—don't you know?'

You shake your head.

It must be something then, in your face, your bitten lip, suddenly, something haunted, because he comes forward and takes you gently by the arm and he sits you on the top step. Quite changed, all of a sudden. Fatherly, authoritative. Asking about your life – England, work, your kids, husband – leeching from you two and a half decades of experience. Telling you all the while about his divorces, his five children, the crazy maintenance arrangements, his job as a high-end property consultant but it never pays enough – two broken marriages and school fees have seen to that – the constant poverty, the ex-wives, the shifting from place to place.

'The one constant – the one true friend in it all – has been Tol.'

You look at him.

He nods.

Then he tells you a story.

Lesson 190

The involuntary thrill that we call 'feeling happy'
does come and startle into vague, mysterious hope
our poor, wondering heart

Of a man who fell in love.

With a teenage girl.

Who asked him once if she could be taught about life.

And so he did. After much resisting, reluctance.

He moulded this rough, raw, scrap of a bush kid, with eyes as knowing as a cat's. Shaped her, learnt from her, cherished her, marvelled at her. Grew to love her, oh yes. He taught her to understand the artist's life; to give him space. It was perfect, it worked. He would never hurt her, he was so afraid of hurting her. He would always be generous to her. His aim was to empower her. A new woman for a new world – so strong and aware that no other man would ever want her, would be afraid of her so she would be his, forever, trapped. As he was.

'He was a writer,' Julian chuckles ruefully, 'with a novelist's eye for the narratives of life.'

'Was? What do you mean *was?*'

Julian brushes aside the question.

The transformation was recorded, in the most beautiful prose, at his desk. You see, by coming into his life this sparky, demanding, stroppy country kid had unlocked him – with her hunger for experience and her enormous curiosity – and miraculously, he was able to write again. He was freed. The words came strong, in a way they never had in his life.

Because of you.

His muse.

Lesson 191

No one can hold the reins of family government for ever so brief a time, without feeling what a difficult position it is: how great its need of self-control as the very first means of controlling others

---

On an afternoon of sullen sky a car drove up. A man stepped out. A valley man. Tol knew it instantly; it was the gait, the shoulders, the face. He also knew exactly who he was – the imprint was clear on his face. You shrink back on the step and shut your eyes, can't bear to hear what's coming next. Before Tol could say anything the man strode up to him and in one enormous fell swoop, punched him hard across the temple before a word had been exchanged.

'It wasn't ...' Dread in your voice.

'Yes.'

You had been seen. That last day you came here. By Colin, your father's old mining mate, who used to look at you with leery, rheumy drinker's eyes. His car had a puncture and his spare tyre was shot and he was walking back into Beddy and he had caught a glimpse of the schoolgirl – the la-di-da convent girl now, Miss Goody Two Shoes who never gave him the time of day anymore – slipping from a gate he'd never given a second glance. Until that afternoon.

And so on that final day – after you came home and shut yourself in your room in splendid shock and exhilaration and release – your father left your house and slipped through Tol's wire gate.

To investigate.

As soon as he saw Tol's face – the awareness, the defensiveness – he knew exactly what had been going on.

The first blow was so savage it knocked Tol unconscious. He lay in the dust as your father crashed and banged his way through Woondala's rooms, bluntly, ferociously, with no respect. In Tol's study he found a manuscript.

The reckless honesty.

The filth.

His daughter, through all of it.

Tol was coming to, reeling in the dirt, trying to get up. Your father came out roaring. With his heavy work boots he kicked Tol in the head and the back and the stomach and he stamped on his hands. Both of them. Stamped and stamped until all the fingers were a bloody, flattened, jellied mess. Stamped out words, stamped out writing, stamped out creativity – all that airy-fairy, namby-pamby good-for-nothing patheticness – stamped out everything he didn't like about this country and this world and this life; everything he couldn't believe existed in his daughter. His *daughter*, for Christ's sake.

An act of extreme and unremitting violence.

Tol was unconscious again, from the brutality of the assault.

Then your father went back through the study and took away every word that was in it. The typewritten manuscript, the only copy that existed; every book, quote, diary, notebook, every narrative arc and worksheet. Because of course Tol had a hopeless memory and wrote everything down, he had told you that once and you had learnt from it.

Your father filled the tray of his ute. Every word. Every stinky rotten filthy perverted word from this godforsaken shithole of a place.

Everything, except several scraps of sentences glued to a wall.

Because he couldn't get them off.

The only words left in this entire place.

Lesson 192

Do not harden or brutalise the child,
and make them virtually disbelieve in love and goodness
for the remainder of their existence

'I still have ...'

'That little housewife's book. I know. Tol told me. It's the only book Woondala has left.'

You both pause in the dark. Julian puts an arm around your shoulder.

'Treasure it,' he says soft.

Your father left this place. His last words? As Tol was stirring in agony in the bloodied dirt. You shut your eyes, don't want to hear them, must.

'Try taking this to the police, you cunt. Just fucking try.'

Because of course Tol couldn't. You were a schoolgirl. He knew the risks.

'But you know what?' Julian shakes his head. 'It's such a crazy thing ... Tol said that as your father was doing it all, as he was ruining all his work, life, opus, there was something about the man that he admired, that he couldn't condemn.'

'What?'

'The love. He did it out of love. For his daughter. His blood. He was literally beside himself, driven mad. It was the only way he could express it. He wept over and over as he was stomping on Tol, "Give her a chance. Let her finish school, you dirty fucker … give her a life. A *chance* …"'

You're weeping now. Julian squeezes your shoulder tight, holding in your sobs.

'And Tol knew that your father was right. He got the gate locked.' A pause. 'And for years he kept it locked.'

'Why?'

He looks at you as if it is obvious.

'To give you a chance.'

Lesson 193

I think I was not quite correct about such a thing
_____

Your world detonating.

With knowing. Realigning.

You had always thought your father didn't love you anymore. Had always thought your stepmother had won, that you had lost that particular battle from the moment she arrived in your life. Had always thought he never cared enough about your study, work, life; it was why he never went to speech nights or father–daughter dances, to formals and school masses.

Because he *couldn't*.

Couldn't talk to those people. Didn't want to be showed up. Didn't understand that world, was *afraid* of it. You squeeze your eyes shut on hot tears. That little, little man, who you once thought so huge, untouchable, heroic. Remembering how he used to talk to you when your stepmother wasn't around – how he still talks to you when she isn't around – remember that, remember it, nothing else.

The purity at the messy, shocking, reeling, cluttered heart of all this. Hold onto it, nothing else.

It is like bursting through the surface of the water, after a drowning, a near-death; bursting through it with a great zooming rush into the air, the light.

Lesson 194

One ounce of kind feeling, tact, and thoughtfulness for others
be worth a cart-load of ponderous etiquette

'Why didn't Tol explain any of this?' you ask, rubbing your
eyes. 'I went mad with it. For years. All the uncertainty, the not
knowing. There was just one measly note that told me nothing,
really. It ate me up.'

'He couldn't tell you. He was too injured, at first. It was only
luck that I found him. I'd driven up to check on the manuscript,
time was running out. I found him on the verandah, a day later.
He'd crawled that far, as far as he could get before collapsing.
He was in hospital for so long. In and out of consciousness. He
refused to press charges, of course. He couldn't write to you.
His hands were no use. He was a cripple. He pleaded with me
to go back to his typewriter, get something to you, anything.
He trusted me to do it. I'm hopeless at these kinds of things. He
wanted you to soar, to live your life strong –' he paused. 'But I
was so furious, at the whole thing; the loss of his manuscript,
his hands. I – I bashed something out.'

'What? But …' You murmur, your mind whirring. Tol, Tol.
'Where is he? I need to see him.'

Julian puts his arms around you. Fatherly, firming.

'Come back tomorrow.'

You take a deep breath. Wipe your hands furiously across tear-stained cheeks. Right. OK.

'Thank you, Julian,' you say, businesslike, firm.

He walks you to your car. Smiles the old smile, from the very first time you met him at this place. As you shut your door he yells out.

'Tol wanted you to have a life. He was mortified. Your father's words really shook him. He's the best person I know. The most generous.'

You nod. 'Yes.'

As you drive past you idle the car. One last question.

'What's his real name?' Because you always wanted to know, and never asked. What on earth was it short for?

'Ptolemy. He *hated* it. It never went down well in an Aussie playground.'

'Ptolemy,' you repeat in wonder and laugh. No wonder he didn't let on.

'We all have to carry burdens from our parents,' Julian grins. 'He wanted to spare you that one.'

You honk your horn in gratitude and speed off, your hand butting the night air in farewell.

Scarcely able to concentrate on the road, veering and wildly correcting yourself as the car sluices off the dirt; stopping abruptly at a roo, its eyes silver coins in your headlights and then driving on with a frantic, churning heart. At all of it.

Lesson 195

The new generation which brightens life with a perpetual hope

_____

To your father, to your jumbly tumbly boys. Your stepmother is out, visiting her sister. You stride in the door of your old home feeling like icy water is washing over you, gasping for breath, voice. You look at your dad – on his fake-leather recliner rocker he's so proud of – with various little men perched on him or scrunched beside him; four cheeky little boys at home, alone, with the run of the house and gleeful with it. Your father's flannelette pyjamas are poking from his trouser legs and all four of them are devouring the Batman movie, *The Dark Knight*, with shiny eyes, you've never allowed your boys to watch it. Even your youngest, Pip, is still up and they're all pleased as punch they've been allowed to stay awake so late, it's the latest they've ever been up in their lives.

You stand there, your heart thumping. So much to say to this old man before you and yet in the heat of the moment, you can't. Just can't. All you remember are Julian's words; that in his violence was a supreme act of love. It was the only way he could express it. Tol had to respect that.

And the sight of all of them together, soldered by blood, your blood, is breaking you.

With happiness.

Because your father only became alive to you, fully human, when you had these kids; he could only relate to you, understand you, when you were a mother. But the intensity of the loving never changed.

And now you understand.

At last.

He told you once – in those reeling days after the locked gate, when he was driving you the three-hour trip back to school – that you must never, ever care for a man more than he cares for you. *Treat 'em mean keep 'em keen and never forget it*, he had ruefully laughed and later you had written his words down. He told you that if anyone ever hurt you he would hunt them down and kill 'em and you saw but did not truly comprehend then that he was scared of the enormity of his love for you, and you held that in your heart for a while but then life took over, and you forgot.

But now.

You understand. That some things in life, you must let go.

Lesson 196

Be very patient with this person; bear their little faults as they must bear yours; make allowances for the unintentional slights, neglects or offences, that we all in the whirl of life must endure

---

You bury your face into the snuffly, lovely, giggly warmth of the boys as you pour them into bed. Your stepmother not only bathed them but washed their hair before she left for her sister's. You smile your gratitude, a warmth towards her nudging through you. It is how she speaks to you, by these solid, simple gestures; how she has been speaking to your father their entire married life.

You do not hate her, at all, oh no. You are intrigued by her. She is a type of woman you didn't know still existed; a woman who has devoted her entire adult life, completely, to one job and one only. *Wife*. A woman from a generation that put themselves last. And what you both know is that you would never want to be her. That you will manage your own life rather than let someone else do it for you. It is unspoken and enormous between you – your difference.

You pity her. She is not educated, not particularly intelligent; your father has told you with relief that she is a simple woman.

You sensed it even at fourteen, the narrowness of her world. Not a reader, no friends beyond family, no curiosity or greed for a wider life. You pity the fear that has dictated her choices in life. Of her husband. Of divorce. Of risk. Of work. Of her watching stepdaughter – suddenly, vividly, hugely, in her life. Who never saw her acutely enough.

Her childlessness. Children of her own never came and you never discussed it with her and can only imagine the vastness of her silent anguish over the years, at the core of her life, and you wish you'd been there for her at some point; that she'd allowed it, that you'd been able to talk about it at least. But she wouldn't have wanted that. She has devoted her whole life to her allotted role within matrimony and she does it with rigorous attention and grace.

You are grateful for her. For your father's sake.

For she is the best type of wife for a man like him.

There is a dignity to it. You curl your body around little Pippy and smile, breathing in deep the smell of his cleanliness.

Lesson 197

Labour is happiness

—————————

A new heart. At last.

Radiant with relief.

You have your father's love. It is like a banner, proud in its breeze, flapping across your wounded soul in this enormous, shifting night. His immense love, and your stepmother can never take that away from you and she knows it as do you, now, and it is enough.

You are free.

You have worked and had children and travelled and lived a life of varied and extraordinary experiences, that a generation ago could scarcely be imagined, and for years you never saw the richness of it. How lucky you are.

But now this.

You are learning gratitude, at last.

And with that comes release.

Lesson 198

Any sort of body can in time be made useful, and agreeable, as a travelling-dress for the soul

Dressing carefully the next morning, as carefully as if you are preparing for a wedding, a formal, the greatest interview of your life. Applying make-up which you rarely do now, changing outfits – once, twice – going back to what you had at the start. No make-up. A simple shirt. The woman you once were. Honest.

Need him to clearly see your face. The living in it. The change. The strength.

But as you drive up Woondala's driveway you are crying, don't know why; a great letting go, perhaps, a floodtide washing through you. Your whole past in this drive and your future. Between the magnificent Slaty Gum by the property's gate and the knife-leafed wattle at the back, you were made, once, you feel that.

A letter is on the doorstep.

Just that.

No Julian. No Tol. No cars. The house as empty as a church.

After the shock, you realise you expected this.

Nothing more. Of course.

Lesson 199

We have come to view life in its entirety, instead of agonisingly puzzling over its disjointed parts

---

A letter, typed. You recognise instantly the intensity of the ink.

How to say this ... I can't meet you. Forgive me. I don't want you to see me like this. My brokenness. Let's remember how we were, just that. It's better that way. Those extraordinary weeks. Don't seek me out, don't worry about me. I am writing. I have found other ways to work. Under other names. It has freed me, in fact.

So. You are back. All changed yet not. A woman now. A mother. Three boys. What a delight! And a good husband. Julian has told me that. He knows these things. You deserve it.

I hope you will write a book. I sensed it from that very first time together in my study. I always had faith in you to write out your questions and your curiosity and your bewilderment. To act with audacity. You are much more honest than me. Which is why you must do this. It is right it comes from you, from your perspective.

Just know one thing. You taught me. No one had ever given me the gift of that. I responded to what you wanted. Thank you for that. Yet I failed you in the end. I could never match you, be honest enough with you. I could never show you my real self. As you did. You had the courage. I didn't.

If I taught you one thing it is this: to live life vividly and with passion. Remember that. We must wring as much happiness as we can out of life during our allotted time on this earth.

So. Turn around. Go home. Seize that happiness and be content with it. Close this chapter, this tiny chapter, in the vastness of your life.

T xxx

Lesson 200

Fear not the world: it is often juster to us than we are to
ourselves

_____

You look up to the roof, reeling in the light, and there it is.
Through your tears, your gulps of wet, your shielding hand.

A shadow.

A movement – at the high window you stood at when you
first came to this house and looked over the valley in audacious
ownership, and felt filled up.

It could have been a bird, a possum, a cloud shift.

But something, definitely, is there.

You run through the house, up the stairs, holding back a sob,
holding back a name. To the wing of padlocked doors but one
is open and you run to it; fingers are just disappearing around
the door frame as it shuts, beautiful useless fingers that tripped
down a back once as speaking as a whisper, hands that have lost
all their strength, are old, but the fingertips are familiar, the
curve of them, the clean lovely moons that you once held in the
cave of your mouth. They stop, for a moment, and you press
your lips to the ring finger – trembling, vulnerable, impotent –
through your tears you feel it.

The moth's first kiss.

Then the hand slips away, and the door is shut.

Lesson 201

Women — whose character is of their own making,
and whose lot lies in their own hands

_____

You turn away.

You walk to your car.

Your thudding heart, your thudding heart.

You do not look back.

Your name, now, Released.

As you power down the road you will never drive upon again.

To the next phase of your life, the next tiny chapter within the richness of all that goes on, that you never appreciate enough.

A phase you own.

No one else. Not your husband, not your parent, not your long-gone lover or your children.

You.

X

'She only comes when she's on top'

James

Lesson 202

She is now mistress over herself — she has learnt to understand herself, mentally and bodily

———————

Back.

To the house held together by thatchers' ladders and coffin lids.

You have changed the intensity of how you live. A gust has blown through your life, flushing it clean. Your perception of how well you are doing is measured by how serene you are feeling at any given time and here, now, you are at peace. With Rexi, who is hooking his hand around your throat as you lie beside him in his bed.

'What are you doing?'

'I'm holding on to you, Mummy, so you can't run away from the boysies.'

You bury your face into the warmth of his neck and smile and breathe deep. Your beautiful son, who makes you laugh so much. All of them.

It is enough.

His firm, soft, nine-year-old hand holding you still as you lie in the voluminous quiet. You've become extremely vulnerable to kindness, it's the quality you now cherish the most. And it's wondrous and moving to see your son transforming into a man. A gorgeous man. Whose kindness astounds you; the generosity of it. He's a much better person than you. He teaches you so much.

Open-eyed.

At last.

Lesson 203

Having chosen, let her fulfil her lot

———————

The urge to return to Australia for good has softened. This is your lot, your life, and you are still with it. Finally. As you have aged you have felt the desire to belong, somewhere, above all, and you belong *here* in this tight, scruffy, imperfect little unit – in this place.

You feel rested too. Pip is finally sleeping through the night and with that comes repairing, an old energy back that you'd completely forgotten about. The balm of solid nights' sleeps. For Hugh too.

You can feel it, something revving.

Lesson 204

By the time she has arrived at half of those three-score-years-and-ten she will generally have become her own mistress

_____

Rushing through the door on a damp Saturday afternoon, laden with midlife-crisis shopping bags. Topshop, French Connection, Zara. You can hear all four of them singing the World Cup anthem around the kitchen table and you head straight into them: they're doing fine. Homework done. Mouths wiped. Lunch consumed, albeit the detritus uncleared but so what?

Hugh eyes the shopping.

'Well, at least you haven't given up,' he remarks drily and you laugh. 'But where's the one from Coco de Mer?'

'What's Cocal din-*ner*?' Jack pipes up.

You pull out a bra, ta dah! Three little boys squirm and cover their eyes in horror. But your husband comes up to you and pushes into your space in silence like a horse at a fence nudging for grass. Strong, gentle, hopeful.

You kiss him back. Hold, and let the holding wash over you, as does he.

Lesson 205

I hold the law of kindness, the alpha and omega of education

You love this man. The knowing washes like a golden balm under your skin, washes through your body as you hold in the kitchen amid a cacophony of chanty, squealy, shove-y boys. Your husband amongst it is in you like the glow of a candle. Quieting.

You know now you are ready to lead a more honest life. A life self-created – or you will disappear. That is your choice as your forties gather pace.

And you have clever fingertips.

Because you were taught, once.

'I want to fuck you tonight,' you whisper.

Hugh steps back in astonishment.

'Boys, straight to bed after *X-Factor*!' he announces. 'You all need an early night. And footy tomorrow. It's about time we all went.'

Boys groaning. Dad rubbing his hands. Mum smiling a smile she hasn't used for a long time, years.

Because you need buoyancy not weight, the older you get. Fun. A loosening. Your clever fingertips trip up Hugh's back, under his shirt, reaping goosebumps.

A giggle in your heart.

Lesson 206

Let all these powers of vital renewal have free play

─────────

Can desire be so crusted over it is gone for good? Buried too
deep to ever be aroused again?

You used to think you never wanted to sleep with anyone
again; that kind of life was gone. You had your children, sex
had served its purpose. You used to think you were broken, that
it was too hard to ever be fixed – adults never get repaired they
get worse, life chips away at them and they carry the damage
throughout their adulthood; it hardens, calcifies, in fact.

But you feel freed. Miraculously.

After years of being the yes woman you have found a voice.
And with that, comes confidence.

You've also noticed that you've put on a bit of weight recently
– and it seems to have woken your husband up. Odd, that. Or
not. As you relax, unclench.

That night you make love with Hugh for the first time in
years. Rusty, like an old lock. You have to force yourself into
working, a remembering, but then it all comes back. And this
time, crucially, it's on your terms – not anyone else's.

Telling your husband what you want. And what you don't

Night after night. Whispering, spilling your honesty, revelling in his astonishment. You want his tongue taut, there, right there, keep going, no talk! *Lift my leg up. Higher. The clit! Now let me go on top.* You teach him, direct, grab his finger and place it exactly on the spot.

A woman he's never seen in his life.

The pleasure in utmost precision.

All of it coming back.

His body is soft from his indoor life, not fat but lacking tone; you do not care. It's not supreme fitness you want, it's the touch. The tenderness. It's always been everything. He never got it.

Until now.

A woman he never knew existed.

That you'd never dared show him.

Lesson 207

Her greater independence in middle life

Now he's coming into bed at 4 a.m. and gently making love – with sleepy, spidery tenderness – because he is finally listening to what you want. Now he is slowly prising you open with a whisper of a fingertip until you are shuddering, endlessly, turning to him then turning from him, pushing him away, alone in your loveliness. Then you want to sleep and he lets you; he wants it too.

You are parents after all: tomorrow, from 6 a.m., the great wallop of life.

It was never like this before. When you had babies to make. When it was so calculating, fraught, businesslike. All that pressure of coming, at the precise moment in the month, pumping the juice from him and then flipping your feet up to the ceiling and praying that gravity would do its work.

Just pleasure left.

The pursuit of it, an endless experiment. You know that now. It is fluid, dynamic, changing, even within a partnership of years, decades. It's possible, if you both allow it. A revelation. You can see now that through the great span of a lifetime there are troughs and peaks, floods and droughts – the less you have the less you want – but then the extraordinary opposite.

Lesson 208

It has fulfilled its appointed course

_____

Mel and you avoid talk beyond banalities at the school gate. You could never do the lesbian things; cripes, the clash of the hormones, twice a month, and God help you if your periods were in sync. But every time you see her there is a smile of secrets, thanking her. For springing you back into life.

Like a steel trap suddenly burst open, you are released.

She knows it. She can see it. She wishes you well, it's in her face.

Lesson 209

Both parties grow out of friendship and cast it, like a snake
his last year's skin — this is a fact too mournfully common to
be denied

Courage now, to face so much.

Life is leaving its imprint on your forehead and you can
see the years stretching ahead of you – of school gates and
speech days and GSCEs with your heart in your mouth and
all the Susans, again and again, with their unthinking crowing
confidence; or insecurity, perhaps, actually – all the Susans you
will have to face throughout life, as a mother trapped in the
glare of their headlights.

Or not.

Has that world cemented so firmly around you that it can
never be cracked apart?

'Sooz, I love you, but you really don't have to give me a rundown
of Basti's achievements every time I see you. He's precious. I
get it. He's a beautiful boy. But they're *all* precious. My boy
as much as yours. I just don't feel the need to say it, darl. I have
to tell you this – gently – alright? It's doing my head in.'

Her astonishment.

The pulling away, from that point. The necessary pulling away.

Your relief.

Because actually, your boy's alright. You know it now, no matter how much she needs to give you her little critique when you pick up Rexi from her doorstep. Your boy is growing up fine. Beautifully, in fact, in tandem with your own happiness firming, your settledness pushing through into all pockets of your lives. And it doesn't matter anymore that she doesn't see it, or does but can't bring herself to declare it. It's her problem. You're strong enough in yourself, as is Rex.

You know now you only want to be surrounded by heart-lifters. Girlfriends who allow you to be yourself. Susan doesn't. In fact, there's a little catch of anxiety ahead of any coffee you have with her. Why on earth do you put yourself through it? You heard at a funeral once that a person's life should be measured in deeds not years; and deeds Susan has done aplenty, you will happily praise her to the heavens, a good kind woman in many respects, yes – you just don't need her entwined in your life anymore.

Not anymore. As the distilling gathers pace.

A lesson you are finally acting upon: some friendships will naturally run their course in life and there is no shame or guilt in that. They are right for a particular time and then they are not. Move on, cleanly, as the souring starts.

It's good for you both.

Lesson 210

Women are but rarely placed in circumstances where they have actively to assume the guardianship or rule of others

_____

Taking control. Blindfolds, handcuffs, vibrators – sometimes two at once. All those things you had reserved for one man and one only but now you can articulate, you have a voice and are not afraid to use it. No blow jobs, and you are hugely apologetic about that – it's just something you've never liked – but Hugh concurs to get everything else. For you it is empowered sex. The balance has shifted: it was always his way in the past.

You laugh at yourselves, the two of you; finish off giggling, side by side, on your backs. How ridiculous and silly and lovely it all is, how amazing that your bodies can still do this. It's like your sex life, as a couple, has burst into colour after years of black and white. He knows now that you will no longer tolerate bad sex. If it is, you don't want it; you'll push him away, you're too old for anything substandard. You've moved beyond youth hostels and Primark and pot noodles and sleeping mats – in middle age you'll only stand for the best.

It has to work. Fabulously. For both of you.

In terms of sex, you have entered a dialogue. Finally. After so many years of marriage.

It has saved you both.

And at night, alone, before Hugh slips into bed with you, you take out your little Victorian book with all its notes, those little nuggets of memory that plummet you back to a time that is burnished.

By what worked. Then, and now.

Heroic sex.

Finally. What Tol was preparing you for. This moment, your entire adult life. You send him a smile, from across the waves, across the world; send a smile to Woondala in gratitude for an awakening, once.

Lesson 211

In growing old, we are able to see the clearing away of knots in tangled destinies

Mel picks up her boy a tad late in the afternoons – on the days her ex or her mother isn't doing it – sauntering always a little behind everyone else. So she doesn't have to engage, perhaps, to become too enmeshed. She has her own life and it's filled up; doesn't need the clutter of the school gate. You can see the zest and serenity of divorced women like her, in control of their lives. You are learning from it.

You tell Hugh you will eat with the kids and leave his dinner on the stove from now on, for when he comes in late, to eat by himself; it's killing you waiting up, having dinner at ten or beyond.

'OK,' he says, with something like relief.

Gosh, as easy as that.

'It'll keep you fresh,' he adds, with a filthy grin.

You burst into a laugh. He's right.

So, just like that, you won't have to hear his loud chewing for five days of the week; one of the many irritations among all the irritations but it's never enough for any type of action. He is a good man. Who delights in preparing his sons' lunch boxes, shoos you off on Saturday shopping treats, insists you take girly nights off *for your sanity* and will even, now, do the boys' nit bath and clip his own head in solidarity – and practicality – because he likes hugging them so much and stray head lice won't be stopping that. It says so much about him.

A *kind* man. To be cherished. Tol would have wanted it.

You cut your own hair and finally dye it, obscuring the grey sneaking in at your temples. Throw away the camel colours, the sand and the chalk, bolden yourself up. Fight the flint of the weather with exuberant colour, purples and greens and reds and pinks. A bit of dazzle on your eyes, a bit of sparkle on your cuffs. Who cares what people think – you are freeing yourself from that too. Seizing joy. Celebrating the wonder of everything around you, the crazy vivid glorious beauty of so much. Becoming that woman who revels in life; who seems like she has sex a lot, three times a day, whether she does or not.

It's in the laugh.

Lesson 212

We have not to construct human nature afresh, but to take
it as we find it, and make the best of it
_____

In the languidness, post-sex, of a lazy Saturday night Hugh
is hearing all about Susan and rolling his eyes – *women* – a
species he knows little of.

'Why on earth are you still friends?'

A not unreasonable question.

'I'm not so much. Anymore. We've drifted apart.'

You tell Hugh how you were forever commenting on the
amazingness of her children, especially her daughter, because
Susan's conversation always cannily steered you into it.

'She's not malicious,' you laugh. 'She just has no idea. It
would never occur to her that maybe I've always dreamt of a
little girl. She's just one of those people with a complete absence
of empathy.' And as you're explaining you're aware that envy
isn't hardening, actually; isn't stewing and festering. It's leaking
away.

As you firm. As you realise the extent of your limitations.
You're never going to get that Prada dress and holiday house in
the Luberon, the vintage Aston Martin and the princess with

her bedroom of fairy wings and tutus. Ah, who cares. Life, as it should be, is a process of simplification. Tol taught you that.

'Let's make one.'

'What?'

'A *girl*.'

You laugh at the ridiculousness. 'I'm far too old for that, mister.' You're on the cusp of menopause, you can feel it.

'Let's try.'

You slam the duvet over your head.

'I need some sleep,' you giggle. 'It's footy tomorrow. Your turn for a sleep-in. Nigh' nigh'.'

Lesson 213

Whether great or small her talents,
she has not let one of them rust for want of use

─────────

But he's got you. Now, feverishly, Googling 'gender selection/
female/diet'. It's extraordinary how much information comes
up. What is repeated, again and again, is dairy: milk, eggs, ice
cream. Yoghurt most of all. To change the lining of your vagina
– its alkalinity – to make it a more conducive environment for
the female sperm. To kill the male sperm off.

You go grocery shopping. Sunday afternoon. You have little
hope.

But a girl. A woman of this new world.

Your mission already is to raise new men – who respect and
value women, who are not afraid of them – and there is the
great chuff of that. But then a girl. Imagine. The world at her
feet, the confidence.

Lesson 214

Happy above all must be that marriage
where neither husband nor wife ever had a friend
so dear as one another

Hugh takes you to Paris. Is aware, after the Australia trip, that you don't really need him – could live quite capably without him – alone with the kids, the old bush girl roaring back. The lack of need keeps him bound, freshly. It's revived the relationship.

You stock up on magazines at St Pancras. An irrefutable sign of middle age: neither of you recognise the starlet on the cover of *Vanity Fair*. Good grief, it has come to this. The world galloping away from you, so soon, so fast.

You both gulp complete like an Indian summer that gleeful, child-free Paris weekend. The room service in bed in front of the telly. Matching bathrobes. The uninterrupted bath. The sleep-ins. The break from the intensity of three little men in your lives.

And in a creamy hotel that Louis Armstrong stayed in once, Hugh asks you what you want. He listens. He complies. You remember what happiness was. You teach him. Show him your vulnerability. The woman Tol wanted all along. Teaching him how to kiss, the last frontier, your way not his. Unlocking your body, and once again in thrall to it. What it can *do*. Touched into light, into life.

'You like sexy sex,' Hugh says in surprise, more to himself than to you.

You smile, he has so much to learn; knows nothing, all those hidden depths like an iceberg under the surface. You stroke his penis, it has returned to its milky velvety softness, so tender, so vulnerable, and you lay your cheek to its warmth in wonder. Because this is the first time in your life you have successfully taught a man. Shaped him. You have confidence now. That is Tol's lesson, it is all coming to fruition. Finally. And it has taken until middle age to get to this point.

What you love about Hugh most of all: that you're comfortable with him, in talk and in silence, and you were never completely comfortable like this with Tol. Affection is what binds you as much as anything, and that's not to downplay the word. There's such a warmth, a cherishing, a delight with your husband – and it's deepening over the years and there's an astonishment at that.

And you know now there can be no sex more profound – more touched by grace – than that which attempts to create a child. The one type of sex Tol never talked about.

The most extraordinary of all.

And the most traditional.

Lesson 215

If man is without occupation, what a poor creature he becomes! – what a dawdling, moping, sitting-over-the-fire, thumb-twiddling, lazy, ill-tempered animal! And why? 'Oh, poor fellow! 'Tis because he has got nothing to do!' Yet this is precisely the condition of women for a third, a half, often the whole of their existence.

So, to writing. Not sure why, just need to now, it is time. Writing this book for Tol, yes, but for Hugh most of all.

For your husband, for all husbands. For your lover, for all lovers.

The anonymous, leather-bound manual beside you that you have carried with you your whole adult life. Joining the ranks, and wouldn't she love that.

Hugh has never known what happened to you during your teenage years; has never twigged. Marriage took you away from that edged awareness but now you have found a way back to it. It *is* possible.

Galloping with your words.

Then commanding *fuck me* in a way you never have in your life.

Waiting on the bed for him. Pulsing, wet, exposed, stripped.

Lesson 216

A principal agent in middle age is a blessing
which rarely comes till then — contentment

_____

Is this, the early forties, the supreme moment of a woman's life?
    The secret, you think: letting go.
    You have finally found the courage.
    To fail.
    Say no.
    Be different.
    Apologise.
    Accept your faults.
    Seize.
    Admit you were wrong.
    Be honest.

And then, and then, two blue stripes on the plastic stick.

Lesson 217

I can bear anything, except unkindness

A music assembly at the boys' school. One by one the parents get up and leave as their child has played. You look around in horror at the diminishing audience, the consummate selfishness. Every child, always, wants to be seen as a success; yet so many of these parents cannot be bothered to give another twenty minutes of their time to a performer not their own. As the recital pushes on, the empty chairs increase. Of course, no one's interested, really, in a child not their own, unless they're relatives or close friends or Godparents – and sometimes not even then.

You have morning sickness, can feel the great engine inside you drawing on every ounce of your energy as it brews a baby and you grip the chair: you will not leave this.

Because of those tiny, aghast faces of the children, five and up, who have yet to shine. Your Jack included, his big moment – and to the middle child who can so easily be lost it means so much, of course. Piano is one of the last group of instruments left, and then violin. You know exactly who will leave and who won't. Susan, of course, sweeping out with her domineering energy as soon as her precious boy has played his flute. Mel hangs on, God love her, and her child was only in the choir at the start. She catches your eye and winks her appreciation at Jack's performance; you wink back, tears in your eyes that he can play anything at all, even if it's the simplest of Bach. More parents leave, and more, until by the end just a handful of adults remain. You rub your belly and rub it, into calm. The last performer sitting on the stage, waiting, has a face that deepens its distress every time she clocks someone else leave, then someone else. She plays beautifully, from memory, the most talented child of the concert. To six parents. You sweep to your feet with wild applause at the end and the rest of the audience follows. What hope have these kids got?

In the chaos of afterwards you tell all your boys how wonderful they are, how loved, how they flood your life with happiness.

Parenting the opposite to your father. Not turning into your parent as you became one yourself; rebelling against him. You say to Jack how enormously thrilled you are by him, how amazing he was. Rexi does too. He's much calmer now, the storm within has passed and you wonder at the great dips and troughs of all their childhoods – how they change so much. What they were at four they are resolutely not at eight; you think you have them down pat and then they slip off, into something else. Just like marriage. It's constantly changing, fluid, dynamic. First one partner in the ascendant, then the other, learning from each other, it's never still. The four of you walk away laughing from the school hall. Everything has firmed, everything.

*

Susan rings late that night to lock you into the face-painting stall at the school fair.

'Wasn't Emma amaaaaazing?' she says, referring to a girl in Jack's class who sang a solo; she'd never give a compliment to your own child, it's a trick she's pulled often before. 'I cried, she was that good.'

You're calm. 'Actually, I cried at my own son.' You smile strong. 'He was amazing. I was so proud of him.'

'Yes,' she says, 'he was.' Taken aback; she has suddenly realised something.

Lesson 218

A solid, useful, available happiness

Your little nugget of a secret at your writing desk in the attic.

Steadying your life like a keeled yacht.

Your manifesto, your instruction manual. It will be written with unflinching honesty; you've opened a door to a reckless, exhilarating new world and you work in a trance of liberation and defiance. You are stepping out of your normal self, becoming someone more brazen and confident, high on hormones and released. Rubbing your belly in glee. This will be anonymous, it is the only way to do it, with your little family so tight and so cherished around you. And when it is done you will walk away from it like a mother who's adopted out a child, you will leave it to make its own way in the world and you will get on with your life.

And one day – you dream – Hugh will find it on his pillowslip.

No idea who it's from. Any woman, and every woman.

But he will learn from it.

Oh yes.

Lesson 219

Deafened with ever-sounding trills of delicious laughter all day,
and lying down at night with a soft sleepy thing breathing at
his side, or wakened of a morning with two little arms tight
around his neck, smotheringly expressing a wealth of love that
kingdoms could not buy

What is healed: the great open wound you have carried all
through your life. For a while there in adulthood you thought
the searing hurt of your father's withdrawal was getting worse,
you had no defences for the pain of his sloppiness; it was
increasing, in fact, as you reached middle age. But finally, after
so long, it is cauterised. And you know now what the greatest
chasm is between two people, out of all the chasms that can
widen and swallow and swamp.

Love withheld, by a parent.

If you want to hurt the most, do the most damage – try
that. If you want to see a miraculous healing, try the opposite.
Love withheld can lock up a life. Lock up confidence, esteem,
strength.

Your father will never say he loves you anymore, never say
how proud he is of you, will never ring you on your birthday or
send a present for Christmas despite you ringing him every one

of his own birthdays and each December 25th. He will never do any of these things, but he did something for you once.

And it is enough.

Lesson 220

We have lived just long enough to trace the apparent plot
and purpose of our own life and that of others sufficiently to
make us content to sit still and see the play played out

Six p.m. Hugh has commanded you disappear. Have a bath,
read a magazine, rub lavender oil into your tummy, do all that
women stuff.

'Leave the boys to their men's business, pizza boxes and beer
cans,' he announces with a cheeky grin, rubbing his hands
in glee and flurrying the boys right up. You retreat upstairs,
smiling as you hear the squeals and thumps and roars rising
below you. A footy's being kicked, you don't mind; all you
want, all you ever want, is their happiness.

You slip out your little manual with its depth charges
threaded through it. Settle your bare feet on the creaky coffin-
lid floor.

It feels like you are painstakingly sewing a quilt up here,
in your little hidden space, a blanket of warmth and comfort,
beauty and secrets – for all women, any women – pouring into
it all the wisdom and the heartbreak, all the ridiculousness and
the ugliness, all the vulnerability and want and exhilaration
and truth.

It's all you've got.

A voice.

And as it's firmed, the world around you is beauty-ing up. The snow outside your window is ragged, undisciplined, dancing in the air in big, blowsy drops and the restless river churns below you in a beautiful ceaseless rush, somersaulting its foam over the rocks. The wind tugs at the tiny attic window that holds firm but protesting on its latch and the roar in the trees sounds like distant surf but the cosiness of your teapot of a house enfolds you strong in its embrace. It is all ravishing, deeply comforting; and right now, enough.

You are finally stepping into the happiness you've spent years backing away from. You didn't deserve it, that is how you always felt; you couldn't possibly just lie back in it and bask. But now.

All surrender.

The laughter tripping through you. As you do exactly what you want.

Lesson 221

Real marriage, with all its sanctity, beauty and glory

That night you feign sleep, face to face with Pip, to try and drop him into slumber. He puts his face so close to yours that you can feel his warm breath and then he touches, wondrously, learning. He touches your eyelids and tries to make them open, your lips, nose, cheeks, then he plants a huge, slightly askew smack of a kiss on your lips.

You want this to go on forever.

Later it is the man who curls around you. Hugh's arm locks in yours, seat belt, he calls it, cupping his child in your belly. Firm in his grip you fall into sleep, nourished. Because what you have with Hugh is evenness, you always know his love, do not doubt it as he does not yours; it is a great constant.

What you have, now, is the seductiveness of shared sleep.

Perhaps it is happiness, perhaps removal, but you rarely think of Tol anymore. Is it a travesty, what you have become, from that girl you once were?

No. Biology took over. Your body insisted you go on this path.

Your breasts ache. Filling, once again, with milk. And this one feels different within you – you are spilling out, widening in a way you never did in the past, a regular Venus of Willendorf, good grief.

Lesson 222

Look up to that region of blue calm which is never long invisible to the pure of heart — this is the blessedest possession that any woman can have

———————————

You begin to bleed.

It begins on a Thursday afternoon. During a huge day of ferrying kids to swimming and piano and play dates, one of those running days where you're constantly trying to catch up. But you carry on. Need to have the kids sorted before you can get to this.

'It might just be one of those pregnancy bleeds,' Hugh says on the phone. 'Rest. Alright?'

By Friday afternoon you are driving yourself to A and E. Are told to go home, put your feet up. The blood is spilling over the soaked pad between your legs, streaking down your legs; the volume is frightening. You wake up on the Saturday after a despairing, hoping, praying night with a sinking heart. So much blood. You wanted this child — this daughter, you just know it — so vastly. Don't fall out!

Back to A and E. The doctor tells you your blood/hormone reading is 13,000 — which means it's still there. Beautiful, radiant, soaring hope. The baby has somehow, miraculously, gripped on while everything around it is falling away. Inside, still, is a ferociously beating heart. Despite despairing clumps of tissue and blood coming out and at one point, on the toilet, a soft rolling 'pop' of a something but the water in the bowl is too murky to get a proper look, and you can't, quite.

All day, hope.

Lesson 223

We are able to take interest in the marvellous government
of the universe

You're admitted into a ward of gyni-complicated women. Are
handed a grey cardboard bowl to catch whatever will come out.
The coldness of the gesture cuts through you. You bite your lip,
staring at it. Right. They want the foetus, their prize; want to
examine it.

By nightfall the nurse confirms you are miscarrying. There
is, of course, nothing that can be done. Nature must take
its course. It's for the best. And now it is as if your body just
wants to flush the alien object out, you bleed and bleed in great
clumps.

A scan confirms everything.

Nothing left.

'Cry, and cry again, love,' the radiographer soothes, her
gentle hand on your belly and then around your heaving,
shuddering back. 'It's a bereavement. Nothing less.'

Oh yes.

The hospital wants you staying but no, you must get out,
there's a family and a house that awaits. It is where you need

to be. You just want to hold your boys at this moment, your beautiful bright boysies, bury your nose into their softness and cuddle them tight, so tight.

As you walk from the fluorescence of the hospital's bright electric doors: an enormous white balloon of sadness inside you, filling you up.

Lesson 224

Marriage ought not always to be a question of necessity,
but of choice

Through it all, Hugh.

Your weeping, as you were wheeled into the ward and were told that your husband was over there, waiting; see, look.

And there he was, yes. Standing, glittery-eyed, holding your overnight bag. The leather bag he bought for a surprise birthday trip to Rome, where he played you a clip from *Roman Holiday* on the DVD player in the cab on the way to the airport and teased *guess where we're off to, guess*? He has packed completely the wrong clothes but never mind, there is so much love in it that you have to laugh. And there is also a cosmetic bag he's scrambled together with absolutely everything you need; it's spot on. Fifty pounds for the TV and the phone rental, your favourite magazines. A Colette book about her childhood of rural happiness that you've never read. So much thought, all of it.

'Thank you,' you say, choked up.

Because you never say it enough.

His disappointment, too. His deflated, telling 'oh' when you say to him that you are miscarrying.

'Bye bye, Bean number four. Hello Bean number five,' he says into the shardy bright.

You laugh and then keen, barely knowing why. Holding him, feeling his weeping through your hands and wanting to swallow his own shudders, swallow his grief, clamping him down with your body.

You're in this together, oh yes.

Lesson 225 – the Last

When the day's work is done

The hour grows calm and quiet like the candle you have lit. You are pulling away from your former life like a ship leaving a wharf, you are sailing far from it. Ahead, the cleanness of a new adventure. You have the shape of your family now, the shape of your life. Hugh and you are not gazing blindly into each other's eyes – you are both gazing out, keenly, at something else. Your three children. Side by side, focused on something else, and that feels strong and calming and right. This is your reality. This is your life. You have chosen it. You are trusting ahead, for what seems like the first time in your life; trusting the void.

You shut your little Victorian volume. It is no longer needed. Your work, for now, is done.

This is the end where now begins.

And how you love writing that.